Praise for *Pro*

"Paul Mason and Don Gold present an organized, no-nonsense, inspiring guide to the most important job in Hollywood—producing. These masters of the large and small screen teach would-be producers and writer/producers a thing or two about succeeding in this business while entertaining everyone with the highlights (and lowlights) of their careers. *Producing for Hollywood* is a must read for all aspiring moviemakers."
— FRED SILVERMAN, former president, ABC, CBS, NBC

"An impressive book filled with practical, current, insightful information, heretofore available only to those who practiced, over and over again, the art of producing. If you only have time to read one book on what you need to know to succeed as a producer and filmmaker, read Paul Mason and Donald Gold's *Producing for Hollywood*. If you have time for two books, read *Producing for Hollywood* again."
— LEONARD B. STERN, chairman of the Advisory Council, *Producers Guild of America*

"*Producing for Hollywood* is a very good piece of work: clear, insightful, and an invaluable roadmap for anyone who wants to take the leap into independent production. It is written by two real pros who've been there and done it and make it clear just how you too can do it."
— DEAN HARGROVE, creator/producer/writer, *Jake and the Fatman, Diagnosis Murder, Perry Mason* films

"Messrs. Mason and Gold have fashioned a very readable and helpful introduction to producing for Hollywood. The newcomer may find the glossary of movie terms and the chapters dealing with when and how the producer deals with the various above the line and below the line elements particularly useful."
— SID SHEINBERG, former president, MCA; president, *The Bubble Factory*

"Hollywood professional[s] give it to you straight—follow it and you'll be on your way."
— DAVID L. WOLPER, executive producer, *Roots*

Producing
for
Hollywood

A Guide for the Independent Producer

Second Edition

PAUL MASON
DONALD L. GOLD

ALLWORTH PRESS
NEW YORK

09   08   07   06   05   04   5   4   3   2   1

Published by Allworth Press
An imprint of Allworth Communications
10 East 23rd Street, New York, NY 10010

Cover design by Derek Bacchus

Page composition/typography by SR Desktop Services, Ridge, NY

Library of Congress Cataloging-in-Publication Data
Mason, Paul, 1930–
    Producing for Hollywood : how to succeed as an independent producer for movies and television / by Paul Mason, Donald L. Gold.—2nd ed.
        p.   cm.
    1. Motion pictures—Production and direction.   I. Gold, Donald.   II. Title.
PN1995.9.P7M36   2004
791.4302'32—dc22   2004005425

Printed in Canada

Contents

Foreword

'**ve always enjoyed watching the eagles fly. In show business, you get
to see a great many beautiful eagles, and they come in all sizes and
shapes. I was producing a television pilot many years ago, with Steven
Spielberg directing. Steven was still young and inexperienced. In fact, the
stars, Martin Landau and Barbara Bain, strongly resisted my hiring him. It
was only with great reluctance that they agreed to trust my judgment.
(We still joke about it.)

The footage was wonderful, and we were all pleased, but heading into
the sixth day, we were three pages behind schedule, and the order came
down from the highest reaches of the infamous Black Tower that this pilot
would have to be completed on schedule. I sat down with Steven during
the lunch break and explained the dilemma—that we would have to make
up the three pages, somehow. He nodded and set up his first shot after
lunch. It was a flowing camera dolly shot that started close on the telephone, pulled back to reveal the actor, and followed him through the
room to the end of the scene. So, instead of filming a standard master shot
with several cover shots, which would have taken about three hours to
shoot, he had, in effect, filmed a difficult, three-page dolly shot in about an
hour. We were now back on schedule. Steven turned to me: "I know how
to do it, but I don't like it." What could I say? *I* thought it was an incredible
shot. I knew then and there that I was watching one of the eagles fly.

I was making a movie for television called *The California Kid,* and we
had hired a young actor by the name of Nick Nolte to play the third lead.

On the second day's dailies, Nick's brother in the film dies, and Nick had to sit on the road and cradle him in his arms. He cried, and it was an exquisite scene. Masculine, moving, dramatic. At that time, Nick was a total unknown. I went to the set and told him how wonderful the dailies were and that I was convinced he was going to be a big star. He stared at me strangely, then mumbled a very shy "Thank you." He was one of the very few actors I've met who did not revel in praise. But there was no doubt that, eventually, he was going to soar . . . and very high.

When I first met Paula Hart, we were making a pilot film for her daughter, Melissa, in New York. Paula was the executive producer for this film, but, in a sense, functioned more as Melissa's mom. Although she was involved creatively, she did not take part in the production process.

The pilot did not sell, but Paula had optioned the rights to an Archie Comics cartoon called *Sabrina, the Teenage Witch* and brought it to Perry Simon, president of Viacom Productions. Perry had always liked Melissa and believed in her talent. He felt it would make a good movie for Viacom's cable network, Showtime.

Paula was, at this time, very inexperienced and nervous and (as she will tell you herself) very afraid of me. We worked together during the making of the movie, and she quickly began to understand the aspects of film production. With the assistance of the Canadian producer, Richard Davis, and the American producer, Alana Lambros, she soon began to bloom. It was during post-production, during the mixing of the picture, as she began to see all the elements coming together, that I could see her beginning to grow feathers.

When the television series of *Sabrina* sold, I hired an excellent line producer, Ken Koch, to work with her, and she soon began to develop into a full-fledged producer, from a creative as well as a financial aspect. But it was while she was producing the film for us in Canada, when she was having difficulty getting the first assistant director (A.D.) to do what she wanted, that her wings really started to unfold. The first A.D. told her, "The director doesn't want to do it that way."

I explained to Paula one of the facts of life: "Tell the first assistant director that it is *your name* on the bottom of his check, and if he doesn't do it your way, there will soon be another first assistant director."

"Can I do that?" she asked.

"If you hired him, you can fire him," I answered.

Paula never looked back. Most recently we did *Sabrina Goes to Rome* in Italy, under the most difficult of circumstances, and Paula soared through it in superior fashion. Another eagle in the sky.

Nora Reynolds was a production coordinator who I hired as my executive assistant. She involved herself in all phases of production that were my responsibility and soon had an excellent grasp of pre-production, production, post-production, and the problems of the personalities that go along with them. After several years, Nora received a much better offer from Paramount Pictures and asked me for permission to leave. I was thrilled to see the feathers growing and gave her my blessing. She was soon hired away from Paramount by NBC and is now a vice president in charge of production.

And then there was the eagle that soared twice.

When we first hired John Travolta to be one of the Sweathogs in *Welcome Back, Kotter,* we paid him $650 a week. We later raised him to $750 a week. Actually, Jimmy Komack, the creator of the show, and I, president of the company, really thought that Larry Hilton Jacobs, who starred in *Cooley High* and played the part of Boom-Boom Washington, was going to be the star of the Sweathogs. But, as we introduced the four kids each week and heard the shrieks from the audience when John came out to say "hello," we realized John Travolta would become a major star.

When John was hired to do *Saturday Night Fever,* my friend, John Badham, who was directing, complained to me that here he was directing his first feature and his star was a TV actor. I told him that I never heard such screaming when a person was introduced since Frank Sinatra's early days. Months later, he called me after filming in New York and told me that it was impossible to record sound, because whenever there was a scene with John, girls somehow found out and stood on the street corners shrieking and yelling. John returned to do another two years of *Welcome Back, Kotter,* even though, at the time, he was the first star to appear in two $100 million movies back to back. He was earning a million dollars per movie, and back in the seventies, that was a lot of money. Our eagle soared for the first time.

John's career hit terrible times after *Moment to Moment* and several other pictures he, and his fans, would like to forget. His career appeared to be in serious trouble. It was at this time that we did a movie together called *Angel Eyes.* John remained, as always, the same solid, wonderful person, aware of his obligations in life and aware of himself as a person, a good friend, and a man not shaken or destroyed by the fact that his career was failing. He remained the same upbeat, positive person, believing that his career was only a part of his life's destiny. My favorite quote of John's is when he was told that one of his pictures was a "disaster."

His response was, "No, that picture was a flop. When a plane crashes, *that's* a disaster." And John has never forgotten the difference between life and films.

And then came *Pulp Fiction*. Our eagle soared again—to even greater heights than ever before.

These are a few of the many eagles I have been privileged to see take to their wings and fly—each in his own way as successful as the others, and each enjoying to the fullest the chance to show their stuff. Sometimes I think it is as much fun watching as doing, and then I realize I am wrong: Doing is a lot more fun.

My collaborator, Don Gold, is a below-the-line eagle. I first met Don in 1968. He was my unit production manager on a television series called *San Francisco International Airport,* starring Lloyd Bridges. It was a most difficult miniseries, with lots of production at San Francisco Airport involving a great deal of process filmmaking and offering a whole host of production problems.

We delivered a superior television product, and we were under budget. The studio was very pleased, and we quickly became known as producers who understood how to develop high-quality products at a very good price. Through the years, Don and I have worked together on many television series, from *MacMillan and Wife* to *CHIPS* to today's television success, *Diagnosis Murder,* starring Dick Van Dyke.

I have always considered Don's knowledge of below-the-line film production—the work of the men and women in the trenches who get the drudgery done—to be thorough and superior. Without the good work of those behind the camera, no actor can succeed in front of the camera. It was for that reason, when I thought about writing a book about film production, that I realized I could not do it alone, because it would not be a total book on film production. It was only after discussions with Don and our agreeing to write this book together that I felt we could offer people interested in total film production a useful tool. I hope it serves as that and more, and I wish you all the joy of soaring with the eagles.

—Paul Mason

Prologue

When a person spends a lifetime in one field of endeavor, he is bound to pick up a lot of knowledge, if only by osmosis—simply by being there. Having spent our entire adult lives in the motion picture industry, Paul Mason and I have been fortunate enough to acquire, and retain, a great deal of relevant, and not so relevant, information.

Making movies is not exactly brain surgery, but it does have its own unique and, at times, complex nomenclature. There are ways to do things in this business, and ways not to do them. In the army, we were told there are three ways of getting things done: the right way, the wrong way, and the army way. It's about the same in the motion picture business.

Every writer has his own individual reasons for writing a book. Our reasons, while assuredly not as compelling as some, are, nevertheless, important to us. It seems that almost everyone has a different story on how they got into the motion picture business. The only common thread is their desire to be in this business.

Paul started as a writer and moved on to producing feature films and hit television series, and is presently a senior vice president at Viacom Productions. I started out sweeping the stock room and handing out double-head nails and gaffer's tape at Columbia Studios. From that rather inauspicious beginning, I moved on to become an assistant director, production manager, executive at Universal Studios, producer, director, and writer. Between us, Paul and I have done just about everything there is to do in this business except act—in front of the camera, that is.

I mention all of this not for self-aggrandizement, but just to let you know where we're coming from. Our only regrets have been that we wasted so many years trying to negotiate the labyrinthine maze that is Hollywood. We had no mentors to guide us past and around the numerous potholes, obstacles, and dead-end streets that make up the dungeons and dragons of the real world. However, we did finally learn our way around, since we rarely made the same mistake twice. But then, we didn't have to—there were always plenty of new ones to make.

So, here we are, nearing the sunset of our checkered careers, which has been much like a Disneyland ride, full of exhilarating highs and depressing lows, but never—thank God—never boring.

Anyway, all of this acquired knowledge is sitting around inside our heads, all dressed up with no place to go. So, maybe it's time, before senility sets in and all of this extraordinary information we have simply melts into one big blob of unrecognizable gunk, to get it down on paper. It seems to us that it would be an unconscionable waste to do nothing with a lifetime of experiences that could save someone from falling into the same traps, bumping into the same brick walls, and tripping over the same stumbling blocks that we invariably, albeit painfully, endured.

And there you have it, dear friends. This book is here to guide you, gently prod you, and save you from the dark corners of celluloid hell. We share with you much of what we have learned through blood, sweat, and tears (my apologies to Mr. Churchill, but if one must steal, steal from the best), and hope that through this knowledge, your career can be a little less rocky. We believe in the old adage, "It's nice to share."

—DON GOLD

The Life of the Independent Producer

The life of the independent producer can be a gigantic roller coaster ride, exalting at the summit of success and wallowing in the depths of despair—almost at the same time.

The most asked question is, "How can I become a producer?" Unfortunately, there is no prescribed method. There are almost as many answers to that question as there are producers. But first of all, we have to define what a producer is, and that is not so easy.

Producers come in all shapes and sizes and with all sorts of extended and convoluted titles: Executive Producer, Supervising Producer, Line Producer, Co-Producer, Co-Executive Producer, coordinating producer (notice I stopped using capital letters), associate producer, and then the one with just the plain, old title, PRODUCER—the guy who usually does most of the work.

Since we are concerned in this book with independent production, we'll concentrate on the independent producer—who he is, what he does, and how he became what he is.

For the most part, independent producers are entrepreneurial. There are three basic attributes that are absolutely necessary if one is to become a successful producer. I will list them in what I feel is the order of their importance. The first is MOTIVATION. The second, PERSEVERANCE. The third, TALENT. I'm sure most of you feel that talent is the most important. But I can tell you from experience that talent doesn't necessarily guarantee success, nor does lack of talent guarantee failure.

MOTIVATION should be an extremely important word in the producer's vocabulary, because one of the most difficult issues you will face in your quest to become an independent producer will be . . . getting started. Maybe that sounds too simplistic, but it is an irrefutable fact. A producer must be strongly self-motivated. There will be no one out there urging you to become a producer. There will be no easy shortcuts, no one to look to for help. All you will see out there is emptiness, and it will be up to you, and you alone, to put the paint on the canvas.

It is amazing how many people dream of becoming a producer, but never have the courage to act on that dream. There is a reason for that, and the reason is a four-letter word: FEAR. That's right, fear. "What am I afraid of?" you ask. The answer is simple. You are afraid of failure. So, you keep dreaming and making excuses why you can't get started right now. But you will start soon, you tell yourself. Unfortunately, soon never comes, and your goals are never achieved.

There is only one way to get past this fear, and that is by confronting it and taking action. That is why motivation is so important. Without it, that first step is never taken. And that is the irony. Because by not starting, you are creating the ultimate failure.

Starting—picking up the phone and making that first call, or writing that first query letter—can be a tough thing to do, even traumatic. I am not minimizing the difficulty of that single act. But I cannot *maximize* enough the importance of it. If you want to be an independent producer, you are not only going to have to fight everyone out there, you are going to have to fight yourself as well. *Don't lose the battle before it starts.*

PERSEVERANCE runs a close second to motivation. In fact, it's damn near a dead heat. If you have a tendency to give up easily, you should really consider another line of work. If you think going ten rounds with Mike Tyson is tough, wait till you try to put a movie project together.

Here is a word to remember: REJECTION. It is something you will either learn to live with, or you will go ahead and take that job in your father's clothing store. Rejection will become a part of your life; you will get to know it intimately. It will stand as a barrier to every hope and dream for which you hunger. Rejection can tear at your very soul, and if you let it, it can chew you up and spit you out.

Rejection is as much a part of the motion picture business as the film itself. It is something that all creative people must learn to deal with. Actors, writers, directors, and yes, producers. Rejection can be vicious and mean-spirited, or it can be benignly innocent. As Don Corleone once said, "This ain't personal . . . it's business." And truthfully, that is an apt description of most rejections. Unfortunately, it doesn't make it any less painful.

As you start on your journey as an independent producer and move toward your initial goal, which will be to raise money for your venture, that nasty word, rejection, will loom up time and time again. Don't fight it, don't rail against the injustice of it, don't make it more important than it is. Instead, learn to embrace it. Rejection can also be a learning experience. What did I do wrong? How did I present myself or my idea? How can I change it so the next person will be more receptive?

Perseverance will help you get through the debilitating morass of rejection. If you want something bad enough, you will fight for it. Regardless of the rejections you will face, you will push forward, you will not toss in the towel, you will not give up. So, that brings up the question, "How many rejections do I accept before I say 'the hell with it' and go back to selling pots and pans?"

That, my friend, is a tough question to answer, because everyone has a different breaking point. To try and put this into perspective, I will relate a personal experience. Over a period of several months, I pitched thirty-five different story ideas for an episode of a television series. All thirty-five were shot down. But number thirty-six made it. So, what if I had stopped after the first twenty or thirty rejections? And if number thirty-six hadn't been accepted, would I have gone on to number forty or fifty? When is it time to say, "Enough already"?

Sorry, I don't know the answer to that. Frankly, I don't think anyone does. All I *do* know is, if one *perseveres,* there is always the chance that one will ultimately reach his goal. On the other hand, if one does not persevere, well then, in that case, there really is no chance at all, is there?

TALENT. Actually, there is not a lot to say about talent. The fact is, you either have it or you don't. It can't be taught; it can't be acquired. That's why I put it at number three on my list. The degree of talent you have is less important than your innate desire for success. I could name a lot of very successful producers who are saddled with mediocre talent, or less. Yes, I could name them, but then, I'd get sued. Suffice it to say, they are out there, many of them—and doing quite well, thank you.

Look at it this way. Everyone has talent to a certain degree. It is not how much talent you have; it is how well you use what you have.

The first problem—or opportunity, as we like to refer to it in this business—for the independent producer is to find a script. That is because the screenplay is the first building block. It is the foundation you will build your castle on. There are two ways to approach this first script. One is practicability, the other is passion. And they are not necessarily incompatible goals. The practical side involves finding or writing a script that will be reasonably inexpensive to shoot and will be an easy sell, not only to your potential investors, but to the distributor as well. For your first project you are not going to attempt *Gone with the Wind*. Nor do you want to get involved with some dark, esoteric story that will have very little mass appeal.

Now, at this point, you may be thinking that you will not prostitute your personal integrity by making something you really don't believe in just to get a movie made. That is admirable. However, it could possibly be the one thing that will keep you from ever achieving your goals. I would venture to say that early on in their careers, Spielberg, Coppola, and Scorsese did some films that they were not too proud of. The main objective is to get yourself into a position where you will, eventually, have the prestige and the clout to do the things you really want to do.

This is not to say that your first project cannot be something of depth, importance, and artistic value. It is, of course, possible. What I am saying is don't get hung up on this. Your immediate goal is to get a film made, to get your name up there, to get a credit, which is a major building block for your career. This is where the passion comes in. You must look at the script you write or acquire as a living, breathing thing. And you must make yourself be passionate about it. This is important for any producer, but especially for someone just starting out. If you do not truly love your project, nobody better be aware of it but you. You must be desperate to get this project up on the screen, without showing the desperation. You must roil with excitement and enthusiasm, because you will have to convince other people—people with money—that your film is the best thing since sliced bread.

It is *essential* that you have a burning desire to do this particular story. Why is it essential? Well, mainly because it will allow you to humiliate yourself in a manner you never thought possible, while confronting all your relatives, friends, enemies, acquaintances, total strangers, lighting and grip companies, camera companies, post-production houses, and indeed, anyone else in the world who can, in any way, help you see your dreams come to fruition.

Once you have that screenplay in hand, you will now face your most formidable obstacle on the road to independent production: MONEY. It is definitely a truism that you can have the best script that's ever been written, but if there's no money, it will never get produced.

That is what makes the motion picture such a unique art form, unlike any other. Even though the finished motion picture is truly art, before it gets to that point, it is strictly business. There is no other art form that can cost millions of dollars to produce—except maybe Mount Rushmore, but that's another story.

To be an independent producer, you must not only be creative, you must also have a sharp business sense. You have to be able to recognize good product when you see it, *and* you have to have the selling ability of a traveling snake-oil salesman.

Like it or not, in the world of independent production, you are going to have to be a salesman. And like any good salesman, you must not only sell your product, you must sell yourself as well. Those two entities are inextricably entwined. In fact, if the truth be known, selling yourself is sometimes more important than selling the product. Investors, as a rule, do not know a lot about what makes, or does not make, a good, viable motion picture. Therefore, quite often, their decisions will be based on who will be involved in the project and, more to the point, who will be handling their money.

You will hear all sorts of stories about independent producers and how they got their pictures made. The only common thread in these stories is money. Now that you have written or acquired the script that you want to produce, put everything else aside and concentrate on one thing and one thing only: FINANCING.

Nothing happens until the cash is in the bank. As a producer, that *must* be your focus. It is at this point that 99 percent of would-be independent producers throw in the towel and give up. Only that very small minority, that 1 percent, will have the tenacity, the guts, the skill, the raw desire to fight for what they want.

If you're part of that 1 percent, it can be done, but don't look for instant gratification. You're in for a long haul, replete with incredible ups and downs and bitter disappointments. Becoming an independent producer is a lot like climbing Mt. Everest. It can be done, but it's damn difficult, and only the toughest and the most dedicated make it to the top. Hopefully, with perseverance and luck, as in most good movies, you will have a happy ending.

The first step in raising money is to analyze the movie you want to make and identify your market. As a first venture, be realistic. Don't try to put together a fifty-million-dollar movie starring Tom Cruise. Unless, of course, you happen to be a close personal friend of Tom's. If that's the case, read no further. Just pick up the phone and call him. Once Tom agrees to do your film, I guarantee you'll have studios knocking down your door to give you all the money you need.

But for the purposes of this book, let's assume you don't know Cruise or Schwartzenegger or Stallone or Hanks or any of the other bankable stars in Hollywood. Let's assume you're just a guy or gal from Des Moines. You're not a multimillionaire, nor do you know any. You've got a job and a family, or maybe you're still in school. But you're a talented writer, or you've found one, and you've got what you feel is a good commercial screenplay. And you want to produce it!

So, here comes the sticky part: ACQUIRING THE FUNDS TO GO INTO THE MOVIE-MAKING BUSINESS.

Now, there are all kinds of movies that one can make: love stories, horror stories, action-adventure, science-fiction, period costume pieces, biographies, detective, high comedy, low comedy, sexually-saturated NC-17-rated, and family-oriented G-rated films, to name a few. You can make a film for a couple of hundred thousand dollars, a couple of hundred million dollars, or anywhere in between.

You will hear some pretty incredible stories about the cost of making movies—people have made features for $10,000 or $20,000 that went on to become big hits. But don't be fooled into trying to emulate this, because in all probability, it never happened.

When you hear of someone who made a movie for $10,000, the real scenario probably went something like this: The producer put up $10,000 of his own money (that's where the ten thousand figure comes from), then borrowed $20,000 from friends and relatives and got another $50,000 in film, equipment, and actor deferments (which means they all get their money out of profits).

So now, that $10,000 film really cost $80,000. But, of course, that's not the end of the story. For a theater-quality release print, one must have a decent sound track, complete with effects and Foley, and a professional musical score. Then, there are the new titles and credits that have to be made, and possibly some re-editing to smooth out some of the rough spots in the film. Maybe a couple of new scenes will have to be shot because of the new editing. The studio or distributor that has bought the rights to this film will have put in an additional two to three hundred thousand dollars to bring that movie up to theater quality, so they can then sell it. What we finally end up with is a ten-thousand dollar film that in reality costs almost a half million.

As we said before, fledgling producers in their first attempt at independent production must have realistic goals. Hopefully, your script will have been designed so that your movie can be shot for less than five million dollars. If not, chapter 4 will explain how to pare down a very expensive story so that it can be produced for the amount of money you have.

Raising one to five million dollars is a realistic goal. At that price, if the finished product is good, your investors should have an excellent chance of making a profit. As a new producer, this is of utmost importance to you. An investor who makes a profit from your first film will be waiting with open arms for your next venture. So will his friends.

THE BIG QUESTION is, how does one go about attracting an investor or a group of investors?

A good salesman convinces his customer that the product is worthwhile and that the investment is reasonably safe. That sounds simple—except when you're talking about motion pictures. Whether or not a product is "good" is completely subjective. And, unfortunately, investing in motion pictures is a notoriously high-risk venture. To sell your product, you must also sell yourself, because, as I said before, you and your product are inextricably tied together.

You must present a sales PACKAGE to the potential investor that will not only enhance his comfort level, but will intrigue him and persuade him, convincingly, to sign his name at the bottom of a check. You will find, as you get deeper into the adventure of raising money, that after all the talk and all the high hopes and all the promises, the toughest thing in the world is to get that signature.

In your pursuit of investors, you should be prepared to spend five to ten thousand dollars, plus innumerable hours, putting together your sales package, or PROSPECTUS. *we can do it cheaper*

I can see all the eyebrows going up. "Where the hell am I gonna get five or ten thousand dollars?" Again, this is where your entrepreneurial skills come into play. There are several ways to finesse that amount of money. You can get a personal loan from friends, relatives, or a bank. You can get a second mortgage on your home. You can sell a piece of jewelry or a painting. And, if you're clever, you can get a lot of the work done on your own computer or on a friend's computer. The object is to explore all avenues.

You will be surprised to see how really inventive you can be. And being inventive is what it's all about. An independent producer cannot be a follower; he *has* to be a leader. He cannot be the one who follows the well-worn path—he must be the one who creates the path.

Now, I'm sure you've heard the old saying, "those who can, do, and those who can't, teach." Not wanting to be part of the latter, we decided that before we wrote this book telling people how to do things, it seemed appropriate that we take our ideas out of the theoretical world and put them into the real world. A test run, if you will, just to make sure that what we write will be based in reality and not on some ethereal academic theorizing.

So, before Paul and I wrote this book, I wrote a screenplay. You will see in the upcoming chapters how all this plays out, in detail, but, in general, here is what I did: First of all, I write a script that I felt would be easy to market, because it was directed at the demographic group that makes up the highest percentage of the movie-going audience, fifteen- to twenty-five-year-olds. The title was "Sex and the Teenage Mind." Two words in the title are there to attract that particular audience, "Sex," and "Teenage." I wrote it with three basic, easy-to-find sets and a minimal number of cast. The ingredients were teenage, sexual angst, a little raunch, and a little nudity. Mix them together with some good-looking kids and voilà, you have an exploitable, low-budget film.

Step One, the screenplay. Okay, that was done. Now, on to Step Two, the prospectus. We did it as described in chapter 2. Frankly, I think it could have been done a lot better, but it sufficed.

Step Three, raising the money. We deal with this in chapter 3. Now, as I said, this was to be a low budget movie . . . I mean a *real* low-budget movie. How does $135,000 sound? That is not very much money for a movie; but, it is still a lot of money when you are looking for venture capital in a very risky arena. I had a business partner in this who found most of the money. How did he do it? The old-fashioned way, he worked for it. He had a sister who put up ten thousand, a couple of friends got together and put up another thirty, I had a relative who put up some more, my partner put in some of his own money . . . and that's how it went . . . small percentages to a lot of people. We also had a couple of friends who wanted to be actors, so, they each put up some money and got a small part plus a percentage for their investment.

Now on to Step 4, which is covered in chapters 8 and 9. First, we hired the director . . . me. I did this for two reasons. One, I work cheap . . . actually, for nothing. You can't get much cheaper than that. Okay, I get a big piece of the action if the movie makes money . . . it is known as betting on the outcome. The second reason was, we had eight days to make this movie. That meant shooting an average of twelve pages a day. Since I had a lot of experience directing television, I felt I was best qualified to do this film. As it turned out, we got a very funny, very good little film and we did it on schedule and on budget.

A film of this kind, with no major stars, will not get a theatrical release, but the sales in home video, television, and cable, both domestic and foreign, will bring us a nice profit. This is important, not just for the money we will make, but for the future. Investors who get their money back and make a profit will be inclined to look favorably on your next venture.

So, there it is, the practical application of what we write about in this book. It can be done. We did it, and we didn't take advantage of any contacts inside the business. We did this film as outsiders would do it, because we wanted to show that it could be done.

Follow the steps outlined in this book . . . we did, and it worked for us . . . it will work for you. You can become the independent producer that you always wanted to be. But, be careful what you wish for . . . it could come true.

2

Developing the Package

Your package is your primary selling tool. Whether you are raising money for a motion picture, real estate, manufacturing, or any one of a thousand other reasons, you will need a prospectus.

Your prospectus *is* your film package, and you will need to assemble the following ingredients: a script, a carefully prepared budget, sketches or photographs of possible location sites, a suggested cast list (stress that you don't actually have these people under contract, even a verbal contract, that the list is simply an example of the stars or personalities you will be attempting to attract), a treatment and/or synopsis, bios of the key personnel, a marketing plan, production schedule, and any charts you can find on current independent movie box office receipts (*Variety* and the *Hollywood Reporter* print them).

Make your binder sturdy, quality stock, conservative. Trying to be too clever or too flashy can have a detrimental effect and actually erode the feelings of confidence you are striving for.

Although there are several different ways to put your prospectus together, the following is one of the more recommended and familiar ways.

Artwork

The first page might be a rendering of the movie poster or ad you envision.

11

Table of Contents

The second page should be your Table of Contents, which should include Executive Summary (Bios), Treatment or Synopsis, Casting Suggestions, Locations, Marketing Plan, Production Schedule, Budget, Legal and Financial Structure, Script.

Executive Summary (Bios)

With today's laptop-publishing capabilities, you can make your bios impressive without being overblown. Hollywood is a small community. Everybody knows everybody, or knows somebody who knows everybody. Don't exaggerate your past positions. A photo of yourself and your co-producer or writer is a nice touch.

Synopsis/Treatment

A synopsis is a one-page, or less, summary of your screenplay. A treatment is a more complete telling of your story, but shouldn't run any longer than five to seven pages.

Cast Suggestions

List the main characters in your screenplay and, underneath each, include the several casting suggestions for each character. List only the two to four star roles. Be realistic in your suggestions. If you're making a two-million-dollar movie, don't list Tom Hanks or Julia Roberts. And be sure that your reader understands that these are *just suggestions* and that you *do not* have these performers tied up. Also, photos are not necessary.

Locations

Photos of possible location sites for the actual filming are usually impressive, because they lend a sense of substance and authenticity to the project. *research*

Marketing Plan

This section is critical to the future success or failure of your project. Making the movie is only part of the scheme. As with any product, it is not enough to just manufacture it; the product must be marketed and sold. Break your plan down into categories: promotional plans; press kits and newspaper exposure; the making and releasing of the picture's trailer; test market plans; sneak previews, if any (possibly in the city or town where the film is shot); poster distribution; how you plan to approach distributors, both foreign and domestic; film markets and festivals you will attend; overseas venues; and ancillary sales, such as home video, in-hotel viewing, and airlines.

Production Schedule

This is, basically, a time line. Investors will want to know how long their money will be tied up and when they can expect to see a return on their investment. The time line begins when the money is in the bank. Pre-production could begin approximately two to four weeks after financing is in place. There can be great variance in this initial time phase, however, depending on the type of story you are doing, the location, and actor and director availability. For example, suppose you are doing a movie that requires snow, and your financing is complete in June. You would have to wait at least four months before you could begin pre-production. Or suppose your movie requires you to shoot in Southeast Asia, and you're funded in October—right at the beginning of the monsoon season. But these delays should not be of concern to your investors. Their money will be safe in an interest-bearing escrow account.

The second phase of the time line is pre-production. The amount of time here will depend on your budget and on the complexity of the story. A high-budget film requiring numerous locations can be in pre-production for six months or more. Generally speaking, a low-to-moderate-budget film would have anywhere from four to eight weeks of pre-production.

Phase three is the production time—how long it takes to actually shoot the film. Again, this depends wholly on budget. In order to properly evaluate the amount of time needed to shoot your movie, it would be in your best interest to hire a qualified production manager to do a script breakdown, schedule, and budget. The cost of this is negotiable. You can figure to spend twenty-five hundred to four thousand dollars for this work. This is part of your initial investment to create the package. The Directors Guild of America will help you to find a qualified production manager.

Budget

The budget is your bible. It is a sacred document that you honor and respect. When you take on the mantle of Producer, you also take on the responsibility of protecting your investors' money. You must always be cognizant of the fact that you are working with *someone else's* money. They have entrusted that money to you, and you are obligated to deliver a good product to them for the amount of money agreed upon.

Therefore, you do not take the budget lightly, and you do not play games with it. A good production manager will develop a budget for you that honestly reflects what your movie will ultimately cost. If you want to make a two-million-dollar picture and the budget comes in at three million, you have only two options. The first is, you raise your sights and try to promote an extra million dollars. Your second option is to rewrite your script so that your film can be made for the two million dollars. There *is* a third option, but it leads to a place where you do not want to go. That is to manipulate your budget so that it will reflect only a two-million-dollar expenditure, even though you know it cannot be made for that figure. This type of deceit has led to the destruction of a lot of careers.

Finally, include only the top sheet of your budget (summary of costs) in your package. It is not necessary, at this point, to include the entire twenty-five to thirty pages of detail. Your top sheet will include all the above-the-line costs (producer, director, writer, and cast) and all the below-the-line costs, which include your crew, equipment, post-production expenses, and miscellaneous expenses, such as contingency, insurance, bonding company, and legal fees.

Legal and Financial Structure

Before putting up his money, the investor will want to know the financial structure of this project, how the percentages are broken down—in other words, who gets what? Will he be involved with a limited partnership or a corporation? What safeguards are in place to protect his investment? What kind of return can he expect from his investment, and how long will he have to wait? These are all questions that need to be answered in your prospectus. And since every project is different, you will need legal advice to design the structure that is appropriate for your particular project.

So, here comes another expense. Again, all part of your original investment in your package. You will need a lawyer who is versed in motion-picture financing. The lawyer will then be able to develop the proper financial structure for your project. Cost for this service is negotiable. If you are paying your lawyer up front, probably a thousand dollars will provide you with all the information you will need for your prospectus. Once the money is raised, then you would be reimbursed for your out-of-pocket costs, and all future legal fees would be charged to the production.

Script

The final element of your prospectus is the script. This is an optional element. Some people like to include it, some do not. Personally, I don't think it is necessary; a treatment is sufficient. Adding the script will make your prospectus rather bulky, and it could be off-putting to some potential investors.

3

Show Me the Money

There are three basic types of financing available to the independent producer: *independent risk capital*, *foreign distribution guarantee*, and *presales to domestic television and home video.* Actually, there is a fourth way to finance your film, and that is through a bank loan. However, this becomes a catch-22 situation. Banks require collateral, but if you had the collateral, you wouldn't need their loan in the first place.

Raising Private Capital

Independent risk capital is the most direct way of going. It affords the producer the least amount of interference in the creative process. Once the money is raised through private sources, you are basically free to make your movie the way you envision it without a lot of outside pressures.

Okay, let's not slide past that phrase, "Once the money is raised," too quickly, because therein lies the crux of the entire financing procedure and, ergo, your whole future in the motion picture business.

I went to a seminar once, at the Directors Guild of America. They had a very distinguished panel of five prominent producers and executives. The subject matter was "How to Raise Money for Independent Films." There were over four hundred people attending this seminar, and as I sat there for three grueling hours, I was struck by the fact that my knowledge of financing was not being advanced one iota. Everyone around me was furiously taking notes—about what, I had not a clue.

The people on the panel were talking in totally abstract dimensions, telling funny and interesting "war" stories, but giving their audience no practical information. At the end of the three hours, there was one overwhelming truth that stood out from the pervasive smog of rhetoric that had blanketed the auditorium. And that truth was—drumroll, please—*find someone with money.*

I kid you not, that was it. Find someone with money. They could have said that in the first two minutes, and I could have enjoyed the rest of the evening at the local bar over several margaritas.

So, let's talk about this "raising the money" issue, because it is at this point that the vast majority of would-be independent producers hit the proverbial wall.

You've done all the preliminaries to this tallest and most formidable hurdle. You have your script, which you have written or have obtained the rights to, and you have your prospectus, which you have invested a great deal of time and money into preparing, and you have built up your confidence as a salesman—no small feat in itself. Now, all that is left is to find "someone with money."

We will now separate the men from the boys and the women from the girls. Somerset Maugham once said, referring to novels, "There are three rules for writing a novel. Unfortunately, no one knows what they are." This also holds true in the world of raising risk capital. It is a world where there are no rules and no holds barred. You do what you have to do—within the limits of the law, of course. Regardless of your passion and desire to become a producer, pulling off a scam and ending up with "Bubba" as your cellmate would certainly be detrimental to your burgeoning career.

Risk capital can be raised from a variety of sources. It can be a group of professionals, such as doctors or lawyers looking for a speculative, high-return investment. Or it can be a wealthy individual, or group of individuals, who have come to a place in life where the risk of making a movie, and the fun of making it, sounds more like an adventure than an investment.

I was involved with a film that was financed by the owner of a major sports team. He liked this particular movie project, and his wife felt it had important social significance. The director was a woman, and she and the owner's wife worked together in the making of the picture—which, by the way, turned out very well. Unfortunately, it was a "message" picture and didn't generate a lot of profit. The owner and his wife never complained, however, and in fact, were proud of their involvement in the making of this film.

Sometimes, financing a film can get more personal than you are comfortable with. I had done a lot of filming in Asia and, consequently, had made a lot of contacts. To digress a moment, remember that word—*contacts*. It is more than just a word; it is an integral part of the motion picture business, and it's as important to your future in this business as talent or luck. Careers can soar to great heights or plummet to the depths because of contacts, or lack of them.

Anyway, getting back to the story. I met a very wealthy Asian gentleman, who, although totally unfamiliar with our business, was somewhat fascinated by it and spent a great deal of time watching us shoot. He would say things like, "I would like to get more involved" and "Maybe I should put some money into a film."

After several months of listening to this, I finally said to him, "I've got a project that's 50 percent funded. Do you want to invest?"

He looked at me for a moment, then reached into his jacket pocket and took out the tiniest checkbook I had ever seen. "How much do you need?"

After he handed me a check for the other 50 percent of the necessary funds, he said, "Are we partners now?"

"As soon as the check clears."

Well, the *size* of the check may have been tiny, but the *amount* wasn't. Sure enough, it cleared, and we made the movie. Now comes the personal part. The real motivation behind his largesse was not his interest in motion pictures or his desire to make a profit from his investment. Oh, no, his motivation was much more devious. What he really wanted was for me to marry his daughter.

Although, I must admit, she was an attractive young lady, marriage was about the furthest thing from my mind. Fortunately, I was able to dance my way around this issue somewhat gracefully—but, then, that's another story.

The reason I relate this anecdote is so you, as an independent producer looking for money, will understand that funding does not always come from predictable sources. And things are not always as they appear to be.

Now, the ugly question arises: "Where do *I* find these people with money? They are out there; I know they are. So, how do I get to them?" My advice to you is to take the "nose to the grindstone, head down and plow forward, damn the torpedoes and full-speed ahead" approach. This is the one that takes guts, gall, chutzpah, determination, courage, and not a small degree of masochism.

It is also known as "beating the bushes."

Here's how it works: You call everyone you know—friends, relatives, acquaintances, and those with whom you have a nodding relationship. If you're like most of us, none of the above will have either the wherewithal, or the interest, to invest in your movie. However—and this is a big "however"—one of these friends, relatives, or acquaintances may have a friend who has a friend who happens to know someone who might be interested.

You see where I'm going with this?

If you do, then you'll see why so many would-be producers simply give up at this point. The task is daunting. You must be willing to put yourself out there, to sell, to plead, to grovel, to promise, to cajole, to compromise, to make a pact with the devil, if need be. Nobody said this was going to be easy!

Everything from this point on revolves around your ability to sell, not only your project, but yourself.

If you keep asking, keep networking, follow every lead no matter how miniscule, never doubt yourself, never lose your self-confidence— then, somewhere down the line, the chance really exists that you will be one of the chosen few, one of that select group of individuals who will grab the golden ring of success.

It can happen in a month, a year, five years . . . or never. That's the chance you take, and only you can decide if the risk is worth it. But you are not just risking the few thousand dollars you have put up. You are risking years of your life and your own emotional well-being. And if you have a spouse, you could be risking your marriage. I don't mean to sound melodramatic, but the motion-picture business is a fertile field for obsession.

Work hard to reach your goals, but never fail to keep your perspective—which is another way of saying, "Don't give up your day job."

The rewards are great for those who make it as an independent producer, but as the saying goes, "If it was easy, anyone could do it." Fighting through discouragement and being able to rebound from bitter disappointment are the attributes you will need to eventually succeed.

Overcoming Sales Resistance

At this point, I think it might be appropriate to discuss some of the resistance you will meet from potential investors. We have said that salesmanship is a big part of the process of raising investment capital, and that salesmanship involves selling yourself as well as selling your project.

Wealthy people with lots of discretionary capital are extremely cautious in how they handle that capital. They didn't get rich by making foolish investments. You will also find that many of them are not averse to taking calculated risks, because in order to get rich, sometimes one has to take those risks.

If you want to separate someone from his money, you must come up with some compelling reasons for him to willingly give up that money. Your prospectus, if it is done properly, should spark some interest on his part. But don't expect anyone to mail you a check because he found your prospectus intriguing.

If a potential investor likes your package, then the real work begins: the face-to-face confrontations. An individual who is considering investing a few hundred thousand, or a few million dollars, will want to look the man, or woman, in the eye and evaluate that person for himself. He will be entrusting you with *his* money, so he will want to know everything about *you* that he can.

This is why it is so important that you be honest and straightforward in everything you discuss. There is an old saying: "If something looks too good to be true, it probably is." You want to sell your motion picture to this individual. You want him to feel comfortable with his investment. You want him to have trust and confidence in you as the producer of this film. But you do not want to get involved with "pie-in-the-sky" hyperbole. Funding a motion picture is a high-risk venture. There is no getting around this fact, so don't make yourself look stupid by telling him there is no risk and he is guaranteed to get his money back, or that he is certain to make a huge profit. The simple fact is, if your investor has gone as far as requesting a meeting with you, he has already done a certain amount of research and is fully aware of the risks involved.

What you have to be prepared for are his reservations about investing in a motion picture and how you can overcome those reservations. What we will discuss now are some of the most common questions that will be put to you by a potential investor and what your responses should be. The fact that many of these questions have already been addressed in your prospectus is irrelevant. He will want answers directly from you.

Questions You Are Sure to Be Asked

If your investor has done his research, which he probably has, one of his first questions to you will be, "Do you have a distributor?" If you have already obtained a distributor, then you simply tell him who that distributor is and relate the details of your agreement with him. If you do not have a distributor in place, then you will need to explain your reasons for not doing so.

Trying to Make Sense Out of Distribution Deals

Although distribution will be discussed in greater detail in chapter 12, I will try to give you some cursory insights into that very complex area of the motion picture business. There are two schools of thought with regard to the distribution of independent films. The first school says you should never go into production until you have a signed distribution deal. The other school says *never* sign a pre-production distribution deal. In a way, I'm inclined to agree with both views. Let me explain. A good distribution deal with a good distributor is a plus. But a bad deal, or an inferior distribution company, is a minus. Even though it could give your investor a level of comfort, it would be a false comfort.

There are virtually no pre-production distribution deals that cannot be abrogated by the distributor if he doesn't like the finished product. So, what you want is to seek a good arrangement with a good company—people who like your movie and are prepared to support it. If not, you are better off waiting until you have something on film that will excite them.

Quite often, when you make a pre-production deal with a distributor, you will have to give up a certain amount of your creative rights. The distributor may demand certain rewrites; he will advise you who to cast and who he will expect to direct. You now have a partner who may not agree with you creatively. It is vital to talk all this out before closing the deal. On the other hand, some distribution companies are very supportive and very helpful. They *do* know what they need to sell a movie. But you need to be aware that if the film turns out to be a bomb because of all their interference, it will still be *your* name that goes up on the screen as the producer, so you will have to shoulder the blame.

If you decide to wait until after your film is completed to sign with a distributor, you might accomplish several things that will be to your advantage and to that of your investors. First of all, you have kept your creative rights intact and produced the motion picture that you envisioned without a lot of outside interference.

When your film is completed, you will be able to hold a screening and invite foreign and domestic distributors, including major studios. They will all come to see your movie. Why not? It's free, and heck, you might even serve sandwiches.

Depending on the quality of your movie, you will have distributors bidding against each other for the rights. But here's the danger: If your film isn't any good, you will not get it distributed. It will simply join the thousands of other movies stored somewhere in Hollywood that will never be shown to a paying audience.

Of course, the fact remains that if your movie is bad, it might not be distributed even *with* a pre-production distribution agreement, no matter what the contract says. Legally, they can open it in some back alley theater and then ship it straight to video.

Finally, there is always the chance that a major studio will pick up your movie on a straight buyout. If a studio sees a well-made film that it feels is promotable, it is to the studio's advantage to pick it up. To make the same motion picture that you make for three million dollars, it would cost any major studio ten million. So if the studio buys it from you for five or six million, it is way ahead of the game, and you and your investors will realize a substantial profit. That's the nicest scenario.

Fighting Off the Horror Stories

Next, your investor will ask you about the horror stories he has heard about films never making a profit, even though they have had huge grosses. He has probably heard the Art Buchwald story regarding *Coming to America,* the Eddie Murphy film for Paramount. Buchwald sued Paramount for plagiarism, claiming the idea for the story was his. He eventually won his suit, but Paramount claimed the movie was still in the red. The film had cost 40 million dollars to produce and, at the time of the lawsuit, had grossed over 140 million. This brought to light something that had long been suspected of Hollywood studios: It is called *creative bookkeeping.*

To counter your investor's fear, you must explain that making an independent film bears no resemblance to how a major studio operates. The costs of your film will be tightly controlled and every expense accounted for. A major studio has the opportunity, if they so desire, to move costs around internally. They also have overhead charges and untold numbers of departmental charges, plus outrageous distribution charges, publicity costs, premiere costs, etc., etc., etc. The independent film is not encumbered with all these ancillary costs. What you see is what you get.

How Much Money Will You Really Need?

Your investor will probably ask you next, "What happens if you go over budget?" Will he be left with an unfinished film, or will you have to come to him and ask for more money? This is a real concern to an investor putting his money into any project, not just motion pictures.

Your answer to him will be that your film will be furnished with a COMPLETION BOND from a reputable bonding company, which will guarantee funds for the completion of your film. "And how does that work?" he will ask. If a motion picture runs over budget, the bonding company provides the necessary financing to finish the film. For this service, they charge a fee of 3 to 6 percent of the film's budget. The fee is negotiable and should be accounted for in your budget. If the bond is not invaded—in other words, you don't go over budget—half of the fee is usually returned.

So, what does the bonding company get out of risking their money? If the bond is not invaded, they collect a hefty fee. But if the production runs out of money, the bonding company, in effect, takes over the film. It now becomes the de facto producer and calls the shots. Which means it can remove the director if it so chooses, or change the script if it feels it will save money, or remove you as the producer. And worse yet, all profits are suspended until the bonding company recovers its costs.

This scenario does not happen often. When preparing your budget, there is always a 10 percent contingency built into it. On a three-million-dollar movie, your actual production and post-production costs would be about two million seven hundred thousand, and you would have a two-hundred-and-seventy-thousand-dollar contingency figure. Also, directors who have worked on bonded films are well aware of the perils involved by invading the bond. If they ever go over budget on a film, they know they are dead meat as far as any bonding company is concerned.

Who is Watching My Money?

The next question will probably be, "Is there any way you can steal my money?" It won't be put to you quite that bluntly, but the meaning will be the same. At this point, you need to explain how the procedure works. Your attorney can lay this out for you in more detail, but simply put, you can tell your investors the following: All investment capital is put into an escrow fund until you are ready to begin pre-production. That money cannot be touched by either you or the investor without the approval of the other. As money is released for the production, all checks must be signed by at least two designated parties, one from the producer's side and one from the investor's side. This insures that the producers cannot abscond with the funds and head for the beaches of Copacabana, and the investors cannot have a sudden change of heart and pull their money out of the project.

Who Can I Trust?

Now comes the big question: "Why should I trust you?" You're pretty much on your own for this one. Trust, we know, is something that is earned. So, the only thing you can do is convince your investor of your honesty, sincerity, and competence. It is a fine line you will have to walk. If you try to tell someone you are honest, they will suspect you are not. If you show them sincerity, they will think it is phony. And if you boast of your competence, they will be certain of your incompetence. The only advice I can give is to be yourself. If you really have the qualities of honesty, sincerity, and competence, your investor will be smart enough to see them.

The Bomb Shelter

Now, the final question he may ask you: "What if the picture's a bomb?" There really is no good answer to this question—at least for you, that is— because you can't tell him that *won't* happen. You are not a fortune teller. All you can do is be honest—oops, there goes that word again. If the movie bombs, he will probably lose a lot of money, maybe all of it. But if he believes in the film as much as you do, and if he believes in you and your ability to pull this off, then the chances are excellent that the film will not only be good artistically, but financially as well.

Dealing With Your Investors

Once you have raised your money, you may think that your troubles are over. Right. *Those* troubles may be over, but now you will be open to a whole new set of troubles. Lucky you—now you have INVESTORS. And who are these people who have placed their hard-earned money into your trembling hands? Well, they can come in all shapes, sizes, races, religions, and from the entire political spectrum, from the far right to the far left and everything in between. And all you have to do as the producer is make sure you don't offend any of them. Because, dear friend, they are holding the purse strings, and your professional life is hanging from those very delicate strings. But sometimes, not offending is easier said than done.

As a producer, you must always be cognizant of the sensitivities of those who are financing your film. The larger the investment group, the less likely you will be bothered with this problem. But if there are only two or three investors, then one must be careful that the wrong buttons are not pushed. Example: If you have a Catholic investor, you will have to think very carefully about that scene in your script that deals with abortion in a favorable light. In fact, you may have to take out the scene altogether. If not, you just may lose an investor.

Or, if your investor is a member of the National Rifle Association and one of the characters in your script extols the virtues of gun control . . . well, you get the picture. Now, you have to decide which is easier, changing the story or finding a new investor. That decision should be a no-brainer. Unless, of course, you have investors waiting in line to take his place. Yeah, sure.

"What about creative integrity?" you ask. Welcome to the real world. Risk capital is hard to come by. Compromise is the operative word. Once you have become a successful producer with a track record of profitable films, then you can exercise your "creative integrity" until the cows come home. Until then, it would behoove you to be reasonable and flexible in your creative demands.

Does this mean you have to abandon all your principals? Not necessarily. Confucius once said (well, he probably didn't, but he could have): For one to eventually enjoy pheasant under glass, in the beginning, one may have to eat a little crow.

In your quest of the ever-elusive risk capital, you may run into that certain gentleman who is sitting on a ton of money and is even willing to give you some of it in order to fund your film. And, as if that weren't enough, he will let you keep total creative control. Wow, a dream come true. Except, there is one little catch—of course, there always is. You see, this guy just happens to have a girlfriend, and she would be just right for the lead in your film—at least, according to him. Heck, she even had the second lead in her high school play, so you know she has to be a good actress.

This situation can lead to a great deal of character development on your part, and I don't mean the character in your film. I mean your own personal character development. Which brings us back to the arena of creative integrity and what you are willing to sacrifice in order to get your picture made. It's a tough call, and one that only you can make. But if you want to be an independent producer, get used to it, because your professional life will be an unending succession of tough decisions. Harry Truman said, "The buck stops here." He was referring to the president of the United States, of course, but it holds just as true for the independent producer. You have the final say. So, you get to accept the brickbats along with the accolades.

Who Gets What?

Now, let's get to the basics of the financial structure of your film when dealing with independent risk capital. There are two basic entities to consider. The first is the financial entity (the investors), and the second is the creative entity (the producers).

Suppose your movie costs three million dollars to produce. The investors will receive 100 percent of all revenue until their three million dollar investment is recouped.

After that, the investors and the producers will split all the remaining revenue, including box office receipts, home video, cable, television, and returns from any other ancillary venues, 50-50 on a pari passu basis. In other words, dollar for dollar. This is standard operating procedure in the independent film world. There are, of course, variations to the above. Some investors will want a 60-40 split, in their favor, naturally. Some will want to recoup 110 percent of their investment before sharing. Others may insist on any deferred monies being paid out of the producer's share. Some will require a stipulation that if a percentage has to be given to an actor, that percentage comes out of the producer's share. All these variations, and others, are negotiable. But if this is your first movie venture and you have interested investors, I don't think I would be too hard-nosed in my negotiations.

Responsibilities

When dealing with independent risk capital, it is important to be very clear as to who will have which areas of responsibility. Quite often, people who invest in movies see themselves as producers and, ultimately, try to take over that position, usually to the detriment of the film and, more importantly, your sanity. One approach you could take when confronted with this situation would be to tell your investor, if he happens to be a doctor, that you promise not perform any surgeries if he promises not to try to produce. Hopefully, he will get the message.

Just make certain that everyone's duties are clearly delineated and that you have retained the film's creative rights for yourself. You will most likely have to cede certain business rights to your investor, and eventually, you'll have to give up some of your rights to a final cut, distribution, and probably even marketing tactics to the distribution company that handles your film.

Knocking at the Studio's Door

There is another avenue open to the independent producer, and that is the STUDIO route. At first glance it may seem like the easiest path to take, but it, too, is fraught with numerous pitfalls. There are some advantages to it, of course, the most important of which is, you don't have to go around scrounging for money. If a studio buys your property, that is taken care of for you.

To properly present a project to a studio, you should definitely look for an agent to represent you. As a novice, you will not have entrée to the upper echelon of executives who are the decision makers. The best you can hope for by presenting your script yourself is to get your property to a low-level reader. Of course, that's better than nothing. But when dealing with a major studio, nothing beats an experienced agent or entertainment attorney.

Getting an agent to represent you is a challenge all by itself. You must be aggressive and persistent. Send your package to twenty different agencies with an introductory letter. There's a good chance that one or two of them will respond. If it's really a terrific script, a lot more will respond.

Just remember, if your agent actually makes a deal with a studio for the script you have written or the one to which you own the rights, you will, in all probability, lose a great deal of your creative control. In some cases, you will be pushed out of the picture entirely. You will make some money, but that could be the extent of your involvement. Major studios spend major bucks on stars and production and will want someone experienced to protect their investment. The upside will be the fact that you will have been involved in the production of a motion picture, and that will certainly open some doors. You have delivered a project. In all future pitches, you will be able to discuss your movie, and executives will listen. You are now a player.

However, if you truly want to be an *independent* producer, never forget what got you in the first place, and keep doing it. The more independent you become, the more studios will want you.

The Entrepreneurial Companies

We discussed how to go about raising private capital and about selling to a major studio. Now, let's discuss another way of getting your film made. There are a multitude of independent, entrepreneurial production companies in Hollywood that deal in low-to-medium-budget films, mainly under ten million dollars.

Most of these companies will look at your package, although you will probably have to sign a "release" first. This protects the company from plagiarism suits. But read this document carefully; all release forms are not the same. In fact, they can vary widely. I would suggest you have a lawyer read it before you sign anything. This may come as a complete shock to you, but there are unscrupulous people out there who are not above taking advantage of the innocent. I know that may be hard to believe, but trust me, it's true.

If one of these companies likes your project, they will option it for a low figure, one thousand to twenty-five hundred dollars for a one-year period, with an option for another year. Then, they will try to put the project together. This means attaching a star—not a major star, but someone in the five-hundred-thousand to one-million-dollar range, depending on the budget of your particular film. They will also try to attach a director, usually a young man or woman who has attracted some attention, but has not yet been offered that "big" picture that will cement his or her reputation.

"Wait a minute," you say. "I was hoping to direct this movie." Bad idea. Unless you are a filmmaker with experience in directing features—and I don't mean student films—you will be doing a disservice, not only to yourself, but to the production company. You need to focus on your producing chores, which will be challenge enough. Trying to direct at the same time is an invitation to disaster. You will not be able to concentrate on your primary function, which is to control the entire production of your film, not just one element of it.

If directing is your ultimate goal, or you wish to become an auteur, learn your craft first. Watch how the professional directors do it before you jump in. Also, since you are not dealing with independent risk capital, but with a production company, it is highly doubtful that they would allow you to take on a dual role.

Once a star and/or a director is in place, the company will then try to secure financing through pre-sales of foreign rights, domestic rights, video sales, and cable sales, as well as seeking private financing. Some companies have revolving loans through banks, which they secure with profits from other films they own.

Each company has its own criteria for what they feel will sell, so even if you get turned down by most of them, there is always one that could say this is what it is looking for.

If your movie is produced, the payoff to the writer will probably be anywhere from seventy-five to a hundred and fifty thousand dollars. If you have written the script or if you own it outright, then, of course, that money is yours. If you own just an option on the script, then that money will, in all likelihood, go to the writer. You, as the producer, will have to make your own deal. Producing fees will depend on your film's budget and on how many producers will be attached. What? You think you will be the only one? Forget it. A company putting up the money will not allow a first-time producer to go off on his own. They will put another producer with you, or an executive producer, or maybe both. Again, it all depends on the budget and on the complexity of the film. Also, as the one who brought in the package, you should be entitled to a percentage of the profits. It would probably be no more than 10 percent at most, but again, this is a negotiable item.

So, who are these companies, and how do you get to them? There are several different ways. The two most widely read industry newspapers, *Daily Variety* and the *Hollywood Reporter* list companies with films in preparation. They also have special market issues during the American Film Market (AFM), the Cannes Film Festival, the Milan Film Festival, and MIFED and MIPED. These issues generally list all companies who buy and sell product. Back issues of *Variety* and the *Reporter* can be obtained by calling the newspaper.

Another method of finding production companies is—and don't laugh—the Yellow Pages. A lot of companies are listed there. But one of the best sources is the American Film Marketing Association, headquartered in Los Angeles. If you write or phone them, they will not only send you a list of all their member companies, they will also include phone numbers, addresses, and who to contact. Now, that is a very important consideration, who to contact. Sending your script to the wrong person in an organization can cost you weeks of valuable time and tons of unnecessary frustration.

Each company will list its top officers and their titles. I don't recommend trying to contact the chairman of the board or the president of the company, unless, of course, it is a very small company and those are the only officers listed. The chairman or the president will probably not have the time nor the inclination to read your script. They will pass it on down the line, until it will eventually get to the right person. But this can take weeks, even months. And in a worst-case scenario, your precious screenplay could disappear altogether.

The key words to look for in the list of officers are DEVELOPMENT, CREATIVE AFFAIRS, and PRODUCTION. In front of these words, you will usually find either VP IN CHARGE OF or DIRECTOR OF. These are the people who are responsible for finding properties and making deals. You want to stay away from titles with the word ACQUISITIONS in them. Generally, these people are looking for completed or nearly completed films.

If you have a low-to-medium-budget project, next to getting your own private financing, one of these entrepreneurial production companies would most likely be your best alternative. But the process is long, tedious and frustrating. Don't look for instant gratification; it doesn't exist. *One Flew Over the Cuckoo's Nest* took eleven years to make it to the screen. Two to five years is about normal. And this goes for films that are financed with private capital as well.

There are so many elements to the puzzle that getting them to all fall into place is sometimes mind-boggling. Putting together a package is anything but an exact science. And the paper needed for all the legal work could level a forest. Unlike a jigsaw puzzle, once you put a piece into your movie puzzle, it doesn't necessarily mean that it will stay. Actors and directors can fall out; investors you thought were locked in can disappear; locations can suddenly become unavailable; events can happen outside your control that make certain scenes in your story, and sometimes the whole story, irrelevant. And these are just a few of the things that can happen. So, when we say two to five years to get a project off the ground, it is truly not a very long period of time.

Other Trails to Follow

As you proceed down the many paths you will have to follow in order to get your movie financed, the term PRE-SALE will periodically pop up. There are several different types of pre-sales, such as FOREIGN PRE-SALES, HOME VIDEO PRE-SALES, including DVDs, which have already overtaken videotape in popularity, and TELEVISION PRE-SALES.

Pre-sales, however, can be a tricky business. As with most things in life, a lot will depend on what you have to offer. If you are doing a low-budget movie with no star power, you may have a difficult time pre-selling your film. It can be done, but it takes a lot more effort. Star power is not the only thing that enters into the equation. Subject matter and quality of product can affect your sale, sometimes positively, sometimes negatively. The point is, don't hang all your hopes on pre-sales. If it doesn't work out, don't get discouraged, just push on to your other alternatives.

A foreign distributor, if he likes your project, can provide you with a GUARANTEE OF FOREIGN SALES. This can be very important to you in securing financing for your film. If the distributor is one of the select group of firms with a strong reputation and a good working relationship with one or more major banking institutions, he can obtain a BANKABLE GUARANTEE for you. This is almost as good as cash, because based on that guarantee, a bank will loan you up to the full amount of the guarantee, if you also have a COMPLETION BOND. Now, that guarantee may not cover the full cost of production, but it will certainly be a good start.

Even if the foreign distribution company that you do business with is not able to get you a bankable guarantee, if it is a well-respected company, an investor may still feel comfortable enough to advance monies based on those implied guarantees.

Most foreign sales people are actively looking for product and are willing to be helpful. But let's face it, it's not necessarily altruistic on their part; it's how they make their livelihood. They need product; that is a given. But they are also deluged with projects, so they are extremely busy and have only a limited amount of time. If they are going to invest that time, and their money, they want to be pretty darn sure that they are investing it in the most viable projects.

It is your job to convince them that your project is worth pursuing.

CASTING is extremely important when it comes to foreign sales. If you can attach an actor, someone who has name recognition with foreign moviegoers, your project will jump to the top of the heap. If there are no names attached, you will start at the bottom. Your foreign sales rep will need to see your prospectus, along with that all-important suggested cast list.

It would be worth your time to meet with CASTING DIRECTORS, the people who actually cast movies. Their ideas for casting your film can be very helpful. You might work out a deal for their involvement if your movie goes forward, as an inducement for them to read your script. Casting directors are also a valuable source of contacts to key agents and business managers.

Clue: Personal conversations with foreign sales people are more important than you can imagine. They regard personal contacts much more highly than do Americans. Additionally, you will learn from them what actors they consider meaningful to the European, Asian, and Latin American markets. This will be a real eye-opener for you. Star names that you think would automatically insure a film's success can have a negligible impact overseas. And some actors, relatively unknown in this country, can be of significant value in getting your picture pre-sold in the foreign marketplace.

An example is Mickey Rourke. His pictures could not generate any U.S. box office, but did phenomenally well in Europe. So well, in fact, that his films showed a profit regardless of what they did in America.

Another actor who comes to mind is Jackie Chan. He was a virtual unknown in this country, but his films were huge box office successes throughout Europe and Asia. It didn't take long for distributors to create a revenue base for Chan in this country. To create this base, distributors knew that Jackie would have to make a movie with a "Hollywood" star—in this case, Chris Tucker. The upshot was a highly successful film called *Rush Hour.* It was so successful that it was followed up by *Rush Hour II,* also very successful. Jackie Chan is on his way to becoming a bankable U.S. star. Antonio Banderas is another example of a foreign star who has become a real power in both the U.S. as well as international markets.

If you can visit the American Film Market (a little pricey, but worth it) or any of the dozens of international film festivals held around the world, it would be helpful for you to see who's up-and-coming in the world marketplace.

Other Pre-Sale Markets

The other major source of pre-sales is the HOME VIDEO AND TELEVISION markets. Making a pre-sale to a major television network is not likely, especially if you are making a low-to-medium-budget independent film. Sometimes, pre-production deals are made for very-high-profile films, but even those are rare. The possibility does exist for making a pre-sale to one of the premiere cable networks, such as HBO or Showtime. This will depend on the story content of your film and the performers attached. Each cable network has its own particular criteria for successful programming, and they are rather inflexible.

You will probably have better luck making a pre-sale to one of the home video companies. But even though these companies are in a constant search for product, it is more difficult to make a home video deal without some kind of distribution guarantee.

Also, you need to be aware that the home video industry has changed considerably in the past few years. There was a time that you could anticipate getting about half of your budget dollars through a home video pre-sale. The market is notably tighter today, although the increased quality of DVDs over the traditional tape has provided the home viewer with a theater-like caliber of projection. It also provides additional entertainment value not available on cassettes, such as interviews with the director and stars, behind-the-scenes footage, and outtakes, to name a few. The producer's involvement with the auxiliary material for a DVD varies. On a big budget film the producer could allocate money to be spent on filming interviews and for additional editing, scoring, and dubbing. On a lower budget film, existing footage would probably be used and the distributor would more than likely control that aspect of the DVD. It may take a lot more hard work to accomplish your goals. Yet, the money is there for those who are willing to put out that extra effort.

Your first duty is to obtain a list of home video and television markets. Then comes the boring part—not only boring, but aggravating, tiresome, and frustrating. You will have to contact each of them, one-by-tedious-one. Your mission (should you be willing to accept) will be to convince them that your project is better than anyone else's and that they would be making an incredibly bad business decision not to get in on this wonderful motion picture venture. And, hopefully, you can do all this without self-destructing.

In Conclusion

So, ladies and gentlemen, future entrepreneurs, future producers, there you have it. The highway is wide open, albeit strewn with potholes, barricades, broken-down vehicles, and of course, broken dreams. But this is the course you have chosen. So what if money is tough to find. So what if you have to call everybody and his uncle—people you like, people you hate, people you don't even know. So what if you have to beg, plead, cajole, badger, make a total nuisance of yourself, put on your best dog-and-pony show. So what?

Show business is your life, or at least you want it to be. Well, this is part of it. Hell, this is *most* of it. As an independent producer, you will spend 90 percent of your time raising money, and 10 percent actually making movies.

Keep your world in perspective. Your focus must be on raising the money. In the real world, in which we all find ourselves, while you are in the process of raising risk capital, you are only a promoter. But when the money is in the bank, then you have earned the right to call yourself a producer.

The Producer and the Writer

In the making of a motion picture, the producer becomes intimately involved with three distinct creative forces: the WRITER, the DIRECTOR, and the ACTOR. In order for a film to have a chance for artistic, as well as financial success, the chemistry between the producer and the other creative entities must be symbiotic. This synergy is orchestrated by the producer. He becomes the driving force behind a cohesive, smooth, running production company. This is not to say that there can never be disagreements between creative people. The mere fact that they are creative provides fertile soil for all kinds of disagreements.

A strong, grounded producer will be able to maintain a good sense of balance and keep any disagreements from escalating into open warfare. It falls upon the man or woman taking on the mantle of Independent Producer to become a paragon of tact and diplomacy, while keeping at the ready an ironclad fist, perhaps cloaked in velvet. The latter, he knows, is to be used only as a last resort, but use it he will when all else has failed.

The first, and probably the most intimate relationship a producer will have is with the writer. This is why it is important for you, as the producer, not only to understand the writer, but to understand *writing.* And not just any writing, but a very specific and unique kind of writing: the SCREENPLAY.

Getting to Know Your Writer

No matter what type of motion picture we are talking about—a one-hundred-million-dollar super-epic or a one-hundred-thousand-dollar black-and-white art film—it all starts with the same seminal creative process: the written word. Before God created the earth, there was a void. And so it was that before the writer created the screenplay, there was also a void. Raymond Chandler, the famous mystery writer, probably said it most succinctly: "The basic art of the motion picture is the screenplay. It is fundamental; without it there is nothing."

Let's start, first, with your understanding of the WRITER. As a producer, your initial contact with a writer can begin in several different ways. A friend of yours brings you a script, or an acquaintance brings you a script written by someone you don't know, or someone sends you a script because they have heard that you are looking for one. Or maybe you have an idea for a story, and you hire or go into a partnership with a writer to do the screenplay.

Whatever the method, or whatever point of development the script is in, you will suddenly find yourself in bed (figuratively speaking, of course) with that strange and unique creature called a writer. So, it is important for you, as a producer, to understand where the writer is coming from, especially the *screenwriter*. In the motion picture business, stars are photographed and drooled over. The director is lionized and thrust onto stratospheric pedestals. Even producers are fawned over and canonized. And writers are . . . Who? What was that? Writer? What does he do?

Somewhere along the way, priorities got kind of screwed up. Most audiences are simply unaware that every word the actor says, every direction the director gives, every production value the producer provides starts with the . . . yes . . . that's it . . . the WRITER. Which reminds me of Rodney Dangerfield's famous line, "I don't get no respect." Well, writers are pretty much in the same creaky boat.

Needless to say, writers can become somewhat touchy when the subject of their worth comes up. And that feeling is understandable, even though they are very well paid for their work. It is just the lack of recognition for what they do that is painful.

Writing is hard work, and it is among the most demanding of the creative arts—and the most unique. It is the only art form that starts with nothing. Think about it. All the other arts have a basis from which to start. Painting and sculpting have models. Musicians, singers, and dancers have music from which to interpret their art. Directors and actors have the written word. It is only the writer who starts from zero. All he has is a blank sheet of paper and his imagination. So, be gentle with the writer. Be cognizant of his or her feelings and peccadilloes, both large and small.

How to Read a Script

Everyone who reads a script reads it through different eyes. The actor reads the dialogue and envisions his own performance. The director reads it, not only for the dialogue, but for the visuals the script presents. The casting director sees only what actor would fit each part. The costumer reads it with an eye for the wardrobe—what challenges and opportunities does this story offer. The propman reads it to see what props he will have to buy or manufacture. And so it goes. *Nobody involved in the making of a motion picture reads a script for entertainment.*

As a producer, it is critical that you understand this fact. Screenplays are unlike any other form of writing. They are written with the express purpose of being transposed to a different medium. A novel, short story, or poem is written only for the reader's enjoyment. Not so with a screenplay. A screenplay is *a book of directions.* It is designed to explain to a lot of different people how to transfer a story from the written page to the motion picture screen. Therefore, a screenplay is written on two very distinct levels: the creative level and the nuts-and-bolts level.

Do not be seduced by a screenplay's NARRATIVE.

The narrative portions of a screenplay, in case you didn't know, are the descriptive passages—in other words, everything but the dialogue. Now, the reason I say don't be seduced by the narrative is because the narrative *does not show up on the screen.* STORY AND DIALOGUE—these are the most important elements in a screenplay, and these are what you should zero in on when you are looking for a script to buy or to option. Some writers will create such sparkling, fresh, clever, and engaging narrative that reading their scripts will be a delight, and you could be charmed into thinking that this is a really great script. Well, maybe it is . . . and then again, maybe it isn't.

Read the dialogue. That is what the audience will hear. Remember, they don't get to read the script. They don't get to enjoy all that clever narrative. All they will know about your motion picture—the characters and the story—is what they hear the actors say.

Buying a script is much like buying any other product. If you buy a home or a piece of furniture that looks great on the outside, but is cheaply constructed with inferior materials, it will quickly fall apart. Approach the script you wish to buy the same way you would if you were buying a home or piece of furniture. Make sure it is constructed properly and that the materials (the story and dialogue) are of the highest quality.

Choosing the Right Script

Selecting the script for your first venture can be a humbling experience. It's like standing over an eight-foot putt in front of a hundred thousand people to win the Masters. The slightest error in judgment, and you not only embarrass yourself, you blow the whole tournament—which, in your case, could be your career. So, you want to be as certain as one can be that you have made the right decision in the selection of a script.

With this in mind, as an independent producer, what do you look for in your search for the perfect script? First of all, you make a decision on what genre of film you want to do, what kind of budget you want to work with, and what market you are going after. You must have a direction and a goal on which to focus. All of these elements must be in sync.

Let's say you want to do a horror film for three million dollars, and your market audience will be early teens through mid-twenties. You find a great script, but it has a ton of computer-generated special effects, and the leading characters are in their forties. You now have some interesting choices to make. You really like the script, so you begin to think, Well, maybe I can raise ten million instead of three, and we'll go after a more mature audience. What you *should* be thinking is, It's really a good script, but I think I'll pass and wait until I can find one I can make for the three million.

This is what I mean by focus. Raising three million dollars is a realistic goal. Upping the ante to ten million could blow you right out of the ballpark. Make a game plan and stick to it. *Find the script that fits your plan. Don't keep changing your plan to fit the script.*

As an initiate in the world of independent producing, I highly recommend that you start with a modestly priced project. High-concept scripts with major stars are enormously expensive. Trying to get one of these very costly projects off the ground, especially when you don't have access to the movers and shakers in this business, is an enormously difficult task. Yes, it can be done, but you can also win the lottery. When you are first learning to swim, you want to start out in a pool of dolphins, not a pool of sharks. You want to be the diner, not the dinner.

High-Budget vs. Low-Budget Films And How to Tell the Difference

As an independent producer, it is important that you understand the basic differences between high-budget and low-budget films, besides the obvious difference, which is money. High-budget films will have at least one of three very necessary elements. These films will be either *actor-driven, story-driven,* or *effects-driven* (and sometimes all three). In other words, they will have major stars such as Tom Hanks, Jack Nicholson, Julia Roberts, or

Cameron Diaz. Or the movie will be based on a best-selling novel or a Broadway play. Or they will have enormously expensive special effects, such as computer-generated dinosaurs, space ships, or natural disasters.

Low-budget movies, by their nature, will not include any of the above. But this is the arena in which you will probably be playing. So, how are you going to entice the ticket-buying public to shell out their seven or eight bucks to see your movie? You can't afford Tom Hanks, you can't afford to buy a best-selling novel, and you can't afford computer-generated imagery. Nevertheless, you have to put something up on the screen that the movie-going public cannot get at home on their television sets.

It all starts with the story. Just because you are not spending a lot of money doesn't mean you can't have a great story. And if you tell that story in an interesting and compelling way, there will be an audience out there that will embrace your film. Unique and creative casting is almost as important as the story. You don't have to have big stars, but you do have to have good actors.

Sling Blade was an example of a low-budget film with no stars, but with really fine actors relating a powerful story. There are, of course, other avenues for you, as a producer, to explore. Sex and nudity can be used as a hook for low-budget films. I'm not talking about pornography, but about a good story that happens to have sexual content. It is definitely a way to go, and can be a major asset when it comes to foreign sales and home video sales.

Selecting the Low-Budget Script

Look for a quality script that can be made for a reasonably low budget, two to five million dollars. "Okay," you ask, "how do I know a film can be made for the money I'm raising?"

There are a few simple rules to follow. The first is, you are not going to try to raise money until you have a script. Having a script means that you have either written it yourself, you own an option on a script, or you own the script outright. If you have taken an option on a script, make sure that some money has exchanged hands, even if it's only a hundred dollars. Don't get a free option and think you have made a great deal. You haven't. The writer can sell the script out from under you, and you will find yourself on very shaky legal ground. Talk to your lawyer about this. Again, expenses for legal advice come under the seed money you will need to get started.

As you search for the right script, don't read it with too many different hats on. Wear your producer's hat only. Your first objective is to find a great script, one that you, as a producer, will want to make into a motion picture. So, read your scripts with only that thought in mind, because if you don't like the script, all the steps that follow are moot.

All right, now you have selected that one script that you can feel passionate about, the one script that you really want to produce. Good. Now, read it again. The first time, you read it creatively. This time you read it from a nuts-and-bolts perspective. All part of the job of an independent producer.

Let's say your game plan is to make a low-budget film for three million dollars. This is the amount of money you feel you can raise. Following are some of the major points you should look at when evaluating the cost of your film.

Cast

Your total cast costs should not exceed one million dollars. The cost of your lead characters will determine how many supporting cast players you will be able to afford. Make a list of the characters in your script. If there are more than thirty to thirty-five speaking parts, look for areas in the script where speaking parts can be eliminated or combined.

Locations and Sets

On a three-million-dollar budget, you will not be able to afford exotic locations such as Paris or Rome or, for that matter, New York City. Moving a shooting company around can be very expensive. You will not only be paying transportation costs, but your crew will be on payroll while they are traveling. On a low-budget film, that is money down the toilet. Individual locations should be kept to a minimum, so you don't spend a lot of time in transit.

Now, the sets within your locations should also be at a minimum. For a low-budget film, you will not be able to afford to build sets, so you must rely on what are called *practical* sets. In other words, if you need a living room in which to shoot, you go out and rent someone's house for the day or two days, or whatever it takes. Here again, you have to analyze the sets in your script. If your story requires a mansion, this can be very expensive, up to ten thousand dollars for a day's shooting. If you need to shoot in a large hotel, the costs will usually *start* at ten thousand dollars. Yachts are also very expensive, as are restaurants, which may have to close to accommodate your company. Of course, you will have to pay for that closure, which means that whatever you have cost them in lost revenue for that day is on your tab. The list goes on and on, but I think you get the idea.

Period of Story

Does your script take place in the present, or in the 1920s, or maybe the 1890s? Anytime you move out of the present, the costs escalate dramatically. Take wardrobe, for example. On a low-budget film, you will spend approximately fifteen to twenty thousand dollars on clothes. That would be for rentals and purchases. If the story takes place in the 1920s, that fifteen thousand could easily escalate to a hundred thousand. That's because almost all of your wardrobe will have to be custom-made.

Automobiles are another example. A modern car can be rented for fifty to a hundred and fifty dollars a day. A 1920s car could cost up to a thousand dollars a day to rent.

If you are renting a home to shoot in, you would probably use the existing furniture, which would be included in the rental of the house. However, if it is a period film, you would have to replace all the furniture with rentals from a rental house that specializes in old furniture. This could run into thousands of dollars.

Are you beginning to get the picture here? Hairstyles are different, which will mean hiring additional hairdressers. If you are shooting in the streets, you will have to hire extra police to block off sections of the street, so that you will not see modern vehicles. I could probably go on for another three pages, but suffice it to say, *if you are making a low-budget film, make sure it is a present-day story.*

Special Effects

There are basically two kinds of special effects in motion pictures, and both are very expensive. Live-action effects are those that are done while the company is filming. These will involve such things as explosions, bullet effects, rain towers, and snowmaking equipment, rigging cars to turn over, rigging people to "fly," sinking boats, and creating boiling "lava."

Effects that are done in post-production are called C.G.I., which stands for Computer-Generated Imagery. The dinosaurs in *Jurassic Park*, the "morphing" in *Terminator II*, some of Jim Carrey's antics in *The Mask*—these are all examples of C.G.I. The cost of this type of technology can literally run into the millions. Need I say more?

Other Considerations

The above-mentioned items are the primary things to look for when analyzing your script for cost. There are numerous other smaller considerations to take into account. Night shooting is much more costly than day shooting. You will need more lighting equipment, a larger crew, and it will take longer to shoot a scene, which means more overtime. Scenes shot in a moving vehicle will take three times as long as the same scene shot in a stationary setting. If you have to shoot in real snow, your company will be slowed down considerably, due to the cold and the difficulty of moving equipment around in that environment.

If all this confuses you, there is a simple solution, which I mentioned earlier. Give the script that you are considering buying to a professional production manager. A production manager will break down your script and give you a preliminary schedule, and from that, he will provide you with a production budget. He will need to know from you the amount of money you want to spend, so he will be able to prepare the correct production schedule. A three-million-dollar budget should have approximately twenty-five to thirty shooting days. Once this is established, he will then create the budget.

On his first run at a budget, a good production manager will take the script literally and put in all the costs relevant to that script. The resulting budget may end up a lot higher than the amount of money you want to spend. At this point, you will sit with the production manager, and he will go over all the problem areas with you.

Now, it is up to you. You will either make the necessary changes yourself, or you will call in your writer and have him do it. Either way, changes must be made if you are going to bring the budget into alignment with the amount of money you have to spend. This is why it is so important for you, as the producer, to understand not only the writing process, but how that process relates to your budget.

Understanding Your Budget

The producer's work is not compartmentalized. His focus cannot be on just one area of the filmmaking process. The producer must have a cognitive, overall, panoramic view of the entire process, because, in fact, he is responsible for the entire process and, ultimately, the final outcome of the motion picture itself.

Before attacking your budget, you should learn its nomenclature. Budgets are something that you will live with your entire life in this business. So, get to know them as well as you know your spouse. The financial soundness of every movie you ever make will depend on how well your budget is prepared. The more intimately you know your way around a budget, the more comfortable you will become as a producer.

Motion picture budgets are divided into two separate parts, referred to as ABOVE-THE-LINE and BELOW-THE-LINE. The above-the-line consists of the creative elements of the film: writer, producer, director, and cast. The below-the-line takes in everything else: the crew, equipment, film stock, developing, post-production, and all the publicity, legal, and miscellaneous expenses.

Adjusting the Budget to Fit the Money Above-the-Line

Cutting the above-the-line costs is a relatively easy task. On a low-budget film, your writer and director are usually hired at guild minimums, so there isn't much you can do with those costs. Look at your cast costs. What you have allotted for leading roles may have to be trimmed back—painful, but necessary. Also, the number of roles may have to be scaled back, with some parts being combined.

That brings us to the Producer category. Now, if you think cutting back on money for actors is painful, wait till you have to take money out of your own pocket. But take it you must. Besides allocating money for yourself, as the producer, there will also be money needed for the executive producers. "What executive producers?" you ask, aghast at the thought.

Let's look at the reality of independent production. You are going to raise money. Those people from whom you have just extracted a few million dollars will very likely want a little gravy on their mashed potatoes. In other words, they will, in all probability, want an Executive Producer title. This will be no skin off your creative nose. They want the title so they can show off to their friends or their wife or their girlfriend, or all three. They will not be producers in any real sense, but for the money they are putting up, they deserve the title. Rarely do these people ever want to be involved in the actual making of the movie.

Another form of executive producer can be found in the person who *finds* the investor for you. This person will receive a "finder's fee" and, in many cases, will also want an executive producer title. Fine, give it to him. You can put as many E.P.s up there as you want. But it will be you that will run the show.

Your first inclination when budgeting will be to allocate a generous salary for yourself. Just be prepared to scale that back as far as is necessary to get your film made.

Adjusting Below-the-Line Costs

Cutting below-the-line (B-T-L) costs is infinitely more difficult than cutting above-the-line (A-T-L). This is where the producer's ingenuity and creativity come into play. Previously, I discussed some of the things to look for when you are evaluating a script you are thinking of buying. Now, we will discuss how to change those expensive elements into something more in keeping with your budget.

The examples I am going to give you are generic, since we have no specific script to discuss. But what I want you to grasp is the concept of changing, redesigning, altering your script without destroying the fabric of the story.

Suppose there is a scene in your script that calls for a party that takes place on a large yacht. The sequence is ten pages long, takes place at night, and requires a couple of hundred extras, all in tuxedos and evening gowns. The major costs here are: the rental of the yacht (about ten to fifteen thousand dollars a day), the two hundred extras in dress clothes, and night shooting, which requires more crew and equipment and slows down the pace of shooting. Ten pages of night shooting would take about four nights to complete.

Okay, a party is essential to your story. But the question you ask is, "Is this *kind* of party essential?" The answer is usually, no. If, however, this kind of party *is* essential, then you have picked the wrong script, because that sequence alone will probably cost you over a quarter of a million dollars to film. Not a lot of money if you're shooting a forty-million-dollar film, but disastrous for one that costs three million.

Okay, so what do you, as the producer, have to change so that this sequence will fit into your three-million-dollar budget? First of all, you change the location. Since you can't afford a yacht, you pick another location for your party that you can afford. Someplace cheap. How about a park, maybe near a lake? Next, you change the sequence from night to day—Sunday afternoons are nice for a party. Instead of 200 hundred extras in formal attire, you will have 50 extras in jeans or shorts. And instead of taking four nights to shoot the scene, you will do it in two days. The costs have now dropped from a quarter of a million dollars to less than seventy-five thousand. Do you get the gist of what is going on here?

Let me give you another example of creative cost cutting. In *Prizzi's Honor,* which was a high-budget film, they used a clever device and saved a lot of money, even though that was not their reason for using the device. In the film, Jack Nicholson had to fly back and forth from New York to Los Angeles several times. To get this story point across, they showed a stock shot of an airliner traveling from right to left for the New York to Los Angeles flight, and then, a stock shot of an airliner flying from left to right for the Los Angeles to New York trip. This was a very simple device, and after the first couple of times it was used, the audience caught on and would howl with laughter, loving the audacity of the storytelling.

When talking of budget cutting, the physical elements you use to actually make your movie cannot be overlooked. The standard for theatrical films is a motion picture camera using 35mm film. There is a huge variance in the cost of renting a camera and of buying and developing film. If you are clever and willing to put in the time and effort, you can get your hands on a motion picture camera at virtually no cost, or a very minimal charge. When I shot my little movie, which I described in chapter 1, we went to one of the premiere rental companies in Hollywood. I told them what I wanted, for how long I would need a camera, and that this was an extremely low-budget movie so there was no way I could meet their standard rental fee.

Now, I was fortunate in that I shot my film in the late spring, which is usually a slow time for rental companies. They had cameras they weren't using and agreed to lend us one, including lenses, free of charge. I was, frankly, surprised, but gratefully accepted. Why did they do this? I'm not sure. But, one reason could be that there were no out-of-pocket expenses for them, and if I did a good movie, I would probably do more, and of course, I would rent from them.

Buying film is another matter. Raw stock goes for about forty-five cents a foot. But you can buy short ends for about a third of that. Short ends mean that you won't get a full thousand foot roll, but you can get four-hundred- to eight-hundred-foot rolls, and you will save a lot of money.

There is also the alternative of shooting your movie on video. But you should carefully consider this before committing yourself to this medium. While you will probably save a lot of money, it will greatly reduce your chances of ever getting a theatrical release, either domestic or foreign. Even if you try to transfer tape to film, the results are seldom theater quality.

There are new forms of video cameras that are far superior to what was previously available. Sony has developed a twenty-four frame digital video camera, that, when used properly, produces quality almost equal to film. In fact, it would take someone knowledgeable in the field to tell the difference. George Lucas used these Sony cameras in *Star Wars, Episode II* to great effect. And while filming the last season of the television series *Diagnosis Murder* for CBS, we used the Sony. Everyone at the network was amazed at the film-like quality of the show.

However, the digital camera does have its drawbacks. The cost of renting one is far more than that for a standard motion picture camera. Also, because it is video, the depth of field is far greater than film, and unless you have a cinematographer who understands how to light for this medium and which lenses to use, you could end up with a film that is flat and uninteresting to look at.

Keep in mind, there is always an alternate way to do anything. Storytelling on film is a malleable art form. When you have lots of money to spend, it doesn't take creative genius to tell your story. It is only when money is very tight that one must become creative to the nth degree. You learn a great deal about creative storytelling when you become involved in television or low-budget features.

I was doing a television show that involved a truck crashing into a busload of people. This was a major story point, but unfortunately, it was also a major stunt that would cost a major amount of money, which, in television, you don't have. So, we did the next best thing. The scene started inside a diner. We hear a horrific offstage crash. People run to the window. Others rush in from outside yelling for someone to call 911. We hear ambulance and police car sirens. We see reflections of fire in the glass. We hear people screaming. The audience knows there was a terrible accident, even though we never actually show it.

"What a terrible cheat," you say. "It would've been much better to see the crash." No kidding. I didn't say the alternative would always be as good. Sometimes it will, sometimes it won't. *But you do what you have to do to get the story on film for the money you have to spend.* As a producer, that is something you better remember. Spending money you don't have is the shortest route to oblivion.

Don't Be Trendy

There is one more thing we need to discuss when it comes to selecting the script that you want to produce. You will hear the word "trend" bandied about a great deal. People love to talk about trends. "The trend is action-adventure." "The trend is romantic comedy." "The trend is teenage gross-out." Whatever it is, there will always be a trend. If you get in on a burgeoning trend, one that is just developing, that can be a stroke of luck for you. But don't count on it.

The truth of the matter is, if you are astute enough to discern a particular trend, and if you happen to come across a script that is in that groove and you love the script—well, hey, all the pieces are falling into place, right? *Wrong.* By the time you buy the rights to the script, raise all the money, cast your movie, shoot it, and do all the post-production necessary to finish your film, that trend you were so clever to figure out will be long gone, and another will have taken its place. And *that* trend, unfortunately, could be about 180 degrees from your movie.

So, the best advice I can give you is to follow your instincts. Go for the best script you can find, regardless of the subject matter (as long as that subject matter will fit into your budget). Who knows, maybe *you* will become the trendsetter. That is a lot better position to be in than trying to get in on the tail end of a trend that is waning.

There is an audience out there for virtually any type of film that is made. If you make a good film and you market it correctly, you will find an audience for it. And more importantly, that audience will find your film.

So, now, like a latter-day Don Quixote, you will go in search of your glorious quest—not to reach the unreachable star nor to beat the unbeatable foe, but to find the one extraordinary script that is absolutely perfect for you.

5

The Producer
and the Director

You have now settled on the script you want to produce. You own the rights to it, a production manager has made a budget for you, and you have raised the money you need to make your movie.

Your next goal is to find the DIRECTOR. Before you think of cast or crew or locations or, for that matter, anything else, you concentrate on finding a director for your film.

Finding the right director can be a formidable task. But it is crucial to the success of your film. You must develop a set of criteria by which to judge the person to whom you will give the responsibility of taking your script and, from it, creating an exciting visual experience.

Directing a motion picture is an awesome responsibility. The director on a film is the captain of the ship. He bears the ultimate accountability for the success or failure of the film, and his word on the set is law. It is at this point that the lines of responsibility in decision making become somewhat blurred.

Resolving Conflicts

"I'm the producer," you say. "I should have the final word on anything that affects my picture." Well, yeah, you should, but it just doesn't always work that way. This is why the selection process is so critical. The director must be able to think independently, yet be in concert with you, as the producer, on all the major aspects of your film. This means you must both be in agreement with the fabric of the story. You both want to make the same film, so you agree on the main story arc, you agree on the subplots and their level of importance, and you agree on the main characters and how those characters should be portrayed.

All of this is done up front, *before* you commit to a director. If there are areas of unresolved disagreements, these areas will not suddenly resolve themselves after a contract has been signed. As a matter of fact, they will only get worse. One of the most destructive things that can happen during the making of a motion picture is a contentious relationship between producer and director.

The producer, of course, holds the trump card, because after the director has had his cut of the film, the producer can usually do pretty much what he wants with it. But the director also knows this, so there are certain things he can do while directing to mitigate changes that he doesn't want. You will hear the term *camera cutting.* This means that the director can shoot a scene in such a way that the editor has no latitude, but must put the film together in a specific way. This is done by stopping a master scene at a certain point, so the editor will be forced to go to a close-up, and by shooting only the amount of close-ups he wants, so again, the editor has no choice but to use that particular film.

These actions are not healthy for the film. They are counterproductive and usually end up hurting the final product. As the producer, it is your obligation to foresee potential problems and head them off at the pass. Directorial conflict is one of more obvious problems to anticipate and prepare for—and one of the easiest to avoid.

You avoid it by never letting the problem occur in the first place. That's why you must be extremely perceptive in your search for the right director. Now, you're thinking: "Hey, if I direct the film myself, I won't have that problem to worry about." You're absolutely right, you won't have that problem. Unfortunately, you will have created a whole mess of *other* problems, most of which are worse than the original problem. This is your first shot at producing. That job is going to be difficult enough without the complications of trying to direct.

By taking on the mantle of producer, you have committed yourself to a fiduciary responsibility to your investors. *This is not film school.* Millions of dollars are at stake here. Millions of dollars of *other people's money.* If this was your own money you were putting up, you would do everything possible to protect your investment and insure a reasonable profit. Your investors will expect, and should receive, the same conscientious effort. It is not only your responsibility, it is your incontrovertible duty as a producer to deliver the absolute best, most professional product obtainable for the money you have to spend.

Choosing Your Director

So, let's discuss how you go about finding the "right" director for your film. In addition to seeing all the movies you can, especially the less expensive ones, the most straightforward approach is to call the Directors Guild of America, West, in Los Angeles and request a copy of their "Directory of Members of the D.G.A." This booklet lists all the members of the D.G.A., what categories they work in, and their credits. Directors' agents will also be listed, along with contact numbers for those agents.

As you go through the list of directors, check their credits for movies and television shows they have done that are in the same genre as your project. Bear in mind that you must select a director not only for his talent and familiarity with your subject matter, but also for the price range within which he will work.

If you are producing a two- or three-million-dollar movie, you do not go after Scorcese, Coppola, DePalma, Beresford, or Zemeckis. For lower-budget films, you should try to get a younger director who has either television or low-budget feature experience. You need a young director with ambition as well as talent. Someone wanting to move up the directorial ladder who will look on your film as a stepping-stone to the big time. Don't worry about him or her using you—you will be using him or her at the same time. Both sides need, and should, get something out of this deal.

You would do well to make a list of four or five directors who you feel will be the best candidates for your film, then place them in the order of your preference. The directors you select may come from the D.G.A. Directory, from recommendations from people you know, or maybe from a movie you saw and felt the director did a standout job. Whatever the source, you will first contact the director's agent. Start at the top of your list, and go after one director at a time.

You do not approach the director personally, even if his phone number is listed in the directory. You call his agent. The first thing you will want to know is the director's availability. At this point in time, you could be anywhere from one to six months away from starting pre-production. This should give you adequate time to find the director you want and to cast the show properly.

If the director you are inquiring about is available in this time frame, the agent will request that you send him a script. This is standard operating procedure. Now, while the director is reading your script to see if he wants to do it, you will not be sitting idly by waiting for his response. On the contrary, you will be actively "checking out" this person.

You want to get all the information you can, because you will be married to this person for the next several months. And, as with any marriage, if you two are not compatible, your life, at least your professional life, can become a living hell. So, investigate carefully.

Look up his list of credits, and check with the producers he has worked with. But don't limit yourself only to producers. Check with assistant directors and production managers with whom he has worked—especially production managers. Assistant directors are sometimes reticent to say anything negative about a director they have worked with. This is because directors in feature films have the right to select the assistant they wish to work with, so the assistant will not want to take the chance of alienating a source of future employment. Unless, of course, the director is a total jerk and the assistant never wants to work with him again under any circumstances. Which, of course, can happen, believe me, I know from personal experience.

The unit production manager will probably give you a more balanced view of the director. U.P.M.'s are usually hired by the producer or the production company and are not beholden to the director. Listen carefully to what the production manager tells you. His perspective will be entirely different from the producer's. And remember, you want to know everything possible about this director.

Another good source of information would be cameramen he has worked with. D.P.s (Directors of Photography) have close working relationships with their directors. They are privy to the director's thought processes as he stages a scene and works out his camera angles. The D.P. can tell you if the director understands the camera or is just faking it. This can be vitally important information for you when producing a low-budget film. A director who doesn't understand camera angles, or what different lenses can do, or is not adept in his staging techniques, can put you behind schedule in a heartbeat.

You should also check with the BONDING COMPANY that you intend to do business with. In order for you to obtain a COMPLETION BOND, which will be critical to your raising the money for your film, the bonding company will have to approve the director. If the director that you are considering has ever invaded a bond—in other words, gone over budget to the extent that the bonding company is forced to take over the picture—that director will be unacceptable, and you will need to move on and find someone else. No great loss, because this is a director you would definitely not want, in any case.

Look at as much film as you can of the director's work. The agent should be able to supply you with this film. If he can't, you can probably find some in your local video store. Also, ask the agent for a list of producers his client has worked for and other references. If the agent can't, or won't, provide you with this information, be suspicious.

Keys to Look For

As you go through this process of evaluating and selecting a director, there are certain key elements that you should look for. As the producer, you will be constantly performing a balancing act, always weighing the creative against the financial. It is a never-ending battle, a never-ending search to get the best product you can for the money you have to spend. It is the bane of every producer, whether he is involved in a mega-million-dollar movie, or a microscopically budgeted art film. Of course, the lower the budget, the more crucial the balancing act becomes.

The director you want for your movie should be a man or woman with a good eye for visuals. He or she must know how to stage a scene effectively and must be able to work well with actors. Your director must also understand story development, have a good ear for dialogue, and have a feel for the proper pacing of a film.

Besides these creative attributes, he must also have a practical side. As the producer, you are responsible for your investor's money. The director you select must also field some of that responsibility. He can deliver great, artistic film to you, but if the cost of it is so high that you run out of money before the picture is complete, nothing but disaster awaits you.

I hope you are beginning to get the picture of what is involved in selecting a director. We have talked about the balance between the creative and the financial elements of a motion picture. I can't emphasize enough the importance of maintaining this balance, especially when you are dealing with low-budget films. Nothing will bury your production faster than an irresponsible director.

Interviewing the Director

Once you have done all your research and settled on the person you want to direct, and that person has agreed in principle to do your film, the interview phase of the process begins. You will meet with the director and discuss your individual philosophies as they relate to this particular project. This will be a sparring session, where producer and director feel each other out, looking for each other's strengths and weaknesses, because, like it or not, your job will be to support his strengths and avoid his weaknesses. He will disagree with you on occasion, but, as the producer, you will want to maintain as much control over your picture as you possibly can. And the director will often be looking to circumvent your control, so that he can make the picture he wants. In short, as the producer, you have to steer everyone in the same direction.

If you are both on the same page from the beginning, it will make for a lot less infighting and maneuvering, and you will both be able to get on with the business of making a good product.

Do not be afraid to ask questions of the director, draw him out, get him to express his feelings about the story and the characters. You will, undoubtedly, have divergent views on many issues, and that is okay, as long as they are worked out up front. The director can bring a fresh eye to your story. As the producer, you have been living with this script for a long time, and as the saying goes, sometimes you can't see the forest for the trees.

Ideas on casting should be thoroughly discussed, as well as the schedule and the budget. Both you and the director must be comfortable in those areas. If he tells you that he can't make the picture in the amount of days you are giving him, believe him. If you really want this director, you may have to make adjustments in your script to accommodate a schedule he can live with. Because once the director signs off on the schedule and the budget, his butt is on the line as far as his reputation is concerned.

If, after your meetings with your potential director, you are not completely comfortable with him or his ideas on story and casting, or, for whatever reason, your gut tells you this is not the person you want to direct your film, then go with your feelings. Move on and start the process all over again. *Don't rush it.* There will be nothing more important to your motion picture than the selection of your director. If you have to delay the start of your film for a couple of more months, so be it. Don't get frustrated and hire any director just so you can get started.

The director you want is out there. It is up to you, the producer, to find him.

6

The Producer and the Actor

You have dealt successfully with the writer of your screenplay. You have dealt successfully with the person who will be the director of your film. Now comes, without a doubt, your most menacing challenge: the ACTOR.

Dealing with actors will test your diplomatic skills to the breaking point. Prepare yourself to deal with individuals who are so unlike anyone you have ever dealt with before, they might as well have come from another planet or astral plane. This is not said in a necessarily pejorative way. It is just that actors are, how would you say, *different* from us average people.

Understanding the Actor

I have worked with, literally, thousands of actors over the years, and if there is one thread of commonality among them, they are, for the most part, a self-involved group. Actors generally view the world only in terms of how it affects them personally. Now, that is pretty much of a blanket indictment, so let me clarify that statement. I do not mean *all* actors. But I *do* mean most of them.

I'm sure you've heard the old saying, "Actors are like children." Well, actually, there is a great deal of truth in that statement. In order for someone to become someone they are not—in other words, to *play a role*—they must be in touch with the part of them that is still a child. Children live in a world of pretend, and actors are privy to that world—

55

at least the good ones are. Unfortunately, for some actors, the distinction between the child's world and the adult world is, occasionally, not all that well defined.

I think it is necessary to understand the mechanics of acting in order to understand the actor. And since you, as a producer, will be spending your entire professional life surrounded by actors, your insight into the world of acting is vital.

Each time an actor takes on a role, he becomes another person, someone who can be totally different from the person he really is. He can become a hero or a villain, a nice guy or the devil incarnate. In order to play that role effectively, he must really believe he is that character, because if *he* doesn't believe it, then the audience won't believe it.

So, an actor takes on a different persona with each role. He immerses himself in that part—he becomes that character. That is what acting is all about. Take any scene out of any motion picture, for example Richard Gere and Julia Roberts in *Pretty Woman.* Now, Richard knows that Julia is not a hooker, and she knows that Richard is not a billionaire businessman. But for that moment, in that scene, they look each other in the eyes as they play their parts, and for them, in their reality at that moment, Richard really is the billionaire and Julia really is the hooker. It takes a unique individual to be able to divorce himself from reality and immerse himself totally in a make-believe world. It is that uniqueness that makes acting what it is—and actors who they are.

Actor Types

There are three kinds of actors in Hollywood. There are *stars,* those who *think* they are stars, and those who *want* to be stars. As a producer, you will be dealing with all three. The most difficult actors to work with are those who *think* they are stars.

The authentic star knows who he is and what he is, as do those who work with him. His position firmly established, he is treated with the proper respect and deference due his station in life. The star, in return, will usually behave himself and not be too much of a pain in the ass, providing all the conditions of his contract are properly met.

The actor who *wants* to be a star is in no position to offend anyone. He'll even be nice to the crafts service guy. Regardless of what you hear, there is hardly an actor alive who, in his heart, does not aspire to be a star. And that includes seventy-year-old character actors as well as twenty-year-old ingenues.

Now, the actor who *thinks* he is a star—he can be a problem. He is the guy who thinks he has everything: looks, talent, and a huge fan base.

Looks, probably; talent, minimal; fan base, zero. Because he is usually very insecure, he can become temperamental when there is no reason. He can be charming one minute and downright nasty the next. There is simply no way of predicting his behavior. The actor who thinks he is a star wants to be treated with the same respect and deference as the true star.

Unfortunately, respect has to be earned, and he has yet to earn it. You have probably noticed, I have referred to the star in the masculine gender only, but everything I have said holds true for the female as well. It just gets a little tiresome saying "him or her" constantly. I hope this does not offend any of my women readers.

Now, I suppose at this point you are dying for me to name names—who are the good guys and who are the bad guys. Sorry to disappoint, but it would serve no real purpose. If I mention the good guys, I have to mention the bad guys. And lawsuits are really an inconvenient pain. The important thing for you, as the producer, is to be able discern and identify the difference. That knowledge will prove critical in how you approach and handle individual actors.

The Hollywood Actor

It would also be helpful for you to understand the real world in which the Hollywood actor lives. There are over fifty thousand members of the Screen Actors Guild. Less than 10 percent of them actually make a living at acting. For the rest, acting is a secondary career, even though most of them will not admit that fact. They are always waiting for that one big break, always trying to grab hold of that carrot hanging from the end of the stick. And while they are waiting and hoping, they sell real estate or pump gas or park cars or wait on tables or teach school. And they call their agents and go on interviews and deal with rejection after rejection.

The life of the typical Hollywood actor is not one of carefree glamour. It's living in small apartments; driving ten-year-old cars; scraping together enough money to go to acting classes; working in small, non-equity theaters at night for very little money, when they can get the job; and desperately trying to maintain their dignity while pursuing careers that can rip their hearts out.

So, why the hell do they do it? Did I happen to mention the carrot? Fame, fortune, and the accoutrements that go with it can be very compelling incentives. Of course, there is also the artistic need that is inside most actors—the need to perform, to be on stage, to be in front of the camera, to be the center of attention.

Working With the Actor

The producer who is aware of what the actor is all about will be in a position to deal with the actor in a constructive manner. The operative word here is *ego.* And this doesn't apply just to actors. Ego runs rampant through the ranks of writers and directors as well. And don't forget producers, who sometimes can boast the largest egos of all.

In dealing with actors, whose egos are usually more fragile than the egos of those behind the camera, the producer needs to take a more oblique approach. For whatever reason, actors seem to have this need to be catered to. Unfortunately, the more they are catered to, the less they are able to do for themselves. But it is not your job, as the producer, to try and change the nature of the beast. It is your job to get through this movie with the least amount of aggravation and disruption as is humanly possible.

Therefore, knowing what you now know about the nature of the actor, keep the iron fist hidden as long as possible. Give in on the small things, so it will not appear that you are always negative. But when the important things come along, you must be resolute and stick to your guns. Especially when you know it is going to cost you money you don't have.

The producer has two major functions in his relationships with actors. First, he must be able to stroke the actor's ego in order to provide a comfort zone so that the actor will be able to perform with a minimal amount of outside interference. In other words, the producer must build a symbolic wall around the performer to shield him from the basic realities of life that the rest of us must deal with on a daily basis. This is not done *just* to protect the actor's ego; it is a vital aspect in providing a friendly arena in which the actor can perform. The more comfortable the actor is, the better his performance and the more efficiently the shooting company will work. Which brings us to the producer's second function with regard to the actor.

Actors have the ability, if allowed to get away with it, to mangle a shooting schedule almost beyond recognition. On rare occasions, this is done with malicious intent. I have seen actors become furious at a studio or producing company because of real or imagined injustices directed against them. In retaliation, they have been deliberately late for work, blown their lines, not come out of their dressing rooms when called, or argued with directors over inconsequential story points or how a scene is being staged.

More often than not, delays by actors are caused simply by their single-minded focus on their individual performances. They concentrate on the micro, losing sight of the macro. The director is the first line of defense against lost shooting time when this situation occurs. However, the director can only do so much. If he becomes too schedule-conscious, he can lose the confidence of the actor, and that becomes counterproductive to the movie as a whole.

This is where the producer must step in. Let's say an actor is having trouble with a certain piece of dialogue, but the changes he wants to make alter the nature of his character, and thereby, the fabric of the story itself. The director will try to convince the actor that he is wrong, but if the actor is obstinate, then the producer must step in and settle the disagreement quickly.

To do this, he or she has two choices: velvet glove or iron fist. Which one the producer decides to use will depend a lot on who the actor is. This is why it is so important for the producer to know his actor well. Some actors will respond better to the subtle approach, where others need to be hit over the head—figuratively speaking, of course. It is usually better to begin with the subtle approach, leaving the two-by-four as the court of last resort. But in the final analysis, what it comes down to is the fact that time is money, especially if one is shooting a low-budget film. Losing an hour of valuable shooting time can have a domino effect on your schedule.

Never deal with an actor in front of the crew. They become an audience, and actors will always do better than you in front of an audience. Get the actor out of his element and into yours, or go to a neutral zone. Things can be said in private that cannot be said in front of others.

As a producer, you will need all of your tact and negotiating abilities. Do not come from a negative place. Acknowledge the actor's viewpoint, and don't immediately try to discredit that view. Then, explain your reasons for not allowing the changes. Be pleasant, but firm. Do not lose sight of the fact that this is *your* picture, not his. If you acquiesce to his demands, and they hurt the final product, *you* bear the consequences, not him.

Don't try to be the actor's friend; it will just muddy the waters. Be fair, be honest, and always be cognizant of what the actor has gone through to get where he is.

Actors like compliments. No, let me re-phrase that . . . actors *need* compliments. Quick story: Many years ago, I was working with Gene Barry on a television series called *Name of the Game.* Gene was known to be a little difficult at times. Actually, he was a pretty nice guy, but he did have his moments of temperament.

Gene also loved good clothes. It was almost an obsession with him. Early one morning, I was told that Gene wanted to see me in his dressing room, that he was really angry about something. When I entered the dressing room, before Gene had a chance to unload on me, I said, "Gene, what a great looking tie. Is it new?" He looked a bit startled, then smiled and said, "Yes, yes it is. Do you like it?" When I told him how great it looked on him, he went into a ten-minute monologue on how he found it and how much it cost, etc. When he finished, I said, "See you later, Gene," and left. He was happy as a pig in a mud hole, and you know, I never did find out what he had been angry about.

The point of the story is simple. Know your actor. Be acutely aware of his strengths and his weaknesses, so you will know which buttons you can push and which are best left alone. The better you know your actor, the better you will know how to deal with him.

The Producer and the Crew

U p to now, we've discussed only the above-the-line members of your shooting company. Now, let's discuss the men and women in the trenches. The people who do the work of physically getting your motion picture made—those usually anonymous people who work behind the camera.

To shrug this off as something that is not important to you, as a producer, could be a catastrophic mistake on your part. Every member of your below-the-line crew contributes something to your film. Some contribute artistically and some by the sweat of their labor, but they all have a vested interest in your film. You may think that it is just a job to them. That all they want is their paychecks and an answer to the two famous questions: "What time is lunch?" and "When do we wrap?"

Sure, to some it will be just a job. But to most people working on a motion picture, the end product is very important to them. The feeling of being associated with a good project, of making a motion picture that will be seen around the world by millions of people, of knowing that they helped put that film out there . . . well, even to the cynics in your crew, even they can't block out that inner feeling of excitement, that rush that comes with being part of an artistic achievement.

I guess that's what makes the art of motion pictures so unique. It is an art form that takes hundreds of people to complete. So, even though you have writers, directors, actors, and producers, nothing gets done without the crew performing the actual labor that gets the images on film.

As an independent producer, you don't necessarily have to have hands-on experience in selecting your crew. You can leave all that to your production manager. But if you want to be a producer who controls his film, who exercises his responsibility to his investors, who really cares about what the finished product will look like, then you should be a producer who takes part in the selection of your crew. You should be personally aware of what each person does on your crew, and you should know everyone's name.

There is a very specific reason for this. The working man or woman on a set usually moves to the rhythm set by the director and the director of photography. If that rhythm becomes too slow, then the work will not get done in a timely manner, and you will find yourself over budget. Having a close relationship with your crew can help ameliorate that situation. You can be the one who steps in and gets things moving—if you have your crew behind you.

There are also a hundred things a crew person can do, if he so desires, to cost you money, and you will never be aware of it. I'm not talking about deliberate sabotage, necessarily, just little things that seem unimportant, but can add up to a lot of additional and unwarranted expense. If a producer is disliked or not trusted, there will be people on the crew who will make "mistakes," consciously or unconsciously. And in the end, it really doesn't matter; it all costs the same.

The first assistant cameraman, who is the focus puller, can miss a shot. He can mention it immediately, which requires doing another take—a small expense—or worse, he can ignore the situation, and you don't discover the out-of-focus shot until you see dailies on the following day. This could require an expensive reshoot, maybe even returning to a location you have already finished. An electrician can plug a cable into the wrong box and burn out the cable. You will have to pay for that. A grip can scratch up a wall while moving it. You will have to pay for a painter to come in and repair the damage. The propman can bring in the wrong prop for a scene. He will have to go back to his truck and find the right prop. This takes time, and of course, time is money.

Much of this unpleasantness can be avoided, simply by you, as the producer, being accessible to your crew. This doesn't mean you have to be Mr. Nice Guy and glad-hand everyone. But the way that you comport yourself around the crew will determine how the crew will react to you. Because you are the producer, you will not be able to give everyone everything they want. You will have to say "no" a lot. The important thing is to treat your crew honestly, fairly, and with respect. If you do, they will treat you with the same honesty, fairness, and respect.

A motion picture crew is a very tight-knit group. While a film is being shot, your crew will see more of each other than they will of their families. As in the army, the rumor mill is constantly grinding out grist for the mill. Also, like the army, there is constant griping. The lunches could be better, there's not enough variety on the crafts service table, they're not getting enough overtime, they're getting too much overtime, it's too hot, it's too cold, too much night work, they're working too short handed . . . and on and on it goes. This kind of griping is not to be taken too seriously. It is standard operating procedure.

The producer, however, should listen to all legitimate complaints and try to deal with them. Sometimes, a very simple change can make all the difference in the attitude of a crew. Like the great sandwich caper. I was doing a movie in which the crew began to complain that they weren't getting enough to eat. Forget that they were being served full breakfasts every morning, and the crafts service table was always fully stocked with everything from donuts and fresh fruit to bagels and candy; they still had to wait until 1:30 for lunch. So, we solved this little problem by putting out sandwich ingredients—deli meats, cheeses, bread, and rolls—at 11:00 in the morning. Did they really need that? Probably not, but the morale shot up, and all the grumbling stopped.

It is not enough for the independent producer just to know who his crew people are. As the producer, you should also have a working knowledge of what each department does, because only then will you know if you are being told the truth about what is going on or if you are being snowed.

Now, you probably have a general idea of what the different departments on a motion picture company are responsible for. But you need to understand the inner workings of each department to fully analyze and evaluate how your money is being spent and whether or not it is being unnecessarily wasted.

The Production Department

Your UNIT PRODUCTION MANAGER will probably be your closest ally, confidante, and walking buffer zone. He (or she) is there to protect your money and control the costs of your film. And he will do it with the tenacity of a pit bull. He is not there to be loved, or even liked, for that matter. He is there to make sure that every dollar that is spent shows up on the screen, and not one cent is flushed down the toilet.

If the director is the creative weight on your scale, then the U.P.M. is the financial weight. It is up to the *producer* to keep the scale in balance. You are the one who will have to make the decision when the director says he needs twenty more extras for a scene and the U.P.M. says you can't afford it. You have to decide if those twenty extras will make a difference to the scene and to your film as a whole. And if you do decide to spend that money, is there somewhere else in the budget that you can take something out to make up for the overage?

Once you have made your decision to spend the money, a good U.P.M. will then proceed to find that money in your budget. Your production manager is actually a de facto producer. He will control all the physical aspects of your movie, relieving you of the responsibility of overseeing the tons of minutiae that occur every day.

The U.P.M. is the focal point for your production. Every department reports to him, and no one is allowed to spend any money over their approved budget without his okay. The smart producer uses his production manager as his point man. When something unpleasant has to be done, he sends out the U.P.M. This keeps the producer insulated from much of the nasty little things that have to be performed in the course of a production.

The FIRST ASSISTANT DIRECTOR is the director's right hand. On a shooting company, if the director is the captain, then the first A.D. is the first mate. His major function is to make sure that the director has everything he needs, when he needs it. The first assistant has the responsibility of holding the entire shooting company together. It is an extremely difficult job, because he must serve several masters without alienating any of them.

It is always helpful if "the first" has a good personal relationship with the director, because he must be able to anticipate a director's needs. He must have the actors ready and on set when they are needed, control the set, keep everyone quiet during rehearsals and takes, notify each department what scenes are coming up, keep things moving so the pace of shooting doesn't lag, and answer about two hundred questions a day from just about everyone on the set.

Now, the first A.D.'s personal balancing act is between the director, the star, and the production manager. He must keep the director happy by giving him what he wants, when he wants it. But if he gives the director too much, the U.P.M. will climb all over him, because he is spending too much money. The first must also cater to the star. He must make sure the dressing room facilities are acceptable, that any special needs the star has are taken care of, and that he doesn't have the star brought to the set too soon, because then, God forbid, the star may have to wait three or four minutes until he is needed.

Talk about your high stress jobs. The first assistant director's job is a world-class ulcer maker. It is physically and emotionally exhausting, but the pay is good, and the smart first assistant can move up to director or production manager or producer.

The SECOND ASSISTANT DIRECTOR works directly under the first. While his job is not as emotionally stressful as the first's, it is definitely more physically exhausting. The second is into work at the first makeup call and goes home after all his paperwork is done, usually after everyone else is on their second martini.

When the first assistant says to bring the actors to the set, it is the second who runs to get them. The second checks all the extras in and out, does all the call sheets and production reports, helps keep the set quiet, works the background action, makes sure the caterer will be ready on time, takes care of the producer's or the star's guests that visit the set, answers the phone, makes sure the actors get their breakfasts while they are in makeup . . . and that is just *some* of the things he does.

The second assistant director's job is just about the worst job on a shooting company. He has to take crap from everybody and just grin and bear it. Yet, it is one of the most sought-after jobs in the industry. *"Why?"* the word leaps out of your mouth. The answer, of course, is that being a second assistant is not a career goal—it is a stepping-stone. It is the best way there is to learn the inner workings of a shooting company—you just want to be sure you move up the ladder as quickly as possible. Being a second is definitely a young person's job, but if you stay in it too long, it'll make you old real fast.

The LOCATION MANAGER works very closely with the rest of the production team, which consists of the director, the U.P.M., and the first and second assistant directors. It is important that you hire a professional location manager, no matter where you are shooting. If you are in an area of the country in which there are no local location managers, bring one in from the nearest production center, and hire a local resident to be his assistant.

It is the location manager's job to scout and preselect all the locations. A good location manager will provide the director and the production designer with several options for each location. Locations will then be selected for their appropriateness to the film. The U.P.M. will also have a hand in the selection of locations, because money will have to be spent to secure these locations.

Personality is a vital ingredient for a location manager, because he has, arguably, the most thankless job in the business. Virtually every complaint registered against a shooting company is fielded first by the location manager. Being able to deal with a sometimes irate public is an absolute prerequisite.

Diplomacy should be at the top of his interpersonal skills, because he will be called on to exercise that diplomacy several times a day. There will always be the guy with the power lawn mower who just happens to want to mow his grass just as you are starting to shoot. Of course, the lawn hasn't been mowed in two months, but he has to do it now. So, the location manager must go up to him and try to dissuade him from mowing at this particular time. Fifty bucks usually works. Then, there is always the nut who will come running out of his home or place of business screaming that we can't shoot there. So again, the ever-patient location manager will politely explain that we have the proper permits from the city, and that, indeed, we can shoot here. Sometimes the pest will be assuaged and will grumble and slink back into his house or store. Sometimes nothing will make him happy, until the policeman comes over and convinces him of the legitimacy of your operation.

A personable, well-liked location manager will be able to get you into places that normally do not allow filming. This is the kind of man or woman you want on your team.

The PRODUCTION OFFICE COORDINATOR is the heart and soul of your production office. She is to a production company what NORAD is to our country's defense system. Virtually every bit of information comes across her desk, and it is her job to channel it in the right direction. Although I refer to the P.O.C. in the feminine, there are, of course, men who do this job, too. It is just that this particular field is dominated by women.

Your P.O.C. will work long hours and, quite often, under considerable stress. Your U.P.M. will look to her for support and backup, because when things get hectic, as they usually do, it is not unusual for some things to fall through the cracks. A good P.O.C. is very adept at plugging up those cracks.

The P.O.C. runs the production office; it is her domain. Part of her duties are to handle all travel arrangements for cast and crew; distribute scripts; photocopy call sheets and production reports and get them to the set; answer phones; type letters; supervise the shipment of film, equipment, and wardrobe; order raw stock; coordinate film runs to and from the lab; do all the filing; handle insurance agreements . . . and that's before lunch.

Needless to say, the P.O.C. must be extraordinarily well organized. If not, she will self-destruct in a matter of days.

The Camera Department

The camera department consists, basically, of a director of photography—also known as a cameraman, cinematographer, or simply D.P.—a camera operator, a first assistant cameraman, and a second assistant cameraman. If you use a second camera, which some companies like to do, especially in action sequences, you will need another camera operator and another first assistant cameraman. If you are working with two or more cameras, or if you are doing a lot of handheld work, you will probably add a loader to your crew.

There is also the Steadi-cam operator, who uses a highly specialized piece of equipment, which is a handheld camera mounted on a counterbalance. This allows the operator to walk, run, or climb stairs without the noticeable bounce and jiggle you would get from a regular handheld camera. Steadi-cams are very expensive to use and can cost upward of twenty-five hundred dollars a day. If you are making a low-budget film, it is unlikely you will use a Steadi-cam very often, if at all.

The D.P. is the head of the camera department, and he is responsible for his crew. This department is probably the most complex and technical department on a shooting company. The D.P. bears sole responsibility for the visual look of the film. He controls the lighting of a set, what lenses will be used, what filters are necessary, and what "stop" will be used. After the director stages a scene, he will usually confer with the D.P. as to what camera angles to use and what coverage is needed. Then, it is up to the cameraman to give the director what he wants.

The D.P. is under a lot of pressure from both sides of the filming process: the artistic side and the financial side. He must provide quality work, yet perform that work within the constraints of the budget. This is part of the balancing act that goes on in all film production. The higher the budget, the more weight is placed on the creative side. Conversely, the lower the budget, the more the weight shifts to the financial side of the scale.

Get to know your D.P. well. Personal relationships can be very important at critical times during the shooting of a film. If you can go to a cameraman as a friend, instead of as a producer, and tell him you are in real trouble and you have to finish this location on time, you will find him much more responsive to your needs.

What if you don't like the cameraman personally, although you like his work? Are you being a hypocrite by courting his friendship? Yes, you could say that. But a producer is called upon to do a lot of things he might not do under normal circumstances. And making motion pictures certainly falls into that category.

Always keep in mind that you carry two major responsibilities with you at all times. Number one, you must produce a good film, and number two, you must protect the investors' money. Because these responsibilities are at the top of your priority list, you will sometimes be called upon to do things that you might consider morally or ethically borderline. So be it. Political correctness aside, you do what has to be done to protect your film and your investor. Live with it.

Next in line to the D.P. is the CAMERA OPERATOR. He is second in command in that department. He is also the person who actually operates the camera during a *take,* not the D.P. A good camera operator not only must have unusually good hand-eye coordination, he must have an artistic sense of composition. He is the only one who is looking through the camera while film is actually being shot, so no matter what he has been told by the cameraman or the director on how to frame a particular shot, he is the one who has to physically do it.

On almost all movie sets today, cameras have what is called a *video tap.* This allows the director and the cameraman to view, on a monitor, exactly what is being shot, as it is being shot. If the camera operator has not framed the shot properly, another take can be made. However, this is time and money. A good operator and a video tap can save you both.

Next in line is the FIRST ASSISTANT CAMERAMAN. His primary duty is keeping a shot in focus. This is a lot more difficult than it sounds. The longer the lens, the less depth of field there is. With a 25mm lens, focus is usually not a problem, but when you start using 75mm or 100mm lenses, then focus can become critical. Add to this a moving camera and moving actors, and keeping them in focus can become a hair-raising experience.

The first A.C. is also responsible for making sure that the camera is set with the proper f-stop and that the right filter is in place. It is his job to reload the camera when necessary and, at the end of a shot, confirm that there are no hairs in the aperture. Sometimes, during filming, a tiny thread can come off the film as it runs through the camera at twenty-four frames per second. This thread sticks in the aperture and can be seen on the printed take as a jiggling line.

The SECOND ASSISTANT CAMERAMAN must do all the paperwork that is necessary so that the proper takes will be printed. He also holds the clapper at the beginning of each take. This identifies the scene number that is being shot and the take number. The good second A.C. can save the producer a lot of money in small ways that usually go unnoticed. Simple things like anticipating a camera reload and having a new magazine close at hand, so he doesn't have to walk back to the truck to get it. And reloading additional magazines with raw stock, so there will be no chance of running short of film. Anything that saves time on a shooting company also saves money.

The Electrical Department

The electric and grip departments work closely with the camera department. The electric crew on a movie consists of a gaffer, best boy (generic term, can also be a woman), lamp operators (or juicers, as they are sometimes called), and a generator operator if they are working on a location.

The GAFFER is the head of the electric department and is also the chief lighting technician. The D.P. usually selects his gaffer, and it is to the producer's advantage to allow him to do this. A cameraman and a gaffer who work well together and have worked together in the past can speed up the filming process without loss of quality. That is because the gaffer knows how the cameraman works and can anticipate his needs.

The BEST BOY is the gaffer's assistant. Besides setting lamps with the juicers, the best boy also ramrods any pre-rigging that needs to be done, makes sure his crew has the correct call times, okays their time cards, and supervises the maintenance of the electric equipment.

The number of LAMP OPERATORS varies with the size and complexity of the production. A high-budget film will work with eight, ten, or however many they feel they need. A low-budget film or a television show will use three or four. If there is night work involved or a particularly difficult location, one or two juicers may be added for those days.

The lamp operators do the physical work of setting up the lights, stringing out the hundreds of feet of electrical cable that are needed, adjusting the intensity of the lights, and adding diffusion. It is tough, physical labor. The lights are heavy, the cable is heavy, and in the morning everything comes off the trucks . . . and in the evening, everything goes back on the trucks. When wrapping up a company for the day, the electricians are usually the last ones out. Except, of course, for the teamsters.

The Grip Department

The grip crew consists of a KEY GRIP, SECOND GRIP, DOLLY OPERATOR, and however many regular GRIPS are needed—on a low-budget feature, usually two or three. Now, "grip" is sort of a strange term. I have no idea of its derivative root. I remember my first day in a motion picture studio—Columbia Pictures, to be exact. I was walking down the back lot when I saw this sign that said "Grip Department," and I thought, "Wow, a whole department just for suitcases."

Well, as I discovered, that wasn't quite the case. There wasn't a suitcase to be found in the whole department. Maybe that term came from the fact that a grip *grips* a hammer, or *grips* a wall to move, or *grips* a century stand. I don't know, but it sounds reasonable. In any event, the grip is the other half of the lighting equation. Electricians set lights; grips set the gobos and skrims that modify the lights.

I can see the next question coming: "What the heck are gobos and skrims?" Gobos are large, rectangular metal frames covered with black fabric. They are used to cut off light from different areas, usually when two lights overlap. Or to cut off a mike shadow. Skrims are diffusion used to lessen the intensity of a light. When diffusion is placed directly on a lamp, the electrician does it. When the diffusion is on a stand away from a lamp, the grip does it. Job descriptions on motion picture sets are very specific. Grips don't touch lights, and electricians don't touch gobos. This holds true in virtually every department on a set. Jobs are *not* interchangeable.

Of course, grips do a lot more than just setting gobos and skrims. They are responsible for operating the camera dolly or crane; setting dolly track; moving wild walls; mounting cameras on cars, trucks, planes, or anywhere else they may be needed. And a hundred other jobs, both large and small, that need to be done every single day of shooting.

Art Direction and Set Decorating

Right up there with the director of photography, in creative terms, is the PRODUCTION DESIGNER. This is a relatively new title, coming into use in the past twenty or so years. They used to be called art directors, but somewhere along the line, some art director felt that "production designer" had a much more dignified and artistic ring to it, and so the term was born. There are still art directors, but they are relegated, mainly, to overseeing the construction of sets that have been designed by the production designer.

Of all the below-the-line personnel, the D.P. and the production designer are most responsible for the physical look of the film. The production designer not only designs the sets that are to be built, he is instrumental in selecting the locations that are to be shot. The producer and the director have a vision of what the film should look like. The production designer makes sure that vision is realized.

The SET DECORATOR and the COSTUME DESIGNER work in close harmony with the production designer, who is the general of this little army. The set decorator and his crew dress the sets that will be used, whether they are on a sound stage or in a practical location. Dressing a set simply means providing that set with furniture, carpeting, draperies, paintings, and all the incidental accoutrements that would be in that particular set.

It is up to the production designer to make sure that the set is decorated in accordance with the design of the set itself. He must also be sure that the color of the wardrobe that the costume designer selects for the actors is compatible with the color of the sets and the dressing. If he has green walls, he doesn't want an actress walking around in a green dress.

The set decorating crew consists of a LEAD PERSON and a SWING GANG. Now, this is not a group that plays 1940s music. These are the guys and gals who do the tough manual labor of moving the furniture and everything else into and out of sets. The lead person is the foreman, and the swing gang is usually composed of three or four people.

The Wardrobe Department

The COSTUME DESIGNER is the head of the Wardrobe department on a film. Although this is, predominantly, a female position, there are many excellent male costume designers. It is their function to design or select the wardrobe that is worn by the actors. If it is a period piece, wardrobe will have to be designed and manufactured or rented from a costume house. If it is a present-day film, wardrobe will usually be purchased from department stores or specialty shops.

The costume designer must break the script down into scenes and continuity, which will chart what wardrobe will be worn in every scene. Since movies are usually filmed out of sequence, the designer must be careful that each actor is wearing the right wardrobe for the scene that he is in.

On a low-budget film, a costume designer is usually employed on a limited basis. She will probably purchase wardrobe for the lead characters. But after that is done, and she and the producer and director have reviewed the wardrobe charts, she will turn over the show to a COSTUMER, who will actually work the set. Most shows will have two set costumers, one for men and one for women.

The Prop Department

The PROPERTY MASTER on your show is in charge of all the hand props. This involves everything from guns to cigarette lighters, wallets to knives, pencils, pens, file folders, etc., etc., etc. In other words, anything that is handled by an actor. The rules regarding what items are props and what items are set dressing are very explicit. Union regulations govern which department handles which items. For example, if a cigarette lighter sits on a coffee table, but is there for decoration and no one uses it, it is set dressing. However, if someone picks it up to light a cigarette, the lighter becomes the propman's responsibility.

If this seems like petty nitpicking, it is. But there is a reason for it. Props or set dressing needed for a scene can sometimes be overlooked. Props thinks that set dressing is going to provide an item, and vice versa. And what happens is, no one provides it. So, by defining the parameters, hopefully these kinds of mistakes will be minimized. You do not want to be on the set waiting for an item while departments argue over who was responsible.

Script Supervisor

The SCRIPT SUPERVISOR is an important cog in the production machinery. The title might be something of a misnomer, because he or she does not actually supervise anything. What the script supervisor really does is follow the action that is being shot and compare it with the written page. Is the actor saying the dialogue correctly, and if not, has the meaning of the scene been changed? Any change must be noted so that the director can either okay it or ask for another take.

The script supervisor keeps track of the actors' movements in a scene. In a *master shot*, an actor may pick up a cup of coffee on a certain line of dialogue. Then, when they are doing that actor's *close-up*, it is important to the film editor that the actor pick up the coffee on exactly the same line. The script supervisor must keep track of all this. He or she also keeps track of all the takes, times each scene, and confirms all *printed takes* with the camera assistant. He also double-checks the wardrobe an actor is wearing. If an actor is wearing a brown jacket in an exterior scene, when he walks inside, he must have the same jacket on, even though the interior scene may be shot a week later.

A script supervisor must be efficient, but he cannot be officious. A director uses the script supervisor as another pair of eyes and ears to help him keep track of what is going on, so he must be able to differentiate between what is important and what is trivial. And he must never argue with the director. He can inform the director of something he feels is wrong, but if the director says it's okay, then he better just let it go.

The Sound Department

The sound department consists, usually, of a three-person team: the MIXER, the BOOM OPERATOR, and the CABLEPERSON. You notice how adept I am getting at nonsexist terms. When I first started in this business, the only women on a set, besides the actresses and extras, were the hairdresser, the wardrobe woman, and the script supervisor. Every other department was 100 percent male. Big difference today.

The MIXER is the head of his department. He is responsible for the quality of the sound of your film. He operates a portable *mixing panel,* which keeps the various audio inputs in proper balance. It is not a particularly difficult job when you are shooting on a sound stage, but the mixer really earns his money when shooting outside or in practical locations. He must then deal with all the extraneous noise from automobile traffic to airplanes, sirens, and dogs barking, along with leaf blowers, lawn mowers, children playing, and the hammering at the house next door.

The mixer must make instantaneous decisions on what he can get away with. If a scene plays great for the camera and the director is happy with the actors' performances, the mixer is loathe to say, We have to do it again, because there was airplane noise. But if he knows that noise is intrusive and can't be filtered out in *post,* then he must say his piece.

If it was a particularly difficult scene, the mixer automatically becomes the most hated man on the set; he knows that before he says anything. But that's his job; it's a matter of shooting the messenger. The director may decide to go for another take, or he may opt to *loop* the scene later. This means that after the film is cut together, they bring the actors back and record their lines on a *looping stage,* then lay the new lines into the film.

The mark of a good mixer is his ability to obtain the highest quality sound while causing the least amount of delay, and his expertise in knowing exactly what he can get away with.

The BOOM OPERATOR is pretty self-explanatory. He handles the microphones, whether they are attached to a sound boom or a handheld fish pole. He must know the dialogue as well as the actors do, in order to have his mike pointed in the right direction as each actor speaks. Otherwise, you will be getting a lot of dialogue that sounds as if it is coming from another room. The boom operator is also responsible for the radio mikes that are used a great deal and have to be placed on the actors in discreet places.

The third man on the sound team is the CABLEMAN. His duties are basically to make sure all the sound equipment is properly hooked up. This position is optional. A company can operate with a two-man sound crew and, on lower-budget films, usually does.

Makeup and Hairdressing Departments

The makeup and hairdressing departments fall into the creative category of below-the-line departments. When you get right down to it, you can have beautiful sets, great scenery, and fashionable wardrobe, but it is the actor's face—ten feet high, up on that screen—that the audience comes to see. And the camera can be brutally honest. The slightest flaw is magnified tenfold, and it is up there for all to see.

The cameraman can only do so much with lighting and filters; the rest is up to the makeup artist. And in many ways, that is exactly what he or she is—an artist. This artist's canvas just happens to be an individual's face.

Stars usually have their own makeup people and hairdressers. They are entrusting how they will look on screen to someone else, and *how* they look can mean their entire career. Because the makeup person and the hairdresser work so closely with the actor, their jobs become very personal. They must not only be good at what they do, the actor must also feel comfortable with them. Remember, they see actors at their absolute worst, like at 6:00 in the morning, after they have had three hours sleep because they went to a party the night before. Now, it is up to the makeup person to make the forty-year-old actress look twenty-five and cover the eye bags and sallow complexion of the sixty-year-old actor—and he or she has about an hour and a half to perform this minor miracle.

When you are doing a low-budget film, you can still run into the problem of a lead actor wanting his or her own makeup person and/or hairdresser. As the producer, you may have to do some negotiating in this area. If you hire the person the actor has requested, you may have to pay more money than you want, because the makeup person will feel he or she is in a good bargaining position.

You will need all your negotiating skills to get around this one. Sometimes this issue becomes a deal breaker. In other words, the actor will not do your movie unless she gets the person she wants. Makeup people work very long hours, so be aware that what may not seem like much additional money can quickly escalate into a thousand dollars a week or more of added expense.

Also, make it very clear that whoever this makeup person is, he or she will be required to make up other actors as well. Otherwise, you will then have to hire an additional makeup person, and this will really put a hole in your budget.

Crafts Service Department

Now, we get to the CRAFTS SERVICE PERSON. This position is usually regarded as near the bottom of the pecking order. This is because the Crafts Service Person, sometimes referred to as the Laborer or Utility Man, does most of the menial tasks. He sweeps up the stage, or keeps the location clean, helps the caterer set up tables and chairs, maintains the snack table, makes coffee for the crew, and performs dozens of other tasks during the day.

His or her main raison d'etre, however, is the ubiquitous snack table. The good Crafts Service Person will keep this table well-stocked the entire day. What he puts on it, of course, will depend, to a great deal, on what kind of budget he has to work with. In other words, will he buy fresh, pre-cut fruit from Gelson's, designer bottled water, and See's Candy, or will he get fruit from Ralph's and cut it himself, Arrowhead water, and bags of individual Baby Ruths and Milky Ways.

If he is clever, he will find ways of buying interesting snack foods and in a large enough supply to keep his table stocked all day. Crews have eclectic tastes, and he needs to cater to all of them. This means donuts and pork rinds, fresh fruit and vegetables, candy bars and cheeses, soft drinks, diet drinks, and fruit juices, and coffee, tea, and cocoa—but especially coffee . . . lots of coffee.

The Crafts Service Person can be a major morale booster on a shooting company. A happy crew is a well-fed crew. So, if he keeps his table clean and neat and well-stocked, you will find your crew will have a lot less to complain about.

First-Aid

Every shooting company, at least in California, will have a MEDIC, or first-aid person, on the set. Even if a medic is not required by law, you would do well to hire one anyway. Hardly a day goes by on a shooting company that some minor mishap doesn't occur. An electrician will burn himself, a grip will drop a piece of lumber on his foot, a propman will cut himself, a set dresser will strain his back. There is always something happening. Rather than having to send a crew member to an emergency room for some minor problem, the medic can usually take care of it right there.

Every once in awhile, a major injury does occur. Someone will fall from a crane, or a special effect will go wrong and an actor or stunt person or the effects man will be seriously hurt. I did a movie many years ago in which a small cannon we were using misfired and blew a hole in the actor's stomach. We were on a location in the desert, and it took almost a half hour before an ambulance could reach us, but the quick thinking of the medic and his expertise saved the actor's life.

From a practical standpoint, the producer needs to protect his company from a potentially devastating lawsuit. By not having a medic on the set, you are leaving your company vulnerable to serious and expensive litigation.

The Transportation Department

The TEAMSTERS are a much-maligned department. But an absolute necessity. Much of the animosity the rest of the crew feel toward teamsters comes from the fact that a driver works for an hour or so in the morning, and then for an hour or so in the evening, and the twelve or so hours in between are devoted to trying to stay awake.

Well, maybe that's a bit exaggerated, but there is definitely some truth there. Every truck must be driven by a member of the teamsters. So, after all the trucks arrive on the location, unless there is a move during the day, there is really not that much for them to do, until it is time to drive the trucks back to the studio at the end of a day. But they are getting paid from the time they come in until the time they punch out. And the overtime can be staggering.

Every production company will have teamsters. Low-budget, high-budget, union, or non-union. Teamsters, in this country, are a fact of life. In many European and Asian countries, motion picture teamsters are almost unheard of. An electrician drives the electric truck, a grip drives the grip truck, and so on. But in the United States, if it's on wheels, a teamster moves it.

One of the producer's best allies can be the TRANSPORTATION COORDINATOR. He is the person who runs the department. He is responsible for hiring the drivers; renting all the rolling stock; finding the picture cars, camera cranes, and lighting cranes; and controlling the costs of his department.

There is a lot of latitude in this department, so keeping a tight rein is extremely important. A driver's starting time can be anywhere from one to two hours before the rest of the crew. That's because he has to check out his truck, make sure it has fuel, and get it to the location before the crew arrives, so it will be parked in the right place and ready for use. A good transportation coordinator will closely monitor each driver's start time. If he can give a driver a fifteen-minute-later call, that fifteen minutes will translate to a full hour of pay at the end of the day because of the overtime.

A producer should thoroughly investigate his transportation coordinator before hiring him. Be sure to get recommendations from at least two or three different sources. Transportation has always been like a loose cannon in this business. The opportunities for shady dealings and kickbacks are plentiful and quite easy for the unscrupulous coordinator to accomplish. There are a lot of good, honest people out there; it is up to you to find them.

Feeding the Cast and Crew

The final category I should mention is the all-important CATERER. The motion picture catering business is a world unto itself. These are the people who travel with the shooting company in their moveable kitchens, much like the old chuck wagons on cattle drives. Only much more sophisticated, of course.

On a normal shooting day, the caterers are usually up about 2:00 A.M. They get all their supplies loaded up and arrive at the location at least an hour before the crew. This gives them time to fire up their grill, make the coffee, and get ready for breakfast.

It used to be that the only people who were provided with breakfasts were the actors and makeup people who had to come in early, and the director and first assistant. Breakfast sandwiches were available at a buck and a half, and coffee was free. Over the years, this procedure has evolved so that now everyone gets a free breakfast, and not just a sandwich. I'm talking about ham, bacon, sausage, eggs, hash browns, waffles, pancakes, breakfast burritos, huevos rancheros, eggs Benedict, hot and cold cereals, fresh fruit, fresh orange juice, donuts, sweet rolls, muffins, bagels and cream cheese, yes, and sometimes lox.

Lunch is equally abundant. Usually two or three different salads, three entrees, three kinds of vegetables, potatoes, rice, pasta, bread, rolls, and at least two or three different desserts. And you, as the producer, are paying for all this. It is part of the price of doing business.

Caterers can make a lot of money off of a production company, so don't be concerned about driving as hard a bargain as you can. A caterer will give you a per person price, which will include breakfast and lunch. You will also be required to pay the chef and his assistant. That is standard practice.

The per person price can vary considerably, depending on what you want and which caterer you will be using. It can range from eleven dollars a person all the way up to fifteen or eighteen dollars. On a low-budget movie, you should be able to find a caterer who will provide good food, and plenty of it, for eleven to twelve dollars a person. Just be careful of the add-ons. Prices should include tables and chairs and all the drinks. Make sure you don't get nickeled and dimed to death with a lot of additional charges for items you thought would be included. Some things, like ice, propane, and gasoline, are justifiable additions.

We have now covered just about every department on a shooting company. There are many more departments when you get to post-production, but we will deal with those later.

8

Phase 1—Pre-Production

The first significant step in the actual making of a motion picture is the start of PRE-PRODUCTION. As an independent producer, you have labored and struggled for months, or years, to get this project off the ground. Now, all the preliminaries are over with. You've got the script you want to make. You have begged, borrowed, cajoled, wheedled, and done everything else, short of mayhem, to raise the money needed to produce your film. And dammit, you have been successful.

So, now the money is in the bank, all the legal paperwork has been done, and you stand on the brink of launching your first production. Your acceptance speech at the Academy Awards ceremony is already spinning through your head. You look around proudly and proclaim to the world, *"I am an Independent Producer."*

Which reminds me of a story. This Jewish guy in New York makes a bundle of money and buys himself a yacht. He gets all dressed up in white pants, a blue blazer, and a yachting cap and takes his mother to see his yacht. As they walk on board the guy says, "This is my yacht, Mamma, and I am the captain." The mother looks at her son and nods. "To you, you're a captain, and to me, you're a captain. But, to another captain, are you a captain?"

So, I ask you: To you, you're a producer, and to your mother, you're a producer, but to another producer, are you a producer? The jury is still out on that one, and you still have a long way to go to prove yourself. You've done okay so far, but the true test lies ahead. The terrifying, stark reality of actually producing a motion picture is staring you in the face. The proverbial ball is in your court. You have no one to turn to. *You* must now make all the decisions.

I can see that look of panic crossing your face. You have gone through all this agony, the thousands of phone calls, the endless hours of desperation, the bitterness of the struggle that finally gets you to this moment in your life, where you stand on the brink of realizing all your dreams. And the thought suddenly strikes you: "I don't know the first frigging thing about producing a movie."

Okay, then, let's get down to the nuts and bolts of producing your movie. I will attempt to guide you through this seemingly daunting process, one step at a time.

First Things First

Before you begin the pre-production process, you want to make sure that you have a director on board. You know how to find the director you want; we discussed that in chapter 5. I want to stress the importance of having a director signed before the clock starts running on the rest of your crew. You do not want to be in the position of scrounging for a director at the last minute and then having to settle for someone . . . anyone. The director is your most significant acquisition. He or she is your crown jewel. Take the time you need to find the right one. It will be time well spent.

The Cast

If you are going after an actor to play the lead and you have a wish list of several performers, any one of whom could play the part, make sure that you close on one of them before you start putting crew people on payroll. You don't want to get into the middle of pre-production and find that the actor you want won't be available for six months. You would then find yourself in the same position you would be in if you didn't have your director signed—scrounging around and settling for someone who you never would have considered using, except that now you are desperate.

To help you in finding a CAST—not just your lead or leads, but all the actors in your movie—you will need to hire a CASTING DIRECTOR. You might be tempted to save the money on a casting director and take on that chore yourself, but don't. It is a foolhardy move in order to save a few bucks, and it will probably end up costing you more in the long run.

Casting directors can be hired on a flat rate or by the week. For a low-budget film, you would be better off making a flat deal. You can figure anywhere from five to ten thousand dollars, depending on the size of your cast.

The actual casting procedure is not particularly complicated. During your pre-production period, your casting director will set up casting sessions for you to read actors for individual parts. Depending on the size of the cast, there will probably be two or three initial sessions, with one *callback* session.

In the initial casting sessions, your casting director will bring in a minimum of three or four actors for each role. He or she will select one or two scenes from your script for the actor to read. After all the actors have been auditioned, then you, the director, and the casting director will discuss each role and make your selections. As the producer, you will have the final say on who is cast, but you would do well to heed the opinions of the director and the casting director. You not only want good actors, you also want cooperative actors, actors who know their lines, and actors who do not carry the baggage of bad reputations.

The callback session is used only if there is some uncertainty concerning a particular role. There may be two strong contenders for the same role, and you are having a difficult time deciding, so you call them back for a second audition.

Your casting director will save you a great deal of time by pre-reading actors, so you will see only the best. As you make your selections, always try to have a backup for each part. Then, if your first choice is not available when you need him, or is too expensive, you will have someone to go to.

Rehearsal sessions are optional, and a certain amount of rehearsal time can be built into the actors' contracts. Depending on the type of movie you are doing, rehearsals can be a major time saver. Even if you only get to sit around a table and read the script together, you would be surprised at how many small, potentially time-consuming problems can be worked out during a read-through. And time spent here is time saved while you are shooting.

Finding Office Space

Once your director and lead actor are set, you have just a few more tasks to perform before you can begin the pre-production phase of your movie. The first task is finding suitable office space. Now, that's pretty basic. You don't have to be an Einstein to figure that one out. But the kind of space you get and where it is located—that you will need to give some thought to. Office space may be somewhat limited, since you will require a short-term lease of only four to five months.

I am referring now to low-budget movies, which I presume you will be making. In order to properly service your movie, you will

do please

require a minimum of about thirty-five hundred square feet of office space, with at least eight individual offices: producer's office, director's office (D.G.A. requirement), U.P.M. and assistant directors, art department, transportation, wardrobe, set dressing and props, and accounting, plus a reception area for your production office coordinator and assistant P.O.C.

If you are making your movie in or around the Los Angeles area, finding suitable office space should not be too much of a problem. Landlords with office space near studio facilities are used to short-term rentals. But timing is everything. If there is a lot of production going on, that kind of office space could be limited. If you are shooting outside of southern California, short-term office space may be harder to come by.

In Los Angeles, you can figure about $1.40 to $1.50 a square foot per month, plus a hefty deposit. I mention this, because you must remember to put this figure in your budget. It is part of your negative cost.

When looking for office space, keep in mind that what you need is something functional; you do not need luxury. Money spent on office space does not show up on the screen, and that is the only thing that is really important—what is up there on the screen. Try to locate yourself central to the support services you will need for your film, such as labs and post facilities. It will save you a lot of travel time.

Once you have obtained your office space, you now have to furnish it. Everything you need, such as desks, chairs, filing cabinets, and lamps will be found at furniture rental houses. You should be able to furnish all your offices for around $1,500 a month. Then, there are the business machines you will need: a photocopier, computers, fax machine, and, of course, a telephone system. Again, everything is rented. Figure another $2,000 a month for those items. These are all budgeted items and must be included in your overall film cost.

Dealing with Guilds and Unions

Your final task before you commit to a pre-production start date is to sign contracts between your company and all the guilds and unions that you will be doing business with. Many independent films today are shot, supposedly, "non-union," but this is somewhat of a misnomer. No movie, except for extremely low-budget, usually amateurish films, are shot without Screen Actors Guild members. An actor who wants to work in film must belong to S.A.G. If he works for a non-signatory company, he can be fined and suspended, which means no mainstream production company will be able to hire him. And since it is his face up on the screen, he can't very well deny the fact that it *is* him up there. So, your company *will* sign a contract with S.A.G.

There is a minimum rate that must be adhered to for all S.A.G. players, but there is some latitude when it comes to low-budget movies. Depending on the negative cost of your film, certain minimums and certain working conditions are negotiable. You will have to sit down with a guild representative and explain what kind of a deal you want.

There are all kinds of deals that can be negotiated. Your lead actor may take no salary up front for a piece of the gross revenue. Other actors may take minimum salaries in lieu of larger deferred salaries, which would come out of first monies in. This is a good deal for both parties. The producer gets to spend more on production, and the actor gets more than he would normally make. This, however, is something you should clear with your investors, because it means that they will have to wait a bit longer for the return on their investment.

You will also have to sign a contract with the Directors Guild of America in order to hire a qualified director, assistant director and unit production manager. It would be a big mistake to try and go non-union in this category. I'd call it penny-wise and pound-foolish. The money you would save in salary and benefits would be spent ten times over in mismanagement. And, more importantly, your film would suffer artistically. D.G.A. will be willing to deal with you in the area of low-budget films. There are different pay scales for different budgets. A five-million-dollar film will pay the full minimum guarantees, but a film with a one-million-dollar budget will have a lower scale, and a film with a two-hundred-and-fifty-thousand-dollar budget will have a still lower scale. No matter what scale you agree on, you will have to pay the fringe benefits for pension and health and welfare. But, these percentages will be based on what the actual salaries are.

Signing with the Writers Guild of America would be necessary only if the person who wrote your script is a member of that guild. If you are the writer, it would probably be in your best interest to join the W.G.A. This is easy to do. The only prerequisites are the sale of a script to a signatory company and the payment of your initiation fee, which at this time is $2,500. Your dues will be 1½ percent of your yearly earnings. It is good protection down the line, when your movie goes to all the ancillary outlets. If you do decide to join, then, of course, you would first have to become a signatory company. W.G.A. is tougher than D.G.A. or S.A.G. on minimum salaries. But lately, W.G.A. has devised a lower scale for lower-budgeted films, and seems more willing to negotiate than in the past.

That leaves the International Alliance of Theatrical Stage Employees (IATSE) and the teamsters to deal with. Virtually everyone else in your crew will be a member of IATSE, with the exception of the drivers, who are teamsters. If you are shooting in a major production area like Los Angeles, New York, or Miami, you may have some trouble trying to go non-union. It's possible you will be picketed, and the union may even try to shut you down. This doesn't happen all the time, but it does happen. A lot depends on how high-profile your film is. IATSE, like the guilds, will make deals with you regarding its members. A lot will depend on the level of production at the time you will be shooting your film. The less films in production, the better your chance of making a favorable deal. IATSE will sometimes allow a lower pay scale, will bend certain working conditions, or will allow fewer crewmembers. These areas are all negotiable, to an extent. But, again, regardless of the deals struck, you will have to pay the fringe benefits.

Teamsters in some parts of the country can be a lot tougher than the IA. Unless you make specific deals up front, you could be subjected to harassment and sabotage. But, oddly enough, you can make deals with the teamsters whereby you use three or four union drivers and the rest can be non-union. But, as I said, these deals have to be made up front.

If production is slow, a lot of union people will work non-union. If they are in a category that is afforded screen credit, they will sometimes use aliases. When things are slow, IATSE will generally turn a blind eye to this sort of thing. After all, people have to make a living.

So, what do you gain by going non-union? Hourly rates are pretty much the same, but what you save is the cost of fringe benefits. These health and pension benefits will amount to about 12 percent of your total below-the-line labor costs. For example, if your below-the-line labor runs three hundred thousand dollars, you would be saving about thirty-six thousand in fringe benefits.

If your movie is under a million dollars, just show the unions your budget and tell them your problems. If they believe you, they will usually leave you alone. But be up front with both the union and your crew. You do not want any surprises during production.

Whether or not you sign with IATSE and/or the teamsters is up to you. As the producer, you will have to decide what is best for your film. Personally, if you can afford it, I feel it is safer all around to go union. You generally get more qualified people, and you don't have to worry about work interruptions or stoppages.

Oops, One More Thing

Sorry. I said dealing with the guilds and unions was the final thing before the start of pre-production, but there is one more thing you have to do. Get your INSURANCE in place.

Every motion picture production must be properly insured. It is essential for your protection, as well as the protection of your investors. We live in a litigious society, and unfortunately, motion picture companies are prime targets for lawsuits.

Make sure that the insurance company you select has had considerable experience with the film business. There are a lot of fine points that only specialists in this field can understand and help you with. If an actor or the director becomes ill or injured and production is delayed, your insurance will cover the costs incurred because of those illnesses or injuries. You must also be covered for accidents and injuries to crew members, and for any onlookers who might be injured by a piece of equipment that falls or by a stunt that goes awry.

Although you cannot be insured for rain delays, if equipment or sets are damaged by inclement weather, that is insurable. If you are using boats or airplanes in your film, they must be covered under your policy. This is very specialized insurance, which is another reason to use an expert in this field.

Errors and Omissions insurance (E&O) must be included in your policy. A distributor will not accept delivery of your film without E&O liability insurance. This provides protection against libel, slander, copyright infringement, defamation of character, plagiarism, piracy and the unauthorized use of titles, formats, ideas, characters, plots, performances of artists or other materials. This is the only insurance application which must be signed by the producer or an authorized member of the production company.

The cost of all this insurance will come to approximately 1½ to 3 percent of the negative cost of your film. So, if you are making a two-million-dollar movie, you must budget in $30,000 to $60,000 for insurance. The difference in cost will depend on the company you do business with and the type of film you are making. Be sure you are aware of the deductibles involved, and review them with your insurance agent. They will vary for the different types of coverage provided. Also, make sure you get at least three bids.

Some of the insurance companies we have worked with are Great Northern, (818) 971-5469 (ask for Greg Jones); Fireman's Fund, (818) 487-6112 (ask for Denise Dimin); Spear, (310) 914-9368 (ask for Tom Alper); and AON Risk Management of New York. Other insurance companies that specialize in motion pictures are Traveler's Insurance, Aetna, and Near North.

Some of the firms you can send your scripts to for E&O clearance are Thompson and Thompson, (310) 273-2900; Joan Pearce & Associates, (323) 655-5464; and Marshall/Plumb Research Associates, Inc., (818) 848-7071.

Finally—The Start of Pre-Production

Pre-production for a low-budget film should last six to eight weeks, depending on the complexity of the project. Now, if you are a little unclear on what, exactly, pre-production is, let me clarify it for you. It is, simply put, getting all your ducks in a row: hiring a crew; selecting locations; building any sets that may be needed; casting your movie; renting all the production equipment, such as cameras, lighting and grip packages, and trucks; finding a lab to process your film; hiring a film editor; checking out the post-production facilities you will eventually need; finalizing your budget; settling on a shooting schedule. And those are just some of the more prominent things that have to be done; the list goes on, ad infinitum.

Now that your director is set, as well as your leading man or woman, you have moved into your new offices, all your guild and union contracts have been signed, and your insurance is in place . . . now you can say, *pre-production has begun.* And with that beginning, you must now set a date to begin PRODUCTION. This is something you should think long and hard about, because once you set a date to begin shooting, that date is locked in, carved in stone. If you budget six weeks for pre-production, every day past that six-week period will cost you money that has not been budgeted and cannot be recouped. It is money that will have to be taken out of the production period, which means it is money that will not show up on screen, and that will hurt the final product.

The importance of this cannot be overstated. Once you commit to a pre-production date, your SHOOTING date automatically locks in. *You are now spending your investors' money.* Protect it vigorously. From now on, *their* profit and *your* future depend on how you handle the money entrusted to you.

How to Hire Your Crew

Now the time has come to begin the hiring process. If you are a smart producer, you have been thinking of this ahead of time. You have networked with friends and acquaintances and researched credits on low-budget movies, and have compiled a short list of four or five people for each department.

Your first step, with the commencement of pre-production, should be the hiring of a unit production manager. This position is key to the everyday operation of your film. The U.P.M. will be your eyes and your ears; he will be an extension of you in all the physical aspects of the making of your movie. A good U.P.M. is a de facto producer, whose main function in life is to control costs, eliminate waste, and make sure every dollar spent shows up on screen. He will also serve as a buffer between you and the crew. This usually turns out to be a "good cop–bad cop" scenario. You're the good cop, the U.P.M. is the bad cop. He really doesn't mind all that much; his role just comes with the territory. And it is an important role in the game playing that goes on during the shooting of a film. Someone has to say "no" to the myriad of requests that cost money. Better him than you. The producer should remain above all the petty squabbling.

Let me state once more that U.P.M.'s, as well as most other members of your crew, can be either male of female. I will use, for the most part, the masculine pronoun, because it becomes tedious to keep saying "he or she." So, again, I trust no one will be offended.

When interviewing for a U.P.M., you should look for certain attributes that are relevant to the position. Experience is vital, especially when working in television or on a low-budget feature. Because money is tight, there is much less room for error. A minor miscalculation can end up costing you thousands of dollars. Also, there is simply no substitution for experience. Being a good, competent U.P.M. requires a lot of years of hard work; it is a long, sometimes tedious learning process. There are nuances that are acquired, as well as hundreds of little money-saving shortcuts that only come with experience.

The U.P.M. should be a people person, because his success, or failure, will hinge on how he gets along with the infinite number of personalities with whom he will have to deal.

Honesty in a U.P.M. is more than a virtue. For you, as the producer, it is an essential. An unscrupulous U.P.M. can skim off a lot of money for himself without you ever being aware of it. Fortunately, most U.P.M.'s are honest, but there are some who work the shady side of the street. In order to protect yourself, insist on references, and then check out those references.

When you talk to the people he has listed as references, be aware of how they answer you. If they praise the U.P.M., that is fine. But, if they say something like, "No comment," run the other way. You will rarely find someone who will say right out, "This guy is a thief" or "He's a terrible U.P.M." The reason is, he can be sued. So, if he can't recommend the person, he will usually say nothing.

The first thing your U.P.M. will do after he has been hired will be to break down the script and make a temporary schedule. From this, he will then create a budget. "But, I already had this done when I was making up my prospectus," you say. True, but that was months ago, maybe even years.

Crew rates have changed, and your script has probably been rewritten several times since then. This new schedule and budget will be a lot more detailed and will reflect all the changes. You will find out, for the first time, what your picture will really cost.

Now, this is where your producing skills may be put to their first test. Suppose you have raised three million dollars to make your movie, but your U.P.M. hands you a budget that shows it will cost three and a *half* million to make.

You have three options to consider. You can go back to your investors and ask for another half million—not a particularly good idea, since they may now look at you as someone who doesn't know what the hell he is doing, which certainly will do nothing to raise their comfort level. You can ignore the U.P.M.'s budget and just plunge forward hoping for the best. Unfortunately, you will, in all likelihood, come to the end of your money before you come to the end of your filming. Or—and this is probably the best solution—you can adjust your script to fit the money you have to spend.

As one of his first duties, the U.P.M. will work out a CREW HIRING SCHEDULE. This will indicate when each department will come on board and how much prep time each department will need.

With the help of your U.P.M., you will want to hire your production office coordinator almost immediately. This is the person who will get your office up and running. She is also the U.P.M.'s right hand and will begin organizing all the paperwork that is part and parcel of a shooting company.

With your U.P.M. and P.O.C. in place, you will next hire the first assistant director and the production designer. Both of these positions should be filled by the beginning of the second week of prep. The director will have considerable input regarding these two positions. According to D.G.A. contract, the director has final approval on who will be his first A.D. He may want to use someone he has worked with before, or he may just want to be in on the selection process. The U.P.M. will usually work closely with the director in finding the right first A.D.

As soon as the first assistant director comes on salary, he will take over the scheduling duties from the U.P.M. As locations are selected and firmed up and script changes are made—which is as certain as the sun rising in the east—the schedule will continue in a constant state of flux. Casting your movie can result in schedule changes, because some performers may not be available on the dates you want them. Also, you may cast a small part that works in two different locations. Unfortunately, those locations are scheduled to be shot a week apart. This means you will have to carry the actor, who has two lines, on salary for a week. So, the first A.D. will start moving his breakdown strips around to try and get that actor scheduled into one or two days.

There are dozens of other variables that will affect the scheduling of your film, such as the availability of certain locations and whether you will be shooting day or night. You may need to accommodate certain physical changes of an actor because of story. Weather can play a factor. Even the story line itself—because of their dramatic value, the director may want to shift certain scenes to a different part of the schedule. The fact is, scheduling changes will be made up until the day you start shooting, and maybe after that.

The director will have to work closely with the production designer, so personality, as well as talent, will come into play. The director will have his reasons for wanting a certain production designer, and those reasons should be taken into account. However, the producer and the U.P.M. should make the final selection in this area. The look of the show is very important, but in a low-budget film, cost control is more important.

The production designer will hire a CONSTRUCTION COORDINA-TOR, who, in turn, will hire his crew of carpenters and painters. How many, and how much prep they need, will depend on your script and the locations you find.

Your LOCATION MANAGER should come on board about the same time as your production designer. In low-budget films, it is unlikely you will be doing much set construction. This means your interior sets will have to be shot in practical locations. In other words, in real homes, stores, warehouses, etc.

Since your location manager is a relatively high-paid individual, your U.P.M. will evaluate exactly when he will be needed. If your film takes place in only three or four locations, then starting a location manager on salary can be delayed for a couple of weeks. The more locations you have, the sooner he should start.

During the first couple of weeks of prep, you, your director, and your U.P.M. will be looking for a director of photography. Although he won't come on salary until about a week before shooting, it is necessary for you to have someone you all agree on committed to your project. That will give him time to notify the rest of his crew, the camera operator and the assistant cameramen, so they will be available when you start production.

The final category the producer needs to be intimately involved with is the choosing of the COSTUME DESIGNER. The costume designer's importance is proportional to the genre of the film. If you are doing a period piece, using a distinctive locale, or making a high-concept film, this becomes a more challenging assignment, and you would need a more creative designer.

In a low-budget, contemporary film, the costume designer's main function will be to purchase wardrobe for the cast, hopefully staying away from Saks, Neiman-Marcus, and Rodeo Drive.

The costume designer should not be brought in until most of your cast has been selected, because only then will she know who she will be shopping for. Once the wardrobe has been purchased and fitted, the costume designer's job is done—at least it is on a low-budget film. A costume designer will usually command a pretty high salary, so you need to use her sparingly. The SET COSTUMERS will take over from the Designer and handle the wardrobe from then on.

Set costumers will usually be brought on about a week before the start of shooting. The U.P.M. will find qualified set people for your show.

The SET DECORATOR will need about three weeks of preparation, and his SWING GANG about a week. The set decorator will be hired by the U.P.M. with input from the production designer, since they will be working close together. The set decorator will hire his own swing gang, usually people he has worked with and trusts.

The PROPERTY MASTER will be brought on either two or three weeks before shooting. This will depend on the nature of your script— how many props will be needed and if there is any manufacturing of props involved. The U.P.M. will usually hire the property master, who, in turn, will hire his own assistant.

The GAFFER, BEST BOY, KEY GRIP, and SECOND GRIP will all get one week of prep, starting at the same time as the cameraman. The majority of D.P.'s have their own preferences of gaffers and key grips, and the U.P.M. will try to accommodate the cameraman in these areas. It all depends on how much these key people want in the way of salary and how much manpower they are used to working with. In low-budget films, union scale is pretty much the norm. As the producer, you will be the final arbiter, but you would do well to listen to your U.P.M.'s advice.

The gaffer and key grip will hire their crews subject to the approval of the U.P.M. Grip and Electric crews will need three or four days in which to get all their equipment together and get the trucks loaded.

Your SOUND MIXER will only need a day of prep to get all his equipment together and check it out. The U.P.M. will present you with several résumés of mixers, from which you will make your choice. Check the résumés carefully and call those people listed as references. The sound department is usually given short shrift on a shooting company. But bad sound recording will make your film appear amateurish. So, take particular care in the selection of your sound mixer.

As with other department heads, your mixer will <u>hire his boom operator</u> and, if necessary, the cableperson.

<u>SPECIAL EFFECTS</u> personnel will be hired by the U.P.M. on an as-needed basis. The number of effects men needed and the cost of materials and rentals will, of course, depend on your story.

<u>MAKEUP and HAIRDRESSING</u> personnel normally need one day of prep in order to get all their supplies together. Unless an actor requests a particular makeup person or hairdresser, the U.P.M. will usually make the decision on who will be hired. If there is a specific request from an actor, the makeup or hairdressing person will usually ask for over-scale, and on higher-budgeted films will, in most cases, get what they ask for. But you are doing a low-budget film. If this situation occurs, it will be up to the producer to make the decision, Should I pay the extra money or risk offending my star by getting a different makeup person?

This is one of those situations you have to play by ear. There are no hard-and-fast rules. A lot will depend on how much clout the actor has and what kind of a person he is.

The <u>SCRIPT SUPERVISOR will get one week of prep.</u> The U.P.M. will confer with the director on this position, because it is the director who will be working with this person on a day-to-day basis. Personality, as well as skill, will be a major factor here. And, of course, the universal question, Will he or she work for the money?

The <u>CRAFTS SERVICE PERSON</u> and the <u>MEDIC</u> will be hired by the <u>U.P.M.</u> and will get one day of prep each.

<u>TRANSPORTATION</u> is the final category. The U.P.M. hires the TRANSPORTATION COORDINATOR. If you have only a few "picture vehicles," you can sometimes get away without a coordinator and just have a DRIVER CAPTAIN. Either way, the U.P.M. will evaluate this and go the cheapest and most efficient way. That is not a contradiction in terms—many times the cheapest or simplest way *is* the most efficient.

The Coordinator or Captain will then hire the rest of his drivers on an as-needed basis. He will also contract for all the rolling stock, which will include <u>grip and electric trucks, prop truck, camera truck, dressing rooms, motor homes, honey wagons (portable restrooms), camera cranes, and anything else with wheels.</u> All this, of course, will be done under the aegis of the U.P.M., who will approve all deals.

During the pre-production period, while you, the producer, are busy casting your movie, supervising the polishing of your script (which is an ongoing process), okaying wardrobe and locations, the U.P.M. is supervising the hiring of the crew and making deals for all the equipment necessary to make your movie.

Selecting the right equipment is almost as important as selecting the right crew. Panavision is the Mercedes-Benz of camera equipment. It is usually a little more expensive than other camera equipment you can rent, but the quality is worth it, and most cameramen will request it. Your U.P.M. will advise you on this. If your budget is such that you really cannot afford the extra expense, he will recommend that you go with Mitchells, which are good, high-quality cameras.

Your U.P.M. and your gaffer will check out the electrical equipment to make sure you are getting first-quality items. Special attention should be given to the generator you will be renting. While you are working on location, electricity is the lifeblood of your shooting company, and the generator is the heart that pumps that blood. If the generator goes down while you are shooting, everything comes to a halt. On a low-budget film, this is tantamount to major disaster. A good gaffer will make sure to get a top-quality generator, and one with enough amps to service your company properly.

During the fifth week of pre-production (providing you have a six-week pre-production schedule), two important events take place. The first is a TECH SCOUT. This is where the producer, director, U.P.M., assistant directors, location manager, production designer, construction coordinator, set decorator, D.P., gaffer, key grip, and driver captain get into a couple of vans and go to each location that will be shot.

At each location, they will discuss the specifics of what is needed. The director will explain the angles he plans to use so that the driver captain will know where to park all the equipment. The less equipment has to be moved during the shooting day, the less time is wasted, and the more time is devoted to shooting the movie.

The D.P. will be able to see from which direction the sunlight will be coming. The gaffer will know what lights will be needed, where his generator will be placed, and how much cable he will need. The grips will see how much dolly track they will need and if they will have to build parallels. The decorator will see if he needs any more dressing, the production designer will find out what signage is needed, and the assistant directors will be able to evaluate if they have enough extras for the scene and if there are proper facilities for feeding the crew.

These are just some of the things that will be discussed during a Tech Scout. And the same scene will be repeated at every location they go to. These scouts sometimes take two days to get through, and sometimes, *long* days.

The second event is the PRODUCTION MEETING. Here, all the keys on the crew, plus the producer, writer (if available), director, U.P.M., and assistant directors gather around a large table and go through the script scene by scene. Now, prior to all this, the director has had individual meetings with wardrobe, props, special effects, transportation, and of course, his assistants. But here at the production meeting is where all the ribbons are tied together. All the unanswered questions are answered, inconsistencies in the script are solved, and confusion regarding any aspect of the script is clarified. This is the place where all the cracks are filled, so that the pesky things that often fall through them can't.

After the Tech Scout and the Production Meeting, the U.P.M. will then fine-tune the budget. You will find that the budgets for some departments have gone up, while others have gone down. Hopefully, they balance out. If not, you must then make your last-minute corrections. As the producer, it will be up to you to decide what stays and what goes. You have a bottom line to meet—you have a bonding company that can take your movie from you if you exceed your budget—so, you make damn sure your budget is accurate and that you can keep the cost of your movie within that budget.

Finally, the director will sign off on the budget and schedule, meaning that he has agreed to do the movie within the allotted time and within the allotted budget. In other words, his butt is now on the line, too.

Okay, folks, that's it . . . *it's showtime.* That momentous, portentous first day of shooting is at hand. All the pieces of the production puzzle are in place. Now, all you need is for the first A.D. to yell, "ROLL IT."

Phase 2—Production

Well, you made it this far. Now the fun begins . . . so to speak. Talk about butterflies in the stomach. The night before shooting begins, you probably won't be able to sleep. You will be going over in your mind every horrible dilemma, every monstrous disaster that could possibly take place. And the scariest part is, there are problems out there of which you are not even aware. So, now you start to worry about the problems that you don't even know about.

But worrying about things that *could* happen will not help. The reality is that shooting your movie will probably fall someplace between Utopia and unmitigated catastrophe. There are going to be problems; that is a given. As the producer, your job now becomes one of *damage control*. It will be up to you to head off problems before they occur, as well as solving problems after they occur. You will never bat a thousand in this ballpark, so don't let that bother you. Your success will be measured on how well you contain the myriad of predicaments that will be placed in your path.

The first morning of shooting, you are on the set at 6:30—barely the crack of dawn. Now, normally, the producer does not have to be the first person on the set. In fact, most producers show up, if they do at all, around 10:00 A.M. But you are not most producers. This is your baby. Your entire future could depend on what happens with this movie. You are not about to leave anything to chance.

This brings up the question of CONTROL vs. INTERFERENCE, and whether or not you know the difference. Controlling and interfering are two entirely different matters. You not only *want* to be in control, you *need* to be. But you want to control without interfering. Granted, it is a fine line to walk, and it is an absolute necessity that you understand the difference. You have hired a lot of capable, experienced people to make your movie. You need to let them do their jobs. However, you are not stupid. Even though you don't have set experience, common sense will alert you to some things that do not seem right to you.

Know Your Problems

The worst thing you can do is to attack a problem without being sure it is a problem in the first place. This is where your relationship with your U.P.M. comes in handy. Suppose the D.P. has said he is ready, but everyone is just standing around . . . nothing is happening. This delay is costing you money. But instead of angrily running up to the first A.D. and demanding to know what the hell is going on, you take the U.P.M. aside and quietly ask him. He will tell you that there was a small tear in the actress's dress, and it is being repaired. It will take about five minutes. Okay, now you know. And like everyone else, you will wait the five minutes, because in this case, there is nothing you can do about it.

But suppose the director is shooting a *master scene,* and after he finishes it, he wants to turn around in the *opposite* direction to do some of his cover shots, instead of staying and doing the cover shots he needs in the *same* direction he has been shooting. What this means is a lot of wasted time tearing out lamps and rearranging furniture, only to have to put it all back again. Now, common sense will tell you to stay in the direction you have been shooting until you are finished in that direction.

All right, as the producer, do you confront the director yourself and demand that he proceed in a more efficient manner? No, you would be better off sending in your point man, the U.P.M., to discuss this with the director. He will suggest to the director that they can save a lot of time by not turning around. That they should stay in the same direction. The director may agree to this, not having been aware of the extra time it would have taken. In that case, problem solved, and you didn't even have to get out of your chair.

However, the director may tell the U.P.M. to screw off, that this is the way he is going to do it. In that case, you *will* have to get out of your chair. You will take the director aside to discuss this matter. You will *not* do it in front of the crew. That would look bad for the director; it would look bad for you; and in the end, it would only serve to hurt the quality of the film.

It is always possible that the director has a good reason for doing what he is doing. Perhaps it is something in the performance level that works better by shooting a particular actor's close shot first. This is a decision you will have to make. By doing it the director's way, it could cost you a couple of thousand dollars in overtime. Is it worth it to the picture? It's your call.

Shooting Has Begun—What's Left for Me to Do?

If a show is properly prepared, it will make everyone's life a lot easier. A mistake made during prep can easily be corrected. A mistake made during shooting can cost you thousands of dollars. This is why so much emphasis is put on the preparation period. Some producers feel that once a show is off the ground, they have done their job. Now they can go out and play golf and come in at the end of the day to watch dailies. Nothing could be further from the truth.

A producer's mere presence on a set can make an immense difference in the attitudes of the actors and the crew—depending, of course, on the producer. I have worked with producers who have created havoc on a set by callously interfering in every department, second-guessing, and generally making themselves obnoxious. They do this in a misguided attempt to assert their authority. But all they do is cause dissension and an unpleasant work environment. And this works against the ultimate goal, which is to get the picture done on schedule and on budget.

The producer's presence on a set, if done right, can be a positive influence. This is the kind of producer you should strive to be: a producer who knows how to lend support, knows how to guide, and knows when to shut up. Every set is different; every director is different; every crew is different. You must be astute enough to sense the temperament of your crew and be able to fit in as one of the interlocking pieces, rather than standing apart from everyone.

Watching dailies is *not* entertainment for the producer—it is work. In fact, it is some of the most important work you will be called upon to perform. This is the film that will eventually become your motion picture. From these bits and pieces that you will see each day, you must be able to visualize how they will fit into the final product. As the producer, you must evaluate each shot that you see, for its individual content.

The questions you will be asking yourself as you view this footage each day will be innumerable. How are the performance levels? Is the director getting the values that were in the script? Are the actors saying the lines the way they were written? Were any plot points missed? Does the director really understand the scene as it relates to the rest of the story? Is there enough coverage for the editor? How is the chemistry working between the actors? Are they believable? How is the camera work? Is the lighting what you were expecting? Is the operator framing each shot correctly? Is every scene in focus? How is the background action? Are the assistant directors utilizing all the extras you have paid for? Is the makeup okay? Is the actress's hair done the way you want? Is the wardrobe what you agreed to? How is the sound? Is it hollow, or are you getting properly modulated voices? Is there too much off-scene noise? Will you have to loop any of the scenes?

Do you see what I am getting at here? Entertainment, it is not. As the producer, you must not only evaluate your dailies; if they are not up to your expectations, you must also do something about it. This could involve discussions far into the night with your director and his assistant.

Because dailies are now telecined directly onto tape, you can view them on a television set in your office or home. It is no longer necessary to go to a screening room. This makes it much easier to discuss each scene, because you can now run your VCR forward and backward as you discuss each take in detail.

Don't hesitate to be completely forthright with your director. If you have concerns, get them out in the open. After the picture is finished, it will be too late. Have your discussions while there is still time to do something about it. Most directors will have their own vision of what their film should be. If you have had discussions with your director regarding *your* vision, *before* you hired him, then both of you should be on the same page.

But although you and your director may have the same vision, sometimes how you approach that vision can vary considerably. If you see the direction he is taking is not what you want, then, for heaven's sake, *speak up.* You are the producer, and although the director's credit may read, "A Film By," it is still *your* movie, and when push comes to shove, you call the shots.

How a Producer Can Change the Destiny of a Movie

Many years ago, Columbia Pictures made a movie called *All the King's Men,* starring Broderick Crawford and Mercedes McCambridge and directed by Robert Rosson. At that time, Harry Cohn was the president of Columbia Studios. When the film was completed, Cohn took it up to Santa Barbara for a sneak preview. Well, the response was somewhat less than enthusiastic.

Cohn decided to take the film over himself. He pulled it from release and put it back into the cutting room. He sent a small camera crew out to shoot inserts and stock shots, and spent a year reediting the film, working in the cutting room with the editor, actually altering the entire story structure. What he ended up with was a totally different motion picture from the one that had been previewed a year earlier.

As they say, the rest is history. *All the King's Men* went on to win the Academy Award for Best Picture, Robert Rosson for Best Director, Broderick Crawford for Best Actor, and Mercedes McCambridge for Best Supporting Actress. Harry Cohn received no credit at all, even though he was almost singularly responsible for the success of this film.

That is what I call a proactive producer. He was in control, and he exercised that control. Cohn may have been a lot of things, mostly bad, to a lot of different people, but he was a Filmmaker. He used his gut instincts to get the picture he wanted up on the screen. Harry Cohn knew what it meant to be a producer, and he never shied away from it.

Just remember, if your film turns out badly, you are going to shoulder all of the blame. Make no mistake about that. Your investors will not be interested in what went on during the making of the movie. They will not care that the director went in a different direction than you wanted him to or that the actors interpreted their roles differently. They will look at you and see someone who failed them, someone who cost them a great deal of money.

Because this is your first film, a disaster like this could also make it your last. Just be sure that this movie is *your* movie—for better or for worse. Since you are going to take the blame for a bad movie anyway, at least make sure it is your movie, and not someone else's.

The motion picture business is sometimes a very idiosyncratic business. If a movie is bad, the producer suffers all the slings and arrows. However, if it is a good film, he only gets partial credit. He must share the accolades with the director, the actors, and the writer. "Not fair," you say? No one said life, or the motion picture business, is fair. It is just the way it is.

And the Problems Keep Rolling In

The life of the producer, during the shooting of a movie, is fraught with problems: huge problems, teeny problems, and everything in between. What those problems will be is anyone's guess. After you finish your movie, you could shoot it a second time with the same cast and crew, and whereas you would not run into the same problems, you would be faced with a whole *new* set of problems.

Manufacturing movies is not the same as manufacturing automobiles. When you make a car, you know exactly how much the car will cost to build, and you know exactly how much you will get for it and what your profit will be. When you make a movie, you hope you know how much it will cost to make, you have no idea how much you will get for it, and you can only pray for a profit.

Just think of all the variables you have to deal with when you shoot a movie. Weather can be a constant nemesis. Rain, high winds, fog—all of these can decimate a schedule. When Steven Spielberg was shooting *Jurassic Park* on the island of Kauai, they were hit with a hurricane that destroyed most of their sets. That cost them a few million bucks due to delays in shooting and rebuilding. Now, *that* is considered a major problem.

I was shooting a TV show at the beach in Malibu with lots of pretty girls in very skimpy bathing suits. When we scouted the location, the weather was bright and sunny. When we arrived to shoot, a heavy blanket of fog rolled in. We shot the scene anyway (heck, this was TV), simply ignoring the goose bumps on the girls. That comes under the category of a minor problem.

Besides weather, there are almost always actor problems to one degree or another. Actors are late; actors get sick; actors don't know their lines. They don't like their dressing rooms; they're not happy with their wardrobe; the assistant director yelled at them; the director is giving more attention to another actor. And the list goes on, ad nauseum. So, you deal with the problems, one at a time, always maintaining proper decorum, at least as long as you can.

On *Miami Vice,* Don Johnson decided he didn't want to be called before noon on Mondays, and he didn't want to work after noon on Fridays, and he didn't want to work at night. So, we learned to live with that by writing him out of scenes and scheduling the shows to accommodate him. If he was on the phone in his dressing room, he wouldn't come out until he was finished, keeping the shooting company waiting for sometimes as long as twenty or thirty minutes. But, what the hell, we had a hit show, and Universal had deep pockets. However, if this was *your* little feature, and *your* money, and your actor kept you waiting like that, what would you do? Think about it. Because it could happen, and you will have to deal with it.

I was doing a television series many years ago called *The Hathaways,* starring Jack Weston and Peggy Cass. It was about a married couple living with three chimpanzees, who were treated like their children. The only problem was, Jack was terrified of the chimps. In one scene, Jack had to take hold of one of the chimp's hands and walk with him. The trainer explained to Jack, very carefully, that when he put out his hand, he should keep his fingers curled downward. Under no circumstances should he put his hand straight out, because that is a sign of aggression to a chimp. Yeah, I'm sure you're way ahead of me. Jack put his hand straight out, and the chimp almost took it off with one bite. Fortunately for Jack, he had quick reflexes and jerked his hand away a split second before it became a chimp hors d'oeuvre. However, that finished Jack for the rest of the day—actually, for the rest of the series. From then on, the producers instructed the writers never to have Jack in immediate proximity to the chimps.

The producer may be called on at any moment to mediate a dispute or to deal with a recalcitrant actor or director, or simply to flex his muscles to get a show back on track. We mentioned that when you cast a show, try to steer clear of actors who bring with them bad reputations. No matter how nice they are when you meet them, once they are on a set, Dr. Jekyll can quickly become Mr. Hyde.

Quick illustration of this: Early in my career, I was a second assistant director on a movie called *From Here to Eternity*, which starred Burt Lancaster, Montgomery Clift, and Frank Sinatra. I met Sinatra when he tested for the role of Maggio, and despite the nasty reputation that preceded him, he was absolutely charming during the whole day of tests. I couldn't believe that this was the same person who had been vilified as angry, unpleasant, with a violent temper. Once shooting started on the film, however, Sinatra's demeanor changed, drastically. He reverted back to what must have been his natural state: nasty, argumentative, and belligerent.

The moral of the story is, don't take an actor at face value. If you have heard a lot of bad things about him, investigate. You don't have to write him off because of rumors, but you should be wary, and you should find out if the rumors are true.

Then, of course, there are other minor, and not so minor, annoyances, like airplane noise, traffic noise, sirens, dogs barking, children yelling, etc., etc., etc. So, you deal with these problems. Airplane noise, you have absolutely no control over, so you wait until the plane is gone. If you are shooting in an area where there happens to be a lot of air traffic, then you must make a decision. If you keep waiting, you may not finish the day's work, which means you would have to come back to that location the next day—very costly. Your only other option is to keep shooting through the noise and loop the scenes later in post—much less costly.

Other interruptions, such as boom boxes, leaf blowers, and jack hammers can be dealt with. Fifty or a hundred dollars can be a cheap pay-off to get rid of a nuisance. Leave those negotiations to your location manager; that is what he does best.

Then, of course, there are the actor illnesses. This can be considered a major problem. Even though your cast insurance will take care of most of the costs, there will usually be a ten-thousand-dollar deductible attached to your insurance contract. So, okay, you pay the ten thousand, glad to get away with only having to pay that. But because you may have to shut down for a few days, a lot of things can happen in those few days that will cost you dearly, and your insurance won't cover those costs.

Suppose, for instance, you were halfway through a scene when you had to shut down, and that part of the scene had been shot in bright sunlight. Now, you come back to finish the scene, and it is gray and cloudy. The cameraman says it will never match. So, that leaves you with three options. You can reshoot the first part of the scene, so it will match the light you have now, or you can go on to something else and come back at a later date, when the sun is out.

Unfortunately, both of those options are costly. Your third option is to bite the bullet and complete the scene regardless of the light. Some of the difference in light can be balanced in post, but there will probably be some noticeable difference. How important is that to you? If you're doing a low-budget film and money is very tight, you would be surprised how insignificant a little difference in light can be.

Well, right about now you are probably wondering, Does anything *ever* go right? Actually, you will find that *most* things go right. It is just that shooting a motion picture is, by its very nature, organized chaos. You are constantly walking a tightrope over a chasm of disaster, but if you keep your focus and your balance, you can get to the other side mostly unscathed.

There are so many opportunities for mistakes to occur that even if you head off the vast majority of them, it still leaves plenty of room for some to slip through the cracks. But don't let all this unduly scare you. You were smart enough to get your film put together; you are smart enough to keep it together. *Common sense* is your most significant ally. Don't be afraid to use it.

10

Phase 3—
Post-Production

Well, you did it. Shooting is complete. Your motion picture is *in the can*. And with all the trials and tribulations, the problems and the mistakes, the worry and the grief, your picture was shot on schedule and on budget. Hard to believe, but it's true. After all the smoke has cleared, you are still standing on the field of battle, unbloodied (well, maybe a little bit bloody), but definitely unbowed.

You now begin to put away the tools of production and turn over the details of wrapping the shooting company to your U.P.M. and Production Accountant. It will take them two to three weeks to wrap up the company. This will involve making sure all the props and set dressing rentals have been returned, as well as all the lighting and grip equipment, the cameras, dollies, and rolling stock. Gradually, everyone will be eliminated from your payroll, and all outstanding bills will be paid. Again, the U.P.M. will control most of this process. Your job will simply be to oversee the procedure.

You may want to keep an office open during post-production, but you will probably reduce your staff to just yourself and someone to answer the phones. If you have leftover film stock, there are companies that will buy it from you for anywhere from ten to fifty cents on the dollar. This will depend on how many full rolls of film you have and how many *short ends*. Also, there are companies that will buy props, set dressing, and wardrobe that you may have purchased. You can even sell your sets if you have built any.

The end of shooting and the closing up of shop can often be a rather melancholy experience. In some ways, it is like the end of a marriage. All these people you have been so close to for all these weeks are gone. Just like that, they are out of your life, moving on to other shows and other jobs. But for the producer, this is not the end. Far from it. You now look forward to the final phase of the filmmaking process. Can you say *post-production?*

Post-production has a life all its own. Sometimes that life will be like a smooth highway, with nothing but sunshine and happiness. But at other times, it can be like a hundred miles of unpaved road in a rainstorm.

It is during the *post* process that the producer must be able to evaluate the picture, as a whole. He must have the ability, and the intestinal fortitude, to be brutally honest when discussing the strengths and the weaknesses of his film. And every film has them. So, as the producer, you will need to reinforce the strengths and minimize the weaknesses of your movie.

There are scenes that seemed so very important when they were being filmed, but now, in the overall context of the movie, they stand out awkwardly, or are confusing, or worse yet, impede the storytelling process. These scene must be tightened, and sometimes, eliminated entirely.

A director may want to keep in a scene even though it no longer works, merely because it was a difficult scene to shoot and he is proud of the fact that he was able to get it on film.

The writer will always argue over the elimination of any of his dialogue, even though trimming helps the pace and makes for a better scene. And the director of photography will want you to keep certain scenes because of the beautiful scenery or exquisite lighting.

As the producer, however, your job is the *overview.* In other words, what is best for the picture as a whole. If you tell too much story, you will bore an audience, which is a cardinal, and unforgivable sin. Many a picture, which could have been a success, failed because it was too long. Cutting ten or twenty or even thirty minutes from a film could make all the difference. Again . . . *it depends on the film.* If your story holds the audience, length is not a problem. It is only when an audience becomes restless that you need to deal with length.

The audience remembers the end of a film most of all. When they get up to leave the theater and talk to one another, a solid, fast-paced ending will usually elicit a positive reaction. An audience will forgive a slow beginning if you have a terrific ending. The reverse is not always true. Under no circumstances, however, will the audience forgive a film for the extra half hour that did not *entertain* them. So, don't be afraid to make the tough decisions. That is what makes you a producer.

There is something about the post-production mystique that can be very intimidating. There are areas of this process that are highly technical, and "Post People" have their own nomenclature, their own phrases, their own terminology. It is really not necessary for you to learn all of this, but you should have a working knowledge of how the process develops and how your film progresses from raw footage to the finished product.

The Film Editor

With the beginning of post, your FILM EDITOR now becomes the most important person in your professional life. He or she will be hired somewhere toward the end of your pre-production period, and he will go on salary on your first day of production, along with an assistant film editor. They will take care of assembling each day's dailies, having them coded, and getting them to the producer, director, and cameraman. As I mentioned before, dailies are now telecined. This is a process whereby videotape is made directly from the developed negative.

Positive prints are no longer needed for editing. The positive print, which you see in the theater, is made only after all the post-production processes are complete. Higher-budget films will go ahead and make positive prints for dailies to be viewed in a screening room, but lower-budget films and television shows will not want to take on that kind of expense for something that is really a redundancy.

The weapon of choice now, for an editor, is FINALCUT PRO. This software lets the editor to edit the movie on his computer. It is fast and efficient and allows the editor to make almost instantaneous changes. Although FinalCut Pro is now being used extensively, it has not replaced the AVID system, which has been in use for several years. The advantage of FinalCut Pro is that it is smaller and faster and can be used wherever there is room for a computer—and it doesn't have to be a computer that is dedicated to only that application.

Years ago, when they had to edit with film on MOVIOLA machines, it was an involved and cumbersome process. The editors would watch the film through a viewer on the Moviola. When they needed to make a cut, they would have to remove the film, put it on a splicing table, make their cut, attach the other piece of film with an adhesive, and then put it back on the Moviola. Now, the whole process is performed with the push of a button . . . zap . . . and it's done. Editing, which used to take months, can now be done in a few weeks. Technology, however, is moving at such a rapid pace that by the time you read this, there may be a whole new way to edit film.

Good film editors are talented and creative individuals. They understand drama, performance, and timing. Editors are artists in every sense of the word and can make the difference between a mediocre film and a great one.

The post-production process really begins with the first day of production, when the film goes to the lab for processing. This is where the editor immediately becomes involved. He is the first one who sees the dailies, and he looks at them with an editor's eyes. How will the scene cut together? Are there enough close shots? Are the actors' "looks" facing the correct screen direction? Does the close-up of one actor balance in size with the close-up of the other actor in the scene? Are there any shots missing?

If he sees anything that bothers him, he will go to the director at once to discuss the problem. Editors are not clairvoyant; they cannot read what is in a director's mind. The good editor will keep an open dialogue with his director, so he will be able to gather insight into how the director perceives each scene.

As scenes are completed, the editor will begin to make rough assemblages. Within a week after the film has finished shooting, he will usually have an assembly for the director to see. By contract with the D.G.A., the director of a theatrical motion picture has the right to supervise the cutting of a film. He gets his shot at editing the film the way he wants. He is closer to the film that has been shot than anyone else, and he wants his vision up on the screen. During this time, the producer may see the film only with the director's approval. Often, when the director is finished with his cut, he will want the producer to view the film with him. It is important that you make the time to do this.

There are very few directors in Hollywood who have approval of a *final* cut. That is something that must be written into their personal service contracts, and only a select few like Spielberg, Coppola, or Scorcese have a prayer of getting that clause in their contracts.

The producer is the person who, in the end, has the final say on what the finished product will look like. After the director has finished his cut, you will take over. Now, you may like what the director has done and not want to change anything. That is up to you. But this is your time to try the changes you would like to see. And don't forget about your investor. He may have a few ideas of his own.

During the editing process, certain dynamics can take place. Because you and your editor have seen all of the footage so many times, this repetitive viewing can become boring and actually create fatigue. At this point, a pair of fresh eyes could be useful. But where do you find them? One way is to hold a private screening for a few people whose opinions you respect and trust.

Objective viewpoints can be a valuable asset. Not being able to see the forest because of the trees may be an old cliché, but there is a great deal of truth in it. Listen to what people say, weigh their opinions, but in the end, do what your gut tells you. More times than not, you will be right.

There may come a time, of course, when the editor is not doing the job you want. Perhaps his timing is not your timing, and his idea of telling a story does not agree with yours. If this ever happens, you may have to bite the bullet and bring in a new editor. But this option should be used only as a last resort.

In thirty years of producing film and television, I have had to fire only one editor. We had a serious disagreement about the way the story of a particular film should be told. He was a talented editor, but I knew the way I wanted my picture to look, and I was not going to settle for someone else's vision. As it turned out, the movie was quite successful.

I knew I had hurt this editor's feelings, but it was a decision I felt had to be made for the good of the project. As a producer, there will be times when you are called upon to make tough decisions. And if you take your job seriously, you will make them.

On the other side of the coin, I remember sitting in an editing room in Tokyo with a lot of footage that, seemingly, would not go together. That editor found a way to tell the story when I couldn't get a handle on it. This is where a good editor can make a good producer look great.

On one movie, my partner and I could not agree on how the picture should be cut. The director and I wanted it one way, and my partner and the distributor wanted it another way. There was a bitter fight, and in order to get most of what I wanted, I agreed to cut one scene from the film. Unfortunately, it was the director's favorite scene. She hasn't spoken to me since. Feelings can run very deep at times like this.

When you have been locked in an editing room for a long period of time, it is important to *air yourself out*. Most editing rooms have no windows, and life gets very cramped and tensions build quickly. Desire for success is strong and the fear of failure is even stronger, so you have to work hard at maintaining your objectivity. If you lose sight of where you're going with your film, it's always a good idea to go back and reread your script and try to remember all the things you loved about it in the first place.

Because a film is so personal, and you will have lived with this story for such a long time, there will, undoubtedly, be certain things you will want to see. Maybe you will like one actor's performance more than another's, so you will edit the film to give the first actor more screen time. Maybe you want the pace of a scene faster, or slower, or possibly, you want to shift the continuity of that scene to improve the story line.

It is truly amazing what can be done with a film in an editing room. You can make a comedy out of a drama, turn a good guy into a bad guy, a lady into a tramp, or a love story into a political statement. I have seen actors totally eliminated from a film without changing the story one iota. Raw footage is almost like a hunk of modeling clay that you can mold into just about anything you want. As the producer, you become the Michelangelo, and the film is your *Pieta*.

While you are working with the editor, you will find that certain INSERT SHOTS will be needed to tell your story properly. If your budget has been put together correctly, there will be an item in the post-production area that will allow money for insert shots.

An insert is a very tight shot of an object, something that an audience needs to be made aware of so that they can follow the story better. For instance: A person is alone in a room, a dark and stormy night; he does not suspect anyone else is in the house. Cut to an insert of the doorknob as it begins to slowly turn. Another example: The killer is leaving the scene of his crime after making sure that nothing has been left behind to identify him . . . except for a glove that fell from his pocket. As he leaves the room, we cut to an insert of the glove lying on the floor.

Once you have entered into the post-production phase of your movie, you will want to hire a POST-PRODUCTION SUPERVISOR. This is the person who will help guide you through all the procedures necessary to complete your film. He or she is a detail-oriented person who will arrange the post schedule; make sure tapes and film get to where they are supposed to be, when they are supposed to be there; arrange for the rental of scoring stages and dubbing stages; and, in general, shepherd the whole post process.

After you have taken over the editing of your film from the director, you can figure another two to four weeks in the cutting room before you will have your movie where you want it. This is strictly an estimate and is entirely dependent on how you, as the producer, view your film, how exacting you are, how much of a perfectionist you are, and how much money you have left.

Once you have finally decided that this is exactly the way you want it, you *lock* the picture. That means no more changes in editing, because once you start the rest of the process, changes become very costly. It is much like building your own house. Once you have agreed to a plan and to the cost, you live with what you have agreed to. If you start changing where a door is going to go or you decide you want another window, it will cost you dearly.

The temptation will always be there to continue tweaking your film as you see ways of improving it. Certain minute changes that don't affect length can be made. For instance, if you want to shorten someone's close-up by ten frames and add those ten frames to another actor's close-up, that can be done, because the length will remain the same.

Post-Production Sound and Music

By now, you and the director have agreed on a composer and a SOUND HOUSE as you enter the final phase of post-production. With your editing completed, or as complete as it can be at this point in time, your Post-Production Supervisor will now schedule a SPOTTING SESSION. Those in attendance at this session will be yourself, the editor, post-production supervisor, composer, and effects editor. You will go through your movie one reel at a time, and you will spot—in other words indicate—where you want music to begin and end in each scene, or if you want music at all in a scene. You will also decide on sound effects—what they should be and where they should go. Since an average film runs nine to eleven reels, you can figure it will take one entire day for sound and one for music, depending on the complexity of the film.

After your spotting session, you will meet with the COMPOSER you have selected to discuss what kind of music you want in your movie. Hiring a composer is much like hiring any creative person. Check out composers of various movies that you like. You will run into some of the same problems hiring a composer that you ran into hiring a director. The person you would like may just be too expensive for your budget. So, you keep looking until you find the right balance between talent and cost.

Once you have met with your composer and indicated some of your feelings on what kind of music you would like to hear, he will then go to his studio and begin to create a score for your film. He will want to take a tape of the film with him for reference. In about two weeks' time, he should come back to you with a demo tape, which will give you a pretty good idea of what the score will be like.

The next item on the post-production list will probably be an AUTO-MATIC DIALOGUE REPLACEMENT session. A.D.R. is another term for "looping." Certain members of your cast will be brought back onto a looping stage, and their dialogue will be rerecorded. Waiting to loop until the picture has been cut is always wise, because then you know exactly what lines of dialogue will be in the finished product, and you don't waste a lot of time and money rerecording dialogue that may eventually be cut out.

When casting your movie, your casting director will include in all the actor deals one day of looping at no additional cost. This is pretty standard in the industry.

Dialogue is replaced basically for one of three reasons. The first is airplane or other extraneous noise that drowns out the dialogue. Even if the dialogue is understandable, when you cut back and forth from one actor to another, the intrusive noise will pop in and out, which makes it very disconcerting for an audience. The second reason is performance level. An actor may have given a wrong reading to a line, which changes the meaning of the line or the scene, and the director did not catch it at the time it was being shot. The third reason is that the dialogue of an actor is so unintelligible that he cannot be understood. You may wonder, and rightly so, why would anyone hire an actor that he could not understand?

I guess I could explain this more easily by relating an experience I had on *Miami Vice.* A very famous rock star had expressed interest in playing a dramatic role in one of our shows. The network was very excited because of this star's prestige and promotional value. So, of course, we hired him. Well, I guess singing and talking are two very different things, because when he opened his mouth to talk, the words were so mumbled, they were almost incomprehensible. But, now we were stuck. All we could do was tough it through and then, in post, bring in an actor to loop the rock star's dialogue. No, I won't say who he is, because that would be unkind. Besides, he is still around, and just as big as ever.

Next comes your FOLEY SESSION. Foley is the addition or sweetening of normal sounds in your picture. These are all sounds that are usually taken for granted, but unless they are specifically laid in, they might not be heard. Things like footsteps. If they are on asphalt, cement, tile, or snow, they all have a different sound. A microphone, seven or eight feet off the ground, picking up dialogue, will only faintly record those footsteps. To make them heard, they have to be added artificially. There are so many other things: the rustle of trees, birds singing in the distance, a car door closing, paper being torn, and the list goes on.

Opticals and Effects

Along with the A.D.R. sessions and the Foley, other things are simultaneously going on in other departments of the post-production process. The OPTICAL department is laying in the *fades* and *dissolves* and any other special optical effects that may be needed. Fades are when the screen goes to black at the end of a scene. Dissolves are when the end of one scene overlaps with the beginning of the next scene. EFFECTS OPTICALS, such as lightning bolts or distortions, as in dream sequences, are being added, along with special sound effects like thunder claps or the eerie sound of a U.F.O.

About this time, you will also start dealing with the MAIN TITLES for your film. There are numerous companies around Hollywood that specialize in creating main titles for movies. Since you will not have a lot of money to spend in this area, you will need the most creative people you can find to give the start of your film a unique, exceptional look. The first images an audience sees on the screen will set the mood for the rest of the movie.

C.G.I.

The term C.G.I. stands for computer-generated imagery, and is presently all the rage. Images can be created by young filmmakers working at their Macs, or by seasoned professionals on very expensive computers known as Henry, DaVinci, Flame, Inferno, etc. Special effects have changed considerably since the stop motion photography of Ray Harryhausen or the exceptional matte paintings of Albert Whitlock.

I was fortunate to work with Mr. Whitlock on many occasions and the matte painting is still a marvelous effect for creating background where none exists.

But now that the effects have become so widespread and complicated, I thought I would ask a friend of ours, Steve Kullback, who was in charge of special effects for us on *Sabrina, the Teenage Witch,* to give you a more complex and detailed explanation of C.G.I. work. Steve, who is presently working at an effects company called Milne FX in Los Angeles, asked his friends Scott Milne and Dan Carrington to help him. Which shows that while everyone knows a little something about effects there is always someone who knows something you don't know, or more than you know. So while I hope the information they have given you is not too technical, always remember our most important adage: The only dumb question is the one you don't ask. Meaning simply, if there is something you don't understand, ask, and if the effect is too complex for you, continue asking until you understand. Meanwhile, I hope that Steve's words are informative to you, as they have been to me.

An Introduction to Visual Effects

Even the savviest consumer of film and television will often ask a visual effects supervisor, what exactly do you do? Despite my having invested more than twelve years in specializing in visual effects, my own father would be hard-pressed to provide an explanation of my work. So here is a stab at demystifying the art and commerce of the process.

Visual effects production is the art of creating imagery, in the service of a story, through artificial means. That is to say, what you are seeing on the screen did not happen in real life in front of a camera. Period. Sure, certain aspects of the image at hand may have been photographed traditionally, but in order to create a visual effect, the elements have been assembled in a process called compositing. Think of it as you would think of putting together the pieces of a puzzle.

My visual effects career started on a television show called *Are You Afraid of the Dark?* for Nickelodeon. I was in charge of post-production for this anthology series, a kind of *Twilight Zone* for kids. In an episode that borrowed from *The Legend of Sleepy Hollow,* a headless horseman was to chase our young hero up to a bridge at night and burst into flames at its foot and then explode. I didn't have a clue as to where to begin, but it seemed logical that our shot would have certain elements. The boy running across the bridge. The headless horseman riding across the bridge. A clean shot of the bridge. If the shot needed to move, we might have achieved this aspect with a motion control camera. As the budget was quite limited, the shot would be static, or "locked off."

The look of the headless horseman was achieved through the very low-tech use of a costume built up in scale so that the neckline was above the performer's head. So then, how to create the illusion that this man on a horse catches fire and explodes? Could we set fire to a stuntman on a horse? Too expensive and dangerous for the animal. Besides the animal needed to burn too. Could we create a computer-generated man on a horse and animate computer-generated fire? Much more easily achieved today, and with a significant budget. Way back in 1991 and on a budget that required we communicate with cans and string, we needed to be cleverer. Or at least cheap. An explosion on the bridge was not going to happen, and besides, it needed to travel with the moving horse. So we set out to shoot what we could. The boy running. The horseman riding. A clean plate. And elements for the reactive light that would have been evident surrounding an explosion. Here we used a 12K with amber gel and shot it pointing in every conceivable direction.

The first thing we needed to do before assembling the pieces of this puzzle in compositing was to pull a matte of the horseman and his horse. That meant creating a white-on-black cutout of the horseman crossing the frame only, so that later it could be filled with another image, in this case fire. By generating this matte, we isolated just the one piece of the image so that when we played the matte back, we saw only the action of the horseman. Believe it or not, this is the same principle behind your local weatherperson appearing in front of his or her weathermap. You have a map. You have a person shot separately for which you generate a matte. You place the matte over the map and fill it with the weather person, excluding the rest of his surroundings. (This is usually done automatically with a chroma key or a blue screen. More on this later.)

In the case of our horseman, we could not have afforded the time and expense of putting a big blue or green screen on the bridge, so we pulled the matte by hand. This is called *rotoscoping*. Here, every frame is hand-drawn painstakingly one by one. This was especially challenging given the horse against the back of the bridge at night was virtually impossible to see on a frame-by-frame basis. One trick we tried was going back to the negative to blow out the image solely to help us find the horse in the dark. That failing, our genius rotoscope artist painted the matte from his imagination.

The next piece of the puzzle we needed was the explosion. Like cooking, the more natural and organic the ingredients you put into the mix, the better it tastes. Here we wanted to create as grand an explosion as possible. Without the funds to hire a pyrotechnic crew and with limitations on where we could even execute such an explosion, we turned to existing movies and acquired a piece of footage that had just the right size explosion. Again, we needed to pull a matte to isolate the explosion from its background. With elements in hand we were now ready to put the pieces of the puzzle together.

In the days before computer-based compositing tools like Flame, Inferno, After Effects, Shake, Commotion, and the like, we made do in a traditional, linear-based online room. Today, the same elements would be loaded into a computer hard drive and manipulated with the motion picture equivalent of Photoshop. In our case we used three videotape machines and an ADO. In the simplest of terms, we layered the elements starting with the boy running across the bridge. Using a soft-edged wipe, we added in the horseman, with flexibility as to how close he could be on the boy's heels. We layered the horseman in, revealing him through his matte, which was gradually softened around the edges to permit a ring of fire to erupt around him.

To create the look of the fire, we filled this soft-edged matte with a fire-colored video feedback. The feedback bled through with a trailing effect by feeding the same video signal in a loop back on top of itself. The result of filling the edge of the matte with the looping video signal provided the same echo you would see pointing a video camera at a monitor showing its own image. It was sheer experimentation that led us to the video feedback technique, but the echoing color looked convincingly like fire beginning to trail off the edge of the man.

As the horseman was to become more and more engulfed, we simply made the soft edge around him bigger until finally we were filling the entire matte with fire-colored feedback. At the climactic explosion moment, we layered the explosion element from the stock, revealing the footage through an ever-growing matte of the horseman. The fire element was easy to isolate from its dark background since the strong contrast of the light was much easier to roto in the dark. On the background layers, we effected the look of light against the background by assembling a reveal or wipe between the clean bridge pass and the variety of takes with the 12K shining its amber-gelled light. Overlapping these layers, and revealing what you want the audience to see and when, is the process of compositing.

So now back to the question of what a visual effect supervisor does. Think of us as you might the architects and builders of your home. The homeowner is ultimately the writer who sets out an initial vision. The architect or visual effect supervisor is the designer who creates the plans, defining the look, style, and approach for execution. The visual effects producer will work with the supervisor and the show's producers to manage the process from a financial and logistical perspective. The contractor, if you will. The visual effects artists are the skilled craftsmen who ply their individual trades. Some are expert roto artists. Others, expert compositors. Using today's sophisticated software, a team of 3D artists can generate every single element we've discussed in a 3D program like Maya or Lightwave or 3D Studio Max. We'll look at these tools a bit closer in awhile, but suffice it to say, the bridge, fire, and even the performers can be 3D generated. You might not want to get too close to the 3D performers just yet, but soon. This approach is how the brilliant artists at Sony Pictures Imageworks created the flying sequences for *Spiderman*. Not only was *Spiderman* 3D, but so were the backgrounds of New York City. Amazing stuff.

What follows is a glossary of terms and an explanation of the role they play in creating visual effects:

2D: Any process using two dimensions in a computer. If you could turn the image over, you would only *see* the reverse of the front. Images are created by drawing with a stylus or the computer's equivalent of a brush and pencil. Here, you can cut and paste collages of existing pictures and photos. Real world comparisons would be painting, airbrushing, drawing, photography, and drafting. Software like Flame and Inferno, After Effects, Shake, and Commotion are 2D compositing tools.

3D: Objects are created or "modeled" by building geometry from curves, surfaces, and basic shapes like spheres and cubes. You can rotate these objects or models in 3D space and look at them as you would a virtual sculpture. Were we to model the horse in 3D, we'd start by creating a computer generated skeletal structure. For *Jurassic Park,* the team at ILM consulted a zoo full of animals for motion studies, and paleontologists to try to replicate an authentic skeletal structure for their dinosaurs. After building this foundation, you then model the muscle mass. Essentially, the process of 3D animation is to build a creature, or object, from the ground up. The team behind *Hollowman* for Sony Imageworks did so much research and development in modeling their virtual human from scratch, they uncovered movement patterns of human anatomy that advanced the body of medical knowledge.

Once you've modeled the bones and muscles, it's onto the process of texturing. Skin for a person, fur for the horse. This texturing process may involve computer-generated painting, shading, and lighting. For a scene with Brad Pitt in *Fight Club* in which the camera gets between him and his girlfriend making love, the French 3D firm Bouef created a model in the shape of Brad Pitt and then "texture mapped," or pasted, a photographed image of him over the top of it.

These textured and shaded objects are then lit with virtual lights as one might light up a stage or room. These lights help place the object in the scene by matching the lighting of the background. A visual camera that can have the same properties as a real camera is then positioned to view the object. One of the real conveniences in the 3D world is creating and animating things that can't exist in the real world and flying cameras around them or attached to them with no movement limitations.

When you do need to integrate a moving object into a moving background or backplate, you must first perform a match move or motion tracking. This is the process of identifying the real camera's movement in space so that you can match the movements of your 3D camera to it. The visual effects supervisor takes measurements on set to help aid this process. The most sophisticated tools for measuring a set employ a laser to scan the topography of a location. Ever wonder how the very unreal "bugs" on *Starship Troopers* appeared to navigate their very real environment?

Batch Render: Setting up multiple sets of instructions to render collectively, so that one will finish and the next will automatically start. See rendering, page 118.

Black Box Technology: A piece of equipment created to do only one thing. Many things in a post-production environment are this type of device. Media converters, sound processors, Da Vinci, telecini, editors, etc.

Bluescreen: A specific color variation of the Keying Process. The common term for "Chroma Keying." By placing a performer or object in front of a chroma key screen, the computer will enable you to generate a matte automatically by electronically eliminating the color of the screen. Ever wonder why sometimes it's a blue screen and sometimes a green screen? It has mostly to do with the color of the object you want to shoot in front of it. On the film *Air Force One*, scale models of the Presidential 747 were photographed on tangerine screen as it presented the best contrast to the plane and its markings.

Compositing: The process of layering multiple images to make a final collage image. In the post-production sense, it is the assembly of many parts, either C.G., film, or video. This also includes blending and color corrections to make it all match as one, homogenous vision. The general term of compositing also may include many other techniques such as keying and matte paintings.

Difference Matte: Creating a matte by having the computer examine multiple images and show what is different or what changed. Imagine a room filmed with a still camera. Then a person walks in. A difference matte can give the artist an approximate matte for the person. This will vary depending on the colors and brightness of the foreground and background elements. If the person is wearing a red shirt and walks into a red room, we would not get much of a difference matte. If the person walked into a blue room, we would. With normal colors that one sees in life, some portions of the difference matte will show well and some areas will show nothing.

Frozen Moment: Taking still pictures from many angles around an object or person moving in space and using these stills to generate a motion picture of a static object. Special rigging is used to hold multiple cameras, sometimes hundreds, all in a smooth circle, line, or camera path around the subject. They are all set off at the same time and these still pictures are then strung together in time and reveal the images of a camera moving around a frozen subject. This process is usually done on a chroma key set (blue screen or green screen) so the subject can be composited over a background and the camera rigging removed. The end cameras can be replaced with motion picture cameras to allow real time to become frozen moment and back to real time. This approach was used in the *Matrix* to freeze Keanu Reeves even though the camera was moving around him.

Matte: A black-and-white image used in compositing. Where the matte is white, a composited image is used. Where the matte is black, we see through to the next layered image or the background. If we were to composite a person over something, the person's matte would look like a white silhouette. Originally used in camera work as covers where the lens was blocked to keep the film from being exposed in certain areas. Also called Hi-Con, Mask, Key, Holdout, and Garbage Matte.

Matte Painting: Combining a painted picture with a film or video image. Originally done with paint on photo-quality glass, and then shot with a camera having a matte on its lens. The matte would save the area where the painting would go from being exposed. Then the painting would be shot with a matte saving the already exposed negative from being exposed a second time. In the computer, we get the same result by compositing a painted picture with a filmed moving image. Also used for set extensions where the filmed image needs to look bigger or more dangerous. Imagine filming a house that is one story tall. Matte painting techniques can be used to extend the house to be a mansion many stories tall and even change the sky to sunset, clouds, or storm.

Morph: Warping two images to matched shapes and dissolving between them. Imagine two faces. Face A is warped to the shape of face B. Face B is warped to start in the same shape of face A and then move to its original shape. Then the two images are dissolved. Originally created for the movie _Willow._ Puppet models of animals and various in-between stages were manufactured and filmed. The images were then morphed to create a smooth blend from raccoon to tiger to ostrich to turtle to other various animals and finally to a woman. The process was used once and then shelved as they did not see any other need for the process. It was later resurrected to become a tool for the industry.

Motion Control: Creating multiple layers for compositing with a computer-controlled camera dolly or crane. The crane or dolly is fitted with motors and sensors. This allows the same pass or camera move to be duplicated exactly through a scene over and over. Imagine an actor with legs playing the part of an actor without legs. If the shot has a moving camera, we need an exact duplicate shot without the actor to place back in the hole created by removing his legs. A motion control camera would record a move programmed by the operator. The "moco" camera could then duplicate the move as many times as necessary. The data recovered with the sensors can also be transferred into computers and used to create 3D virtual cameras so composited images or 3D models move perfectly with the real camera.

Pin Registering: Using special cameras and telecini that hold a film frame exactly by alignment with the film pinholes. This is to make multiple passes of film perfectly aligned. Normal cameras and telecini only hold the film in approximate position and as the film flows over the gate, it will float around to a small degree. However, as multiple passes of the film are then composited together, things will not move with the same float and will be obvious that they are layered parts by their motion alone. Unfortunately, pin-registered equipment is much more expensive, may be much slower, especially in the telecini, and is more restrictive in the filming rates and camera sizes.

Plates: General term for filmed images used as backgrounds or layers in compositing. Also called clean plates or back plates.

Pleasantville: A term coined from a movie that mixed black-and-white and color in the same shots. This can be done on-set, but is very restrictive. Creating the black-and-white portion in post is much easier overall, but usually requires significant rotoscoping of mattes for those portions.

Rendering: Once you provide the computer software with its set of instructions, this is the process of sitting and doing seemingly nothing while the hardware executes those instructions.

Render, 3D: In 3D, things are built in wireframe and hardware shaded samples. Surfaces and lighting are not fully shown until the model is rendered and an actual picture is created. Depending on the complexity of the setup or 3D model, rendering an image can take from less than a second to days, just for one picture. Multiply that by twenty-four or thirty for one second of motion and it adds up.

Render Farm: Many computers, set up to render images, generally twenty-four hours a day, seven days a week, with no one sitting at the computer to use it for anything else but rendering. Software can control rendering so an operator sets up a job, and the software takes it and breaks it down into a smaller part for each available computer.

Resolution: In the computer, all pictures are created by colored pixels (one small square). For better picture quality, more pixels are used.

Standard NTSC television, as we work it in the computer, is 720 × 486 pixels. High Definition is up to 1920 × 1080 pixels, about six times clearer than standard television. Film projects go up from there with IMAX being 4000 pixels wide or more. The downfall is that the higher resolution, the longer things take to work with. The computer ends up spending time to create each pixel. So if HDTV is six times clearer because it has six times the pixels, it takes six times longer to work with. Film goes up from there. If your project took one hour to render in standard definition TV, it would take six in HDTV, and over a day in IMAX.

Rotoscoping: Painting on a moving image. Similar to cartoon animation where someone has to draw a character and paint in that character, frame by frame, by hand, over dozens to hundreds or thousands of frames to make it move when played back. It is very time-consuming. However, in some cases, it is the only way to achieve the desired results. It can be used to actually draw something on the image or to draw a matte to use in compositing for something that cannot be keyed.

Split Screen: Blending two images, generally to have one actor play two parts in the same scene. The scene is shot twice with the actor playing the separate parts. The scenes are then composited together to make the two actors look like they were in the same place at the same time. For complicated crossings and interactions, the actors may need to be shot on blue screen to allow better layer control. For less complicated interactions, or where blue screen is impossible, rotoscoping may be required for overlaps and interactions. If the camera is moving, a motion control rig is needed.

Stabilizing: Tracking the movement of an image and fixing a given position in the frame to one point on the screen. It can be used to remove bumps and camera jiggles from an image. It can replace the need for pin-registered cameras and telecini, therefore saving cost and time.

Test Render: Doing a render at a lower resolution for a quick but poor quality sample. If you are rendering film resolution, a full resolution render could be days of machine time. This allows problems to be found out before the investment of long full term machine time.

Tracking: Having the computer follow an item of interest within an image. We select a portion of an image and the computer finds that small picture within the subsequent frames of the sequence. Imagine a camera driving by a billboard. We can track the corners of the billboard and using this information, move another picture exactly with the billboard as we drive by. This can then be composited on the original image to make a different billboard.

This process can also be done in 3D to add 3D models to the image and have them move correctly with a camera move. The computer tracks multiple points in the image. With tracking points in the foreground, middle ground, and background, the computer can figure out what movement the camera made. This can then be applied to a virtual camera and 3D models can be rendered with the same move to exactly match the filmed image. Imagine a camera moving in a room. The computer can track the room. An artist can build a soda can and place it in the virtual room in a position that would place it on a table. The rendered soda can would then be composited over the filmed image to create a soda can sitting on the real table with matching shadows.

Warp: Stretching and pulling an image to reshape it. Imagine a picture on a sheet of rubber. You can grab the rubber at points and stretch it as desired and the image will change by stretching and compressing with the rubber sheet. This has been used to make animals talk and change footage of President Kennedy to have him say a story-specific line in *Forrest Gump*. Also the major portion of Morphing.

Wire/Rig Removal: Digitally erasing safety cables, tow dollies, hanging and flying rigs, gimbals, and puppet rods. This can be done in combination with blue screen or just as good old-fashioned rotoscoping. There are even software packages out there that specifically predict what should be behind the wire or rig in moving shots by tracking the image over time.

Wireframe: The construction and preview-viewing mode for 3D creations. This is the quick way that a computer will show 3D objects. They look like drafting in 3D.

Re-Recording

By now, the composer has finished writing his score, you have listened to the demo tape and have made your suggestions. Now, the music is ready to be recorded. Your Post-Production Supervisor has rented the recording stage, the composer has hired the musicians, and the big day arrives. You will, undoubtedly, want to be at that recording session. Not to supervise, but just to enjoy. Music, done right, can be an enormous help to a movie by defining the mood of a scene. But it should never be intrusive or over-powering. If you become more aware of the music than of the action taking place on the screen, then the composer has gone too far.

On many smaller-budget movies, composers use syncleviers or other machines that create music synthetically. Some of these scores are very good. In cases like this, you can hear the score at the composer's work room. Sometimes a synthesized score will have real instruments added to it; it's only a matter of money.

Now your film is ready to DUB. At this session, all the sound elements are put together. The various original tracks are now recorded onto a single magnetic stripe, with the dialogue, music, Foley, and special sound effects all being blended together. This is a *domestic* mix. You will also want a *foreign* mix, in which all the sound, except dialogue, are blended on a single track. The reason for this is, when your film is dubbed in a foreign language, all the music, Foley, and sound effects will remain intact, even though the dialogue will be replaced.

Low-budget movies usually mix in about a week. Major films can take months. But watching all of these elements finally come together is one of the great highs of producing. It is a rush that will never leave you.

The Final Process

Next, your film will be color timed. This is the process where the color is *balanced* in the negative, eliminating too much blue, red, or yellow. Your film is then ready for the final process in its evolution from raw footage to finished motion picture: NEGATIVE CUTTING. A special negative film cutter is hired for this process. The original negative of your film will be cut to match the edited version you have been working with. Then, POSITIVE RELEASE PRINTS will be made from this negative.

There are dozens of technical processes that will occur within the overall framework of post-production that I have laid out for you. To detail each one would take a technical manual. Suffice it to say, this overview will allow you to follow and participate in the process. It will be a learning experience.

Some producers love post-production and become deeply involved. Others want to be involved only in the editing process, or in the music, or in the final dub. It is strictly up to you how much you, as the producer, want to involve yourself in post. But, in my opinion, to be a truly creative, well-rounded producer, one should embrace the post-production process with the same passion and vigor as the shooting process.

One last piece of information that can be very helpful to you. On the next four pages is a POST-PRODUCTION FLOW CHART, with account numbers that match the accounts in the sample budget in appendix E. This chart was made up by John Sprung, who is presently director of technology at Paramount Studios. It has always helped me to see the film as it went from A to Z.

This chart is for delivery on video. If you were to deliver a print, you would cut the negative *after* the movie was locked, and then make prints for theatrical distribution.

A Video Post-Production Flow Chart, with account numbers:

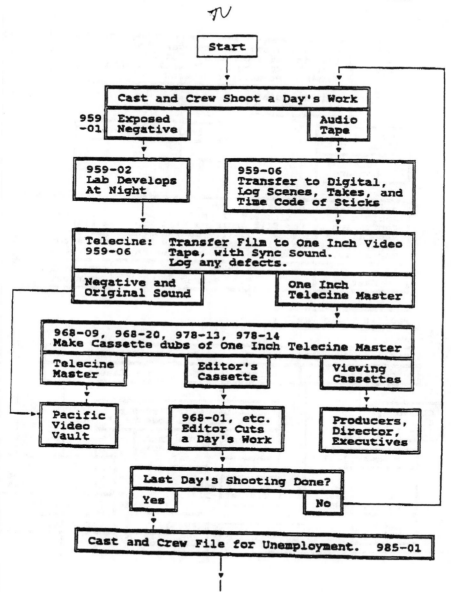

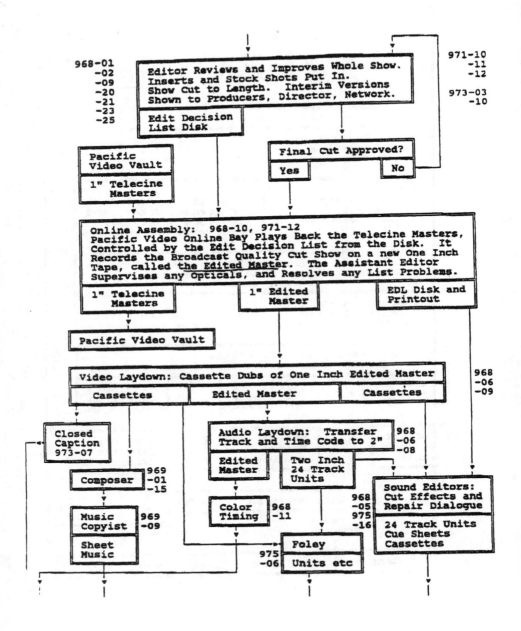

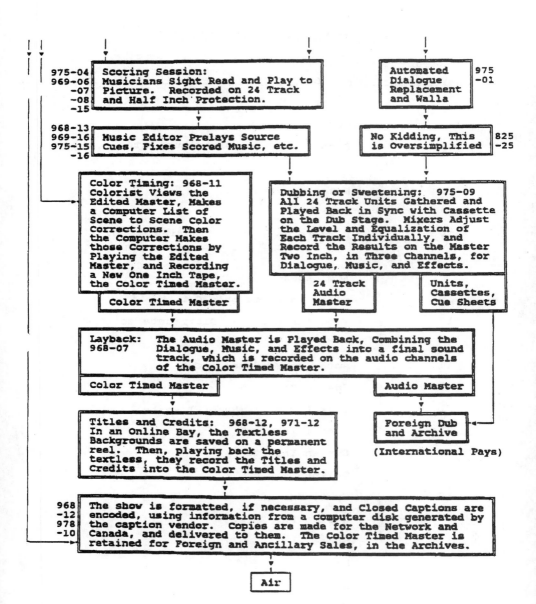

975-04
969-06
-07
-08
-15

Scoring Session:
Musicians Sight Read and Play to
Picture. Recorded on 24 Track
and Half Inch Protection.

Automated
Dialogue
Replacement
and Walla

975
-01

968-13
969-16
975-15
-16

Music Editor Prelays Source
Cues, Fixes Scored Music, etc.

No Kidding, This
is Oversimplified

825
-25

Color Timing: 968-11
Colorist Views the
Edited Master, Makes
a Computer List of
Scene to Scene Color
Corrections. Then
the Computer Makes
those Corrections by
Playing the Edited
Master, and Recording
a New One Inch Tape,
the Color Timed Master.

Dubbing or Sweetening: 975-09
All 24 Track Units Gathered and
Played Back in Sync with Cassette
on the Dub Stage. Mixers Adjust
the Level and Equalization of
Each Track Individually, and
Record the Results on the Master
Two Inch, in Three Channels, for
Dialogue, Music, and Effects.

Color Timed Master

24 Track
Audio
Master

Units,
Cassettes,
Cue Sheets

Layback:
968-07

The Audio Master is Played Back, Combining the
Dialogue, Music, and Effects into a final sound
track, which is recorded on the audio channels
of the Color Timed Master.

Color Timed Master

Audio Master

Titles and Credits: 968-12, 971-12
In an Online Bay, the Textless
Backgrounds are saved on a permanent
reel. Then, playing back the
textless, they record the Titles and
Credits into the Color Timed Master.

Foreign Dub
and Archive

(International Pays)

968
-12
978
-10

The show is formatted, if necessary, and Closed Captions are
encoded, using information from a computer disk generated by
the caption vendor. Copies are made for the Network and
Canada, and delivered to them. The Color Timed Master is
retained for Foreign and Ancillary Sales, in the Archives.

Air

GENERIC SCHEDULE TEMPLATE *

DAY #	EVENT
1	Shoot
7	Wrap
9	First Cut - Distribute to:
11	Notes on First Cut
	Edit
14	Director's Cut - Distribute to:
	[CGI Locked]
15	Notes on Director's Cut
17	Producer's Cut - Distribute to:
19	Notes on Producer's Cut
20	Insert Day
21	Lock Picture: (Shoot Inserts)
22	(Shoot Inserts)
23	Cut in Inserts
24	Online
25	Spot: FX; Music
26-30	Music; FX; Foley
31	Score
32	Mix
33	Layback
34	DELIVER

11

Filming Outside
the United States

There is always the possibility, especially in today's global marketplace, that you will have to, or want to, shoot your film in a foreign country. The factors that would enter into this decision would be, first of all, where your story takes place. Then, where the financing has come from. If you have foreign investors, they may want all, or part of your film shot in their country. Some of the reasons for this could be related to their tax structure, or to distribution contracts, or to the fact that they might feel they would have more control over the film.

If your story takes place in the United States, you still may want to take advantage of currency exchange rates, foreign government tax incentives, or lower wages paid to local crews. At this moment, the Canadian dollar is worth sixty-two cents against the American dollar. That, in itself, is a big incentive to shoot in Canada.

Advantages and Disadvantages

Whatever your reasons, analyze very carefully the advantages and disadvantages of shooting in a foreign country. Sometimes, the money you think you will save can end up being just a mirage. After you factor in the cost of airfares, hotel expenses, per diems, and other special transportation costs for yourself, the director, cast, and the crew you will have to bring with you, it could end up costing you more. And not just in money, but in aggravation, sleepless nights, and ulcers due to the different laws and regulations you will suddenly have to deal with.

Depending on what country you will be shooting in, you will most certainly have to bring some crew people with you—probably a D.P., a sound mixer, and a makeup person, to name a few. Most industrialized countries have competent motion picture crews, but their highly technical positions, for the most part, still do not come up to our standards. And actors are very sensitive about who will make them up. If you have any kind of name actors, they will almost invariably insist on their own makeup person.

Beware the Laws and Customs

Once you leave the borders of the United States, you are subject to the laws of the country in which you are filming. This is a fact of life that you, your crew, and especially your actors must be aware of. *Do your research.* Know the laws and the customs of the country you are going to be shooting in, including their income tax laws, censorship laws, import and export laws, and the problems of local production. I am not overstating the case when I say that your knowledge of those laws and customs could mean the difference between the success and failure of your project.

Be especially aware of the drug laws in the country to which you are going. Most foreign countries are not nearly as lenient as the United States when it comes to prosecuting drug offenders. Getting caught with any kind of illegal drug, even marijuana, can get you a long jail sentence and, in some countries, the death penalty. This is no joke. Fooling around with drugs in foreign countries is like playing Russian roulette. Even if you, yourself, have nothing to do with drugs, if one of your actors gets caught using, all your film could be seized, and you could be thrown out of the country.

Inadvertently offending someone in a foreign country, particularly an official, can cost you dearly. Permits can inexplicably be delayed, import or export papers suddenly get lost, and the cooperation you need in order to get into some locations can vanish into thin air. And the worst part of it is, you can be totally unaware of what you did.

I went to Japan once to prepare a film. I knew that the Japanese had this thing about business cards, but I didn't know how serious they were. I went into a meeting with twelve men, all from the same company, and every one of them requested a business card from me, and every one of them gave me their card. After two or three of these kinds of meetings, I ran out of cards. I ended up offending a lot of Japanese businessmen, until I was able to get more cards Fed-Exed to me.

Knowing local customs can not only save you money, it can save you a lot of embarrassment. While shooting a film in Madrid, we issued a call sheet for the first day's shooting for a 7:00 A.M. crew call. The next morning, I showed up exactly at 7:00 in order to greet my crew. Unfortunately, I was the only one there. Some of the crew began straggling in around 8:00, and by 9:00, everyone had finally shown up.

I wasn't aware of the fact that in Spain, people don't have dinner until eleven o'clock at night. The earliest they come to work is 9:00 A.M. I asked my local coordinator why he didn't mention this fact to me when he saw the call sheet. He said he didn't want to embarrass me. Like I wasn't embarrassed standing all alone on a street corner at 7:00 in the morning! Needless to say, from then on, our crew calls were at 9:00 A.M.

Tax laws can become very complicated in certain countries. You will need to know what your actors and crew will have to pay in income taxes in the country in which you are working, and every country is different. It will be one amount in Canada, another in the Philippines, and another in France. You need to know the tax laws, so you will be prepared to deal with them.

Actors are particularly affected by these laws. Suppose you are paying your star five-hundred thousand dollars, and the country you are shooting in requires him to pay a 20 percent income tax to the country. That is one-hundred thousand dollars he will have to come up with before he can get out of that country. While this money is usually applicable to his U.S. taxes, the actor and his management will still complain vociferously.

One way of partially getting around this problem is to *bifurcate* the actor's contract. This means that the amount of money the actor makes can be divided into four separate portions. The first portion would be for the performer's participation in development and pre-production, the second portion for his performance in the film, the third portion for his help in post-production, and the fourth portion for exhibition and publicity.

What this does is reduce the actor's tax obligation to the foreign country to that amount he receives for actually performing in the film. So, instead of paying one-hundred thousand dollars in taxes, he will pay only twenty-five thousand dollars, or 20 percent of one-hundred-twenty-five thousand dollars.

Be sure you review everything with an attorney who is proficient in the laws of the country you want to shoot in. And make sure that your actors and their agents are agreeable to whatever arrangements you make before you hire them. You don't want any last-minute negotiations where the agent tells you his client won't go unless you pay the taxes for him.

Importing and exporting regulations can be frustratingly complicated if you don't follow proper procedures. Do your homework, and be sure to hire a local person who is conversant in that field. The film commission in that country can be a great help in finding the right person for you.

Censorship laws are rigidly enforced in many countries. Some of these laws are politically oriented, and some are morally or religiously oriented. Whatever the case, you would do well to adhere to the letter of these laws. Do not try to be cute. Bureaucrats in many foreign countries are not known for their sense of humor.

One time we were going to be barred from shooting a film in Sri Lanka because the "natives" in our story were cannibals. Officials there were deeply offended and told us, in no uncertain terms, that the people of Sri Lanka were not cannibals. Fortunately, our local producer explained to the censors that, yes, the people in our story *were* cannibals; however, the story did not take place in Sri Lanka, but in a mythical country. The explanation was accepted, and we were allowed to shoot our film. Oddly, though—or not so oddly—the movie never played in Sri Lanka.

In a foreign country, it is important to be straightforward and aboveboard in all your dealings with officials and bureaucrats from that country. Even though the temptation to cut corners or play loose with some of their laws may present itself, *don't*. It will usually come back to bite you.

There was a very well-known producer/director who shot a film in an Asian country. He showed the government officials one version of the script, then proceeded to shoot a different, much more risqué version. He managed to get out of the country one step ahead of the "sheriff," but now he is persona non grata there.

You may not be so lucky. Consequences to this kind of game playing can be more immediate and far more devastating. Your film could be confiscated in midshoot, and you could be thrown out of the country. This could mean a loss to you of hundreds of thousands, even millions of dollars, and, in a worst-case scenario, you could end up doing time in a "Turkish" prison. Not a happy thought.

Problems Are "No Problema"

Then, of course, in many foreign countries, you will face the dreaded "no problema" syndrome. Whether it is a Spanish-speaking country, or French, or Malaysian, or Farsi, the syndrome is always the same. You will ask for certain things—a piece of equipment, a specific location, a certain prop—and you will be told, "No problem." A bit of advice: Whenever you hear that phrase, you can bet the farm that there *will* be a problem.

We were shooting a film in Puerto Rico, and while scouting the locations, I met with the man who supplied all the electrical equipment. He showed me the generator we would be using, and while it wasn't the latest model, it looked well-maintained, and he assured me there was (musical sting) "no problema." Naïve and innocent as I was, I believed him.

On the first morning of shooting in Old San Juan, I was informed that the generator wasn't working, and they would have to order a spare part from the mainland. "How long will that take?" I asked guilelessly. "Maybe two, three weeks, more or less." This is said to me while I have an entire shooting company standing there waiting to start lighting the first scene—with no electricity.

I felt the jaws of disaster opening to swallow me, when the generator man uttered that now famous phrase, "no problema." He then proceeded to climb the nearest utility pole and tie into an overhead power line. We now had all the electricity we needed. And that's the way it went for the rest of the shoot. Wherever we were, the generator man just climbed the nearest utility pole.

I found out later that the generator hadn't worked in years, and this was the way they provided power. They just don't mention this little fact ahead of time, because they don't want to scare production companies away.

In Jamaica, you simply never count on anything. I have found that the further south you go, the more laid-back the populace. We were in Ocho Rios shooting a movie for Showtime, and I needed two cars for the next morning. We selected the cars and told the Jamaican transportation captain we would need them at 7:00 A.M., because they were in the first shot. "No problem, mon. They will be there; my two cousins will be driving."

Do I need to go any further? Yeah, that's right, they showed up about 10:00. They really couldn't understand why I was so upset. "Hey, mon, big night, big party . . . cars are here now." The fact that it cost us about twenty thousand dollars in overtime just didn't seem to concern them all that much.

So, how does one go about dealing with "no problema"? There is no fail-safe way, but you can help ease the pain by hiring a local producer in whatever country you are working. Local producers can be enormously helpful in this area, since they know the laws, the customs, and the idiosyncrasies of their government. They can also find the best crews and equipment and lead you to the locations you will want.

Then, of course, there are the pay-offs that are often de rigueur in many foreign countries. This is a fairly common practice and not necessarily illegal. In many parts of the world, it is simply a way of doing business. Your local producer will prove himself invaluable in this area. He will know who to pay off and with how much money. Sometimes, these negotiations can be delicate and painstaking, and virtually impossible for an outsider to conduct.

However, you should check out your local producer very carefully. You want the *mordida* paid to the right people; you don't want it ending up in *his* pocket. The best way to check out a local producer is to contact U.S. producers who have worked in that country and follow their recommendations.

First Contact

When entering a foreign country, the first thing you should do is contact the FILM COMMISSIONER. Most countries, and large cities within the countries, have Film Commissions. It is their job to help you in any way they can, so that you will want to shoot there. But there's a danger here, also. Because they want to attract business, they may not be entirely truthful in their representations of what they have to offer. Beware the hyperbole. Always be pleasant and polite, but make your questions pointed. If they are vague about certain things, pin them down. You want information, but you want *correct* information. The personal approach usually works the best. Take them to lunch or dinner, and they may level with you . . . after a fashion . . . usually.

Finding Extras

Hiring BACKGROUND EXTRAS in certain countries can be tricky at times, depending on your story and the type of extras you will need. I was shooting a film in Australia that was substituting for North Carolina. We needed African-American extras, but we were told there were very few blacks in Australia.

That night, I took a friend, and we went to all the bars we could find. I approached each and every black person I saw, gave them my card, and asked if they would like to appear in a movie. The next day we were inundated with "African-American" extras.

While shooting in Italy, we had a scene that required Japanese extras. We faced the same problem: a dearth of Japanese in Rome. So, we went to the local Chinese and Japanese embassies and recruited their employees.

We have done the same thing, only in reverse, in Sri Lanka and other Asian countries, when we needed Caucasian extras. Hotels and embassies provided us with what we needed. The point of all this is, when working in foreign countries, you will be called upon to use every bit of ingenuity you possess. If you are clever and are willing to explore uncharted territory, you will be able to overcome almost any problem you are confronted with.

Protecting Your Currency

When shooting in a foreign country, at some point your American dollars will have to be changed into the currency of the country in which you are shooting. But be careful, because exchanging currency in foreign countries can become a sticky situation. One hard and fast rule is, never bring too much money in at any one time, even if you are offered a special rate. It is better to convert your money on an as-needed basis.

The principal reason for this can be described in one word: *inflation.* Some countries are subject to double-digit inflation monthly, even weekly. I was involved with a production that was being shot in Brazil. A Brazilian banker negotiated a very special deal for us, buying cruzeiros at half price. Our American company purchased all of their local currency up front, from the banker. Unfortunately, runaway inflation severely eroded the cruzeiro the first two weeks we were there, which led to financial disaster. In this case, the American company had deep pockets, and we were able to complete our movie. But if we had been a small independent film with a fixed cash flow, we would have lost everything.

While making a film in the Philippines, the American dollar was equal to four pesos and twenty-five centavos when we arrived in Manila. Somewhere in the middle of filming, the local currency was devalued to twelve pesos and fifty centavos per American dollar. Because we only brought production money into the country on a weekly basis, we suffered almost no financial loss.

Researching the Foreign Country

Before you travel to a foreign country, you would do well to thoroughly check out that country. One place to start would be the FILM LOCATION EXPO, which is held each year in Los Angeles at the Downtown Convention Center. Check with the Los Angeles Film Commission for exact dates. Dozens of countries have booths at this Expo, and you can travel around the world without ever leaving Los Angeles. You will be inundated with brochures, pictures, and information on countries from England to Singapore, Hungary to India, and South Africa to Russia, as well as numerous states and cities in the United States.

At the Expo, you will learn how to contact the Film Commissions in foreign countries. Make sure you do. The information you will get from them will be invaluable in determining which country you should go to.

Another good research source is international film festivals. At the time of this writing, there are more than two hundred and fifty film festivals held around the world. So, there is probably one near you. There is a partial list of festivals at the end of this book, or you can contact the Film Commission in your locale. If the festival has the word "international" in front of it, try to go.

You will be able to meet and network with foreign producers, who will provide you with a lot of inside information on shooting outside the United States—information that can be vital to the success of your production. You may also meet producers who are willing to cofinance your film. These will probably not be dollar-for-dollar shares of the budget. Instead, they are called "below-the-line" deals.

The foreign producer will agree to provide a local crew, plus certain elements of production, such as lights, grip equipment, and the construction of sets. You will still have to pay for raw stock, and you will need to bring your cast and some key crew personnel, but this is a good way to get your picture made. Also, having a deal like this in your pocket can ease the process of raising capital in the States.

Deals of this nature can be made by working out a split of territories for distribution rights. Each territory in the world marketplace has a value. Some go for millions, others for a few thousand. A good way to analyze what the cofinancing deal is really worth is to confer with a foreign sales person and determine the value of the territories that your cofinancing partner wants, because he *will* want some territories in return for all the goods and services he will be providing your production. You can compare the value of what you will receive in crew and equipment to the value of the territories he wants, and this will give you a fair dollar value.

When you are doing this kind of a trade-off with a foreign producer, make sure the equipment he is providing is up-to-date and in good working condition, especially cameras and the lighting package, including the generator. Remember Puerto Rico.

In Malaysia and Sri Lanka, I have worked with Chandran Rutnam and the Film Locations Services Company and found their equipment to be excellent, especially for Asia. If you're working in the Philippines, you can get equipment from Charlie Wang in Hong Kong, or from a company called RSVP in the Philippines, run by Oli Laperal.

The point is, there are people in many countries who will be willing to talk cofinancing with you. It is your job to find out who they are, and then approach them with your deal. Whether or not you make a deal will depend on how much money, or goods and services, you want and what you are willing to give in order to get what you want.

If you are able to make a cofinancing deal, you will be in a good position to approach a FOREIGN SALES DISTRIBUTOR who could help you fill in the financial gap. For instance, if your film is budgeted at two million dollars and your cofinancing partner will provide five hundred thousand in crew, equipment, and services, the foreign distributor could pre-sell your movie in various markets for a million dollars. This would leave you with only five hundred thousand to raise in risk capital, and investors would have a high level of comfort knowing that your film is already three-quarters financed.

Select your partner carefully, and qualify him as soon as possible. Who is his primary banker? What is his source of financing? Can your attorney satisfy you that this is a bona fide situation? Check with your bonding company. They know who's real and who isn't.

Don't allow anyone to market your project until you have a clear and concise understanding of what your potential partner intends to do. Make yourself crystal clear with each company you talk to. If you are gathering information and haven't decided who you're going to work with, *say so*. Tell them you'll get back to them. If you are going to be talking to other companies, tell them that. You may as well. They'll find out anyway.

Check and Double-check

Since 9/11 it is very important to be especially careful about security. And you want to make sure you are dealing with good, reliable local producers as well as the U.S. Consulate in checking out the problems that might come about during filming. It is wise to check with insurance companies and even companies that bond pictures because they are very current, regarding problem places in the world.

12

Distribution and Marketing

Now that your motion picture is finished and ready for the world to see, you will be moving into a whole new arena, into the final leg in your *Journey from Screenplay to Silver Screen.*

Before that final leg, however, there is one more piece to the production puzzle that must be put in place. Actually, it comes under the heading of "sales tool." And that piece of the puzzle is the TRAILER—two to three minutes of film that grabs an audience and creates an anticipation and a desire to see your film.

The cost of making a trailer will be factored into your original budget. Since you will be using actual footage from your movie, the major cost of producing a trailer will be editing time for film, sound effects, and music. For a low-budget film, a good, exciting trailer should be produced for under ten thousand dollars. You will probably end up hiring a professional with the ability to synthesize, hype, and sell concepts.

This is the area where marketing savvy really comes into play. Your trailer *must* be directed at the audience you want to attract. If you attract the wrong audience, two very bad things will happen. First, word of mouth will virtually kill attendance. And second, the audience that would have liked your movie will be put off by the trailer. As the producer, you must work in concert with the trailer experts to create a sales tool that will not only tell your story, but will generate a compelling desire for your target audience to see your movie.

Getting your movie into the marketplace is every bit as important as the production of that movie. It makes no difference how good your film is; if it is not marketed and distributed properly, it will not be successful. That is a fact of life. So, everything you have gone through up to now, all the hard work and ulcer-producing aggravation, the sleepless nights, the chaos, the craziness and the triumphs—all of it now hangs in the balance. And whereas, up to this point, you have had almost total control over your destiny, you must now be prepared to relinquish some of that control to the experts who will get your film out into the global marketplace.

Distribution Deals

A theatrical film project is normally designed with the intent that DOMESTIC THEATRICAL DISTRIBUTION (United States and Canada) will provide the principal source of income from the marketing of a motion picture. Typically, about 80 percent of domestic theatrical rentals (distributor's share of box office gross) are accrued in the first year a film is distributed, and 20 percent in the second year. In the case of *market-by-market* release, the rentals are more typically accrued 60 percent in the first year and 40 percent in the second year.

There are a wide variety of exhibition arrangements. As a rule, the theater owner ("exhibitor") takes in the admissions paid at the box office ("gross box office receipts") and retains a portion of those receipts. The share retained by the exhibitor generally includes a set amount per week to cover his fixed operating expenses, or "house nut," plus an escalating percentage of receipts. The balance ("gross film rentals") is remitted to the distributor.

Some other methods of distribution are "four-walling"; regional, or platform distribution; and boutique, or small, specialized distribution. Four-walling means that you rent theaters, yourself, in which to play your movies. In other words, you are doing your own distribution. The upside is, you get to keep every dollar that comes in at the box office. The downside is, you must come up with the capital for theater rentals, prints, and advertising. This can get expensive, and you should consider this as part of your budget when raising money, if you plan to four-wall.

Some people consider four-walling beneath them, but years ago, a company called Sun Classics turned the technique into an art form. They are the ones who gave us *Chariots of the Gods, In Search of Noah's Ark,* and *Grizzly Adams,* to name a few. Sun Classics became a multimillion-dollar company through four-walling.

Regional, or platform distributors will sell on a larger scale, but not nationally. Boutique distributors will sell to small, very specialized locales, depending on who they feel their target audience is.

Do not dismiss the small distributor. Even if your picture gets only a limited or narrow distribution domestically, foreign buyers will be impressed. The truth of the matter is, they believe that if a picture is distributed in the United States, it is worth more overseas. In fact, sometimes their contracts will stipulate that a picture must have been distributed in the States for them to distribute in their homeland.

Limited distribution can also work in your favor on another level: It's called word-of-mouth. A case in point is a very-low-budget film called *The Blair Witch Project*. The releasing company opened this movie in only two select locations, one theater in New York and one in Los Angeles, and let the word-of-mouth build. As it did, they widened the release until it was national. The original cost of the film was about thirty thousand dollars. They put a lot of additional money into post to sweeten the film, and then eventually poured about ten million dollars into prints and advertising. All this paid off handsomely. At last count, the film had passed the one-hundred million dollar mark. And that was just the domestic gross.

The original *Friday the Thirteenth* film cost seven-hundred-fifty thousand dollars to produce and grossed over thirty-five million dollars domestically. It was not a good movie, even for its genre, but then, it didn't have to be. The marketing ploy used for this film was ingenious. Knowing they didn't have a particularly good film, the distributors launched an incredible television advertising campaign. Using the most shocking visuals they could extract from the film, they built a taut, horrifying trailer, which they ran incessantly in prime time. Public response was more than they could have hoped for. They reached their target audience, which was the fifteen-to-thirty-year-olds, and the movie became a runaway success, spawning several sequels.

Agreements between the distributor and the producer, or owner, of a film can vary considerably. Under some common distribution contracts, the distributor receives a 25 to 35 percent distribution fee, plus recoupment of costs incurred in distributing the film. These costs relate, primarily, to prints and advertising. Only after these costs are recouped does the producer begin to share in the "gross film rentals."

In other types of distribution agreements, the producer may be granted a percentage of "gross film rentals" at the same time the distributor is recouping his fees and costs. The producer's percentage escalates after the distributor has made back his investment. The distributor will negotiate a minimum amount of money that he will expend on prints and advertising. If the picture is doing well, he will usually up the ante.

The distributor will customarily negotiate with you for the license right to exhibit the film for a period ranging from ten to twenty years. But regardless of whether the contract is a "gross" or "net" deal, the distributor will be recouping his investment at a faster rate than the producer will be recouping his.

Outright Sales

Another avenue to investigate is the selling of your movie to a major studio, such as Universal, Fox, Paramount, Warner Brothers, Columbia, or Sony. There are also major independents with close studio ties, such as Miramax, Revolution Studios, and Searchlight. These studios are in the business of distributing films they have either made themselves or have financed. But, on occasion, they acquire a completed film from an independent, if they feel it is something they can market profitably.

As I explained in chapter 3, the same film that you make as an independent for three million dollars would cost a major studio ten million to make. So, if they can buy your film for six million, then everybody makes a profit. This is called a BUYOUT. But even though they make you a flat deal for the buyout, you may still be able to negotiate a small percentage of the net profits after the gross has reached a certain figure. This protects you in the event your picture catches fire and becomes a huge hit.

There is also an arrangement known as a NEGATIVE PICK-UP, where you make an agreement with a distributor prior to the start of your production. At this time, they will give you a contract agreeing to purchase your picture, when it is completed, for a set price. This type of arrangement can be of enormous value to you in financing your film. A negative pick-up is, for all intents and purposes, a guarantee. And you can take that guarantee to the bank—it is rock-solid collateral.

If you go this route, there will be certain banking-related costs, such as interest. Remember, you are getting a production loan from the bank at, probably, three to five points over prime. The loan will be outstanding from the time you begin pre-production until you deliver the *answer print* to the studio. Therefore, you will have to factor in the interest costs for that period of time into your production budget.

Distribution, especially wide distribution, is an enormously expensive proposition, often costing the distributor as much as twenty to thirty million dollars for a higher-budget film. These types of films would also need one to two thousand prints. For smaller pictures, of course, the demand would be from maybe thirty prints on up, depending on the distribution plan. The point is, whether dealing with a high-budget or low-budget picture, distribution is costly, and the distributor must have faith in the project, or he is not going to risk investing his time and money.

Every week, *Variety* and the *Hollywood Reporter,* two of the preeminent trade papers, print distribution revenues. There is a listing of each and every distribution company putting out movies: the amount of prints in circulation and the amount of gross domestic revenues. These are the companies that are in business right now, and these are the companies that you should contact about your film.

Foreign theatrical rentals are commonly accrued at 40 percent in the first year, 50 percent in the second year, and 10 percent in the third year. The Foreign Distributor may act as a sales agent, or he may hire subdistributors on a territory-to-territory basis. It is also possible for the producer to negotiate with the distributor for an advance guarantee against a percentage of gross film rentals for each territory. The producer then does not receive any further payments until all distribution fees and expenses are met and the advance has been recouped. When the distribution contract calls for both domestic and foreign theatrical rights, the contract is said to be "worldwide."

Ancillary Sales

In the United States, the producer can sell commercial broadcast rights to the six operating networks: CBS, NBC, ABC, FOX, UPN, and the WB. Syndication rights are sold to independent stations in individual markets. Pay television rights include Cable (both Premiere Channels and Basic Channels), Direct Broadcast Satellite, Microwave, and other services paid for by subscribers.

The right to license broadcast network and other television markets may be part of the domestic theatrical distribution contract, which the distributor then uses as a possible offset of costs in the event the picture does not perform as expected in theatrical release.

Although the sequence of licensing can vary widely, as a rule, rights to theatrical features are sold first to pay television for an exhibition period, then to broadcast network television, then back to pay television, and finally, syndicated to independent stations. Therefore, the film generates income resulting from television licenses over a period of approximately seven years.

The right to distribute your film in HOME VIDEO MARKETS may also be included in the domestic or worldwide distribution contract. The market for videocassettes and DVDs for home use has expanded rapidly, and this expansion is likely to continue as ownership of VCRs, and especially DVD players, continues to grow.

Home video markets in foreign territories have been increasing at an exceptionally rapid rate, due to the relative lack of diversified television programming in those countries. Consequently, the prices paid for the right to market videocassettes and discs in these foreign markets has been increasing in recent years. Film industry analysts predict continual growth in the video market in both the United States and foreign territories for the foreseeable future.

Your distribution contract may also include provisions for your distributor to act as sales agent for non-theatrical and non-television markets. These markets include in-flight viewing and closed-circuit venues, such as hotels and motels, schools, public libraries, community groups, the armed forces, and ships at sea. And let us not forget the Internet. Baby steps are already being taken in the airing of feature films and television shows on the Internet. How the distribution and marketing of film in this new media will be accomplished is still up for grabs.

Besides the exhibition of your film to viewing audiences around the world, distribution contracts may also include the rights to license music from the score of your picture, which includes sheet music and public performances of that music.

And let's not forget merchandising and promotional tie-ins, which is a billion-dollar industry. Your distribution contract will probably include the rights to license merchandisers to manufacture and sell such products as video games, toys, T-shirts, posters, and other gifts. And finally, rights may also be licensed for novelization of the screenplay and related book rights.

Retaining rights is a difficult art. You will be dealing with companies who are specialists in getting the better part of the deal, and you are not in a very good position to make powerful demands—not yet, anyway. To protect yourself and your future earnings, it is absolutely vital that you retain an attorney. Not just any attorney, but a theatrical attorney who is knowledgeable in entertainment contracts and knows what the latest deals of division are all about. It's important to be current when you are discussing dividing up the profits.

Don't feel you must go with the top-ranked firms. What is really important is that you feel you are being personally represented. Some of the smaller legal firms are just as good. Go with someone with whom you feel you can have an honest business relationship. Someone who will return your phone calls is a good start. Having your phone calls returned is of major importance, because it tells you that they regard you as an meaningful client.

13

The World of Television

This chapter is dedicated to those hardy souls who wish to dive head-long into shark-infested waters with the elusive hopes of finding that tiny pearl of success in a vast bed of oysters . . . in other words, television programming.

Television is a much more complex arena than feature films when it comes to putting a project together, because you are at the mercy of so many entities over which you have no control. Not only don't you have any control, you will never even know who or what some of these entities are.

But if you are determined to enter this field of endeavor, let me, at least, give you some guidelines and point you in the right direction. Years ago, there were three networks to deal with, and that was it. You either sold to NBC, ABC, or CBS, or you didn't sell. Today, there are six networks, five premiere cable channels, and at least half a dozen basic cable channels that produce original dramatic programming.

That's good news for the producer or writer who is looking to sell his product to television. But the downside is, every network and cable chan-nel has its own criteria for what they want to exhibit. As a producer, you need to do your homework, so you, or your agent, don't waste a lot of time trying to sell your product in the wrong market.

The only advantage television has over feature production is the fact that you don't have to raise any money. Outside of documentaries and after-market sales of theatrical features, nothing is produced on spec for network television or cable programming. One does not raise money to make a pilot film or a movie-of-the-week, and then try to sell it to a network or a cable channel. That is what is known in the parlance as *ass-backwards.* Network- or cable-company approval of a project is an absolute necessity before any work can begin on that project.

To Agent or Not To Agent

In dealing with television networks and cable channels, you will definitely need the services of an agent. Just make sure that the agent you sign with is conversant with all the facets of television deal-making. It can become very complex, because you are not selling a program to be shown one time. A television show's afterlife can involve everything from syndication to foreign theatrical releases to media not yet invented.

A good agent will be aware of what type of programming each network or cable channel is looking for. You can do some of your own research simply by watching the shows that are telecast. You will find that some outlets are slanted heavily toward sitcoms, others toward drama or reality shows, some will prefer edgier shows, others are more family-oriented. Know your market before you start submitting.

The basic areas of television programming are: one-hour dramatic series, half-hour sitcoms, two-hour movies-of-the-week, miniseries (which can run from four to twelve hours), game shows, reality shows, soap operas, investigative journalism programs, and documentaries.

Getting Your Show on the Air

Before you decide to attack the fortress that is network television, you need to understand some of the mechanics involved in trying to get a show on the air. First of all, we will eliminate soap operas and investigative journalism programs from our discussion. These shows are done in-house, by networks, using their own staff producers. Let's also eliminate documentaries. If you have a great documentary, you may get it sold to one of the basic cable channels, but there simply is not much money there.

When discussing episodic programming, which are the one-hour dramas and half-hour sitcoms, we must divide them into two distinct arenas. The first is creating the series, and the second is writing for existing series. Selling a new series idea is definitely the most difficult nut to crack.

There was a time in this business when practically anyone could get his idea to a network executive or a production company executive. The world is a good deal more complicated today.

If you haven't dealt with network programming, let me give you a brief primer on how it works. Normally, a PRODUCTION COMPANY will produce a product (movie-of-the week [M.O.W.] or series). The network will pay a LICENSE FEE for the right to run the M.O.W., or each episode of a series, twice. Cable channels work on a different premise. They still pay a license fee, but it is usually based on a time element. In other words, they can run a show as often as they want within a specific time frame. The production company pays the difference between the license fee and the cost of production. Then, after these initial runs, the ownership of the M.O.W. or the episodes revert back to the producer, who will be free to sell his product to whomever he wishes.

To complicate this process, most networks and cable companies have their own production arms, which, of course, are in competition with independent producers and major studios who are in the business of providing product to those very same networks and cable companies.

The M.O.W.

Movies-of-the-week are probably the best opportunity for an independent producer to break into the television market. If you have a script and you couldn't raise the money needed to make a theatrical film, then MOWs are a whole new market to explore. So get in there and pitch. But before you do, check out what each network wants to see, what audience they are reaching out for. It does no good to pitch a sci-fi movie to Lifetime, or a women's-issues picture to the Sci-Fi Channel. If you're pitching to VH1, it better be about music, and if it's UPN, it will need lots of action.

It helps to have an agent to guide you through the labyrinth of pitching, packaging, and selling an M.O.W. Or, if you know a producer who has access to the networks and cable channels, you could work out a coproduction deal with him and eliminate the agent.

A few years ago, I did a movie for Showtime. It was the writer's first sale. He lived in Oklahoma, but he had a friend in Los Angeles who knew a producer. The friend brought the script to the producer, who liked it and, in turn, brought it to Showtime, where he eventually made the deal.

There are no hard and fast rules on how to sell M.O.W.s. At one time, networks would never buy from a completed script; they only wanted to see treatments. Now, it is a mixed bag. Some will want to see scripts, others only treatments, and some will take pitches. It is one of those things you have to play by ear, because the rules will change as often as you change your underwear.

Selling the Series

Now, let's say that you, as an independent producer, have a series idea you would like to sell. It would be extremely difficult, if not impossible, for you to go to a network, directly, to sell your idea. Even if you could get to a programming executive who liked your idea, the chances of your little company producing the series would be nil.

The reason for this is simple. Any company producing series for television has to have very deep pockets. Virtually no series today is made without deficit spending. A one-hour episode costs one-million eight-hundred thousand dollars to shoot (which, by the way, is about average), and the network pays a license fee of one-million two-hundred thousand dollars (also about average). If the show is made on budget (which doesn't happen too often), the producer is in the hole by six-hundred thousand dollars. Multiply that by twenty-two episodes, and you come up with a shortfall of over thirteen million dollars for a season.

The producer hopes that within a couple of years, through syndication and foreign sales, he will come out with a profit on his series. But someone has to come up with that deficit, and be prepared to carry the debt load, until he can turn a profit.

Your goal should be to get your project to a viable production company. If they like your idea, they will get it to the network. If the network likes your idea, the creative process begins in earnest. *Never* write a script, or pay to have a script written for you, for a pilot film. Series ideas are not sold from screenplays; they are sold from PREMISES. The premise simply tells what your series is about, who the characters are, and how they interact with each other. Just make sure your premise is no more than five or six pages. Most executives have a very short attention span.

If the network buys your idea for a television series, they will pay the producing company to hire a writer who they approve of to write the pilot screenplay. If the screenplay is approved, then the green light will be given to shoot the pilot film. After the pilot (which the network has paid for) is finished, then they will decide if it is worthwhile to them to find a time slot for it. The odds of your actually getting a series on television starts out, at inception, at about ten thousand to one and drops, at completion of pilot, to about a hundred to one. Well, I guess it's better than the lottery . . . but not much.

It would really be a waste of your time and effort to try and sell a miniseries, unless, of course, you own the rights to a best-selling novel. This is because virtually all miniseries are produced from novels. Offhand, I can't think of any miniseries that has been produced from original material.

The Reality Show

With the success of reality shows, it is now possible for anyone to present a concept that they have filmed with a home camera or cut from a magazine article. In selling a reality show, the concept is everything and the presentation is not important. Additionally, reality shows are a good way for lesser-known talent to break into the industry because it isn't always necessary to have a big background and be a major showrunner. The question here is whether or not you can show the buyer that you are capable of delivering the required amount of shows with this concept. In fact, where reality shows are concerned, it is often a plus if the show has an amateurish look. COPS is the most obvious example.

Nevertheless, you are still in the rare atmosphere of having to compete with people who are known to the buyers and with whom they are more comfortable. And the stronger you can make your presentation—whether it is on camera, stills, digital, or whatever means you can invent to make your concept worthy of their attention and . . . more than that, to make them believe that this is a concept that will attract an audience—the better off you will be. In reality shows, as in all other forms of entertainment, you must also have a good idea of what it will cost to make these shows on a weekly basis, or even on a strip (or daily) basis. It does not do you any good to have a show that costs you three-hundred thousand dollars an episode if the Weblet buying your show is only going to give you fifty-thousand dollars per episode. And while the general concept of reality shows allows them to be made for much less than the average television sitcom or drama, you will quickly discover that one-hundred thousand dollars doesn't go very far, even when making cheap, down and dirty reality shows.

But start with the concept and the presentation. If you can find a buyer, he will be pleased to introduce you to people he feels will be able to help you produce your show at the desired budget.

The Art of the Pitch

At some time in your sojourn through the Faustian maze of the television world, you will probably be called upon to PITCH a story. If you are not a writer, but have obtained rights to a property, you will be the one who will have to pitch the story to a network or cable executive.

There are some basic dos and don'ts inherent in the art of the pitch. First of all, know your story. Your pitch should sound effortless, as if you were telling a story to a friend. Maybe inside, your stomach is churning, but on the outside you must appear cool and collected. If you know what you want to say and you have practiced it long enough, the words will roll out easily.

Keep your pitch short. No more than five to seven minutes. *Do not* go through your story scene by scene, describing individual scenes and discussing each character. People want to hear the story arc—beginning, middle, and end—and who the main characters are. Don't worry about leaving things out. You want to hook the person's interest. If you do that, he will then ask you questions. At that point, you can elaborate. Or he may challenge you. That is not bad either, because it shows he is interested. Don't be defensive, merely explain your position. If he doesn't ask any questions and says, "Thank you very much, we'll think about it," just say good-bye. It will be the last time you will see him.

One way to begin your pitch is with a LOG LINE. Many executives feel that a good story can be boiled down to a couple of sentences. If you were pitching *ER,* you could say, "This series is about life-and-death struggles in a big-city emergency room, and the doctors who deal with people in need on a daily basis." Then you could go on to tell what the series is about in more detail.

Whatever you do, don't editorialize, hype, or apologize for what you are about to say. Just about the worst thing you can say is, "This is really a funny story" or "You're gonna love this." I can guarantee you that it will *not* be funny, nor will they love it.

Pitching is an art form that takes a great deal of practice. Some people will be, just naturally, more proficient than others. But if you know your material and, more importantly, believe in it, you can be successful.

Working in television can be as exciting, and as frustrating, as working on feature films. In television, the writer is king; in big movies, it is the director. But in the world of independent movie-making, the producer still reigns supreme. And as the differences between television and features narrows and the marketplace widens, I would go wherever I could produce my product. Keep your projects ready at your side. They are the soldiers you will send into battle.

Epilogue

I guess from here on in, it's up to you. You've chosen a tough profession, but one in which the rewards, both financially and emotionally, are extremely high. You have the opportunity, as an independent producer, to be in that unique position of satisfying your artistic needs, while at the same time satisfying your more basic needs, like food, clothing, and a roof over your head.

Without discouraging you, we have tried to give you a realistic view of the life and the world of the independent producer. As with any life endeavor, a person gets out of it what he or she puts into it. There are no shortcuts, no simple answers, no easy way . . . in other words, *no free lunches*. This is a business where hard work and perseverance, coupled with ambition and talent, can lead to success—*but* it is *not* a guarantee. And that, dear friend, is because Lady Luck plays a major role in your personal drama.

Like it or not, there is much to be said for being in the right place at the right time with the right property. But if you are not properly prepared for that moment when the "stars are aligned," then all the luck in the world ain't gonna help.

So, there it is. Preparation and luck, luck and preparation. They go together like love and marriage and the horse and carriage. You are going to need both, and one is no good without the other. But in the total balance of your career, you will, in the long run, do better with a *lot* of preparation and a *little* luck, rather than the other way around.

We have given you the tools you will need to become the independent producer you want to be. It is up to you how those tools are used. The motion picture business, like most art forms, is not stationary. It is ever-changing, always evolving. And because it is a business as well as an art form, the pressures of new technologies will be propelling this business forward at warp speed in the new millennium.

The best advice we can offer you is, learn to live with the heartaches, the disappointments, and the failures, so that when the time comes, you will be able to savor the triumphs. We wish you the best. We know the road is difficult, because we have been there. We also know that dreams can come true, because we've been *there,* too.

Example of Film Partnership Proposal

*Note: This section is designed to show one way of formatting a film proposal. All monetary figures are for example only.

TABLE OF CONTENTS

I. CORPORATE MARKETING POSITION

For investment purposes, the entertainment industry is normally typified as a high-risk venture, requiring sizable amounts of capitalization, with a slow payback period and a potential for a large upside return. For these reasons, many alternate forms of investment are recommended (and justly so) for the appropriate needs of the investor, or group of investors. It is with these factors in mind that the following creative proposal has been specifically developed.

Therefore, it is our intent to enter the theatrical marketplace in a viable, yet conservative manner; as will be noted in the following pages. The key from this investment standpoint has been to:

1. Minimize risk
2. Maximize the upside potential
3. Speed up the payback period
4. Maximize the investor's equity position

Specifically, this project is recommended, as it consists of producing and directing the distribution of a theatrical film, directed toward the primary theater-going demographic.

This project also offers some significant benefits which normally are not available to a new theatrical venture; that is, the position, expertise, and reputation of the key personnel involved. Although it is hard to assign a dollar value to these individuals, it does insure effective, aggressive, and knowledgeable production and business experience in a very competitive and somewhat closed business environment. The key factors these individuals lend to the project are:

1. Sound and profitable production experience
2. Access to skilled production and cast members
3. Strong relationships with the guilds and unions
4. Strong banking and legal experience
5. Effective management experience
6. Network and pay TV relationships
7. Proven distribution background and negotiating ability
8. Sound marketing experience, broadcast, advertising, and campaign development
9. Highly successful track records

In reviewing the following pages, please note that these are realistic and conservative projections, attainable figures based on the specific production value, ingredients, and dollars allocated for prints, advertising, publicity, and time of year released. We base this on past performance of similar pictures and feel these figures are conservative in that they represent the downside potential.

Also, please note that a network and pay TV pre-sale is included. We ultimately do not recommend this course of action as a way to maximize total dollars, but realize the need for timeliness of the investor's recoupment. Upon funding of the package, the networks will be approached in securing a pre-sale for this film.

II.   FILM TITLE

1.   SYNOPSIS AND CREATIVE POSITIONS

A short synopsis of your film, how you feel this film will be marketed, and to what type of audience it is directed.

2.   CREDIT LIST

Executive Producer:

Producers:

Director:

POTENTIAL CAST LIST

List of principal acting roles and actor(s) suitable for each role.

Character Name: Actor(s):

3.   DISTRIBUTION ASSUMPTIONS

The following figures reflect assumptions for this film based upon the following criteria:

(1) Pay TV pre-sale (fourth quarter) of $.5 million, with escalators based on box office performance.

(2) Network pre-sale (fourth quarter) of $1 million, with escalators based on box office performance.

(3) Wide domestic release during the January/February period, utilizing approximately 700 release prints, with a substantial broadcast, print, and radio campaign.

(4) Total estimated expenditures for release prints and advertising (initial release) is $4.5 million. A first-quarter release is recommended due to availability of theaters (due to Christmas product coming off the screens), lower broadcast costs, increased inventory, and decreased competition with the marketplace.

(5) We recommend that a single and/or soundtrack album be promoted in the market prior to Christmas. Second, that utilization of cast for national public appearances tours begins in January.

(6) Merchandising items will be developed for entry into the marketplace prior to Christmas.

(7) Ninety percent of revenues will be collected during the first twenty-four-month period, the balance of ten percent over the subsequent three-year period.

(8) Positioning and campaign development would occur concurrent with production and post-production.

(9) Delivery of the <u>answer print</u> during December.

4. PROJECTED REVENUES (in millions)

		TOTALS
DOMESTIC BOX OFFICE (theater gross)	$18	
FILM RENTAL (distributor's gross)	(9)	
LESS DISTRIBUTION EXPENSES	(3.5)	
NET TO DISTRIBUTOR		$ 5.5
LESS 35% DISTRIBUTION FEE		(2.0)
DOMESTIC DISTRIBUTOR'S NET TO PRODUCER (before negative cost)		$ 3.5

NETWORK	(net of commission)	$ 1.5	
PAY TV	"	.85	
FOREIGN THEATRICAL	"	6.2	
SYNDICATION	"	.9	
VIDEO	"	1.1	
*ANCILLARY RIGHTS	"	.85	
NET TO PRODUCER (additional revenues)		$11.4	
BALANCE BEFORE DISBURSEMENTS			$14.9
LESS NEGATIVE COST			(3.5)
NET PROFIT			**$11.4**

*Includes cassettes, army, navy, 16mm, airlines, cruise ships, etc.

5. RESEARCH

Domestic Film Rentals of Related Films*:

One Flew Over the Cuckoo Nest (1975)	$77,772,481
The Shining (1980)	35,000,000
When a Stranger Calls (1979)	11,400,000

Network Rating of Related Films:

	Network	Date	Rating	Share
The Eyes of Laura Mars	NBC	10/1/81	16.3	29
Audrey Rose (repeat)	NBC	6/14/82	15.4	28

*Film rental figures adjusted to current dollars.

III. FILM PARTNERSHIP DEAL STRUCTURE

1. The partnership will produce one motion picture tentatively titled: *TITLE OF FILM.*
2. The investor will provide a total of $2.8 million to cover all costs of production.
3. For financial consideration, the investor will receive 50 percent equity in the partnership.
4. The partnership will allocate $60,000 for advertising and sales materials and related expenses as needed.
5. Return of investment (negative cost) will be paid back before distribution of any profit participation.
6. As soon as the investment monies have been repaid, profit participation will be divided on an equity basis between investors and producers.
7. An outside agency, mutually agreed upon, will monitor and disburse all payments.

IV. PRODUCTION SCHEDULE

FILM TITLE OF FILM

Monies in place March 31st

PRE-PRODUCTION: April, May
PRINCIPAL PHOTOGRAPHY: June, July
POST-PRODUCTION: August, September, October, November
DELIVERY: December

V. PRODUCTION BUDGETS

ANYWHERE PRODUCTIONS, INC.
BUDGET MASTER SUMMARY REPORT

RUN DATE :

EXEC PROD:
PRODUCER :
UNIT MGR:
SCHEDULE :
COMMENTS :

SCRIPT DATE:
NO. OF DAYS:
SHOOTING DAYS:

PRELIMINARY BUDGET #

Acct#	Category Title	Page	Total
600-00	STORY	1	$0
610-00	PRODUCER	1	$0
620-00	DIRECTOR	2	$0
630-00	CAST	2	$0
640-00	FRINGES	2	$0
650-00	TRAVEL & LIVING	2	$0
670-00	AGENCY COMMISSION	2	$0
640-00	**Total Fringes**		$0
	TOTAL ABOVE-THE-LINE		$0
700-00	EXTRA TALENT	3	$0
705-00	PRODUCTION STAFF	3	$0
710-00	CAMERA	4	$0
715-00	SET DESIGN	4	$0
720-00	SET CONSTRUCTION	5	$0
725-00	SET OPERATIONS	5	$0
730-00	ELECTRICAL	6	$0
735-00	SPECIAL EFFECTS	6	$0
745-00	SET DRESSING	7	$0
750-00	PROPERTIES	7	$0
755-00	WARDROBE	8	$0
760-00	MAKEUP & HAIRSTYLISTS	8	$0
765-00	PRODUCTION SOUND	9	$0
770-00	TRANSPORTATION	9	$0
772-00	PICTURE VEHICLES	10	$0
775-00	LOCATION EXPENSE	10	$0
785-00	PRODUCTION DAILIES	11	$0
790-00	LIVING EXPENSE	12	$0
795-00	FRINGES	12	$0
798-00	FACILITIES FEES	12	$0
795-00	**Total Fringes**		$0
	TOTAL PRODUCTION		$0
800-00	EDITING	13	$0
801-00	POST-PROD VIDEO EDITING	13	$0
810-00	MUSIC	14	$0
820-00	POST-PROD SOUND	14	$0
830-00	STOCK SHOTS	15	$0
840-00	TITLES	15	$0
850-00	OPTICALS, MATTES, INSERTS	15	$0
870-00	FRINGES	16	$0
870-00	**Total Fringes**		$0
	TOTAL POST PRODUCTION		$0

Acct#	Category Title	Page	Total
910-00	ADMINISTRATIVE EXPENSES	16	$0
920-00	PUBLICITY	17	$0
940-00	FRINGES	17	$0
940-00	**Total Fringes**		$0
	TOTAL OTHER		$0
	TOTAL ABOVE-THE-LINE		$0
	TOTAL BELOW-THE-LINE		$0
	TOTAL ABOVE & BELOW-THE-LINE		$0
	GRAND TOTAL		$0

ANYWHERE PRODUCTIONS, INC.
BUDGET MASTER SUMMARY REPORT

RUN DATE :

EXEC PROD:
PRODUCER :
UNIT MGR:
SCHEDULE :
COMMENTS :

SCRIPT DATE:
NO. OF DAYS:
SHOOTING DAYS:

PRELIMINARY BUDGET #

Acct#	Description	Amount	Units	X	Rate	Subtotal	Total
600-00	STORY						
600-02	STORY - CONSULTANTS						$0
600-04	WRITER'S FEE						$0
600-10	WRITER SECRETARIAL						$0
600-11	PROGRAM FEES						$0
600-13	SCRIPT COPY						$0
600-14	ABANDONED SCRIPTS						$0
600-25	RESEARCH						$0
600-81	ROYALTIES						$0
600-95	OTHER						$0
600-97	WGA PH & W						$0
						Total For 600-00	$0
610-00	PRODUCER						
610-01	EXECUTIVE PRODUCERS						$0
610-02	PRODUCERS						$0
610-04	ASSOCIATE PRODUCERS						$0
610-10	PRODUCERS SECRETARIAL						$0
610-12	PRODUCERS LIVING EXPENSE						$0
610-45	PRODUCERS ENTERTAINMENT						$0
610-95	OTHER						$0
						Total For 610-00	$0

Acct#	Description	Amount	Units	X	Rate	Subtotal	Total
620-00	**DIRECTOR**						
620-01	DIRECTOR						$0
620-07	CASTING DIRECTOR						$0
620-08	CASTING ASSISTANT						$0
620-09	CASTING EXPENSES						$0
620-81	ROYALTY						$0
620-95	OTHER						$0
620-97	FRINGES-PENSION H & W						$0
						Total For 620-00	$0
630-00	**CAST**						
630-01	PRINCIPAL PLAYERS						$0
630-02	SUPPORTING CAST						$0
630-04	STUNT COORDINATOR						$0
630-05	STUNT PLAYERS						$0
630-09	TALENT LOOPING COSTS						$0
630-20	OVERTIME						$0
630-31	CAST LIVING EXPENSES						$0
630-95	OTHER						$0
630-97	SAG PH & W						$0
						Total For 630-00	$0
640-00	**FRINGES**						
640-01	A-T-L FRINGES						$0
						Total For 640-00	$0
650-00	**TRAVEL & LIVING**						
650-31	CAST TRAVEL						$0
650-32	CAST LIVING EXPENSE						$0
						Total For 650-00	$0
670-00	**AGENCY COMMISSION**						

Acct#	Description	Amount	Units	X	Rate	Subtotal	Total
670-00	AGENCY COMMISSION (CONT'D)						
670-01	PACKAGE FEE						$0
						Total For 670-00	$0
640-00	Total Fringes						
						Total For 640-00	$0
	TOTAL ABOVE-THE-LINE						$0
700-00	EXTRA TALENT						
700-01	STAND-INS						$0
700-02	GENERAL ATMOSPHERE						$0
700-10	CAR/MILEAGE ALLOWANCES						$0
700-11	WARDROBE ALLOWANCES						$0
700-20	CASTING COMMISSIONS						$0
						Total For 700-00	$0
705-00	PRODUCTION STAFF						
705-01	UNIT PRODUCTION MANAGER						$0
705-02	FIRST ASSISTANT DIRECTOR						$0
705-04	SECOND ASSISTANT DIRECTOR						$0
705-05	SECOND 2ND ASST DIRECTOR						$0
705-08	SCRIPT SUPERVISOR						$0
705-09	PRODUCTION ACCOUNTANT						$0
705-10	ASSISTANT ACCOUNTANTS						$0
705-11	PRODUCTION COORDINATOR						$0
705-14	PRODUCTION ASSISTANTS						$0
705-17	TECHNICAL ADVISOR						$0
705-89	CAR ALLOWANCE						$0
705-90	BOX/COMPUTER RENTALS						$0
705-95	OTHER						$0
						Total For 705-00	$0

Acct#	Description	Amount	Units	X	Rate	Subtotal	Total
710-00	CAMERA						$0
710-01	DIRECTOR OF PHOTOGRAPHY						
710-02	CAMERA OPERATORS						$0
710-03	FIRST ASSISTANT CAMERA						$0
710-04	SECOND ASSISTANT CAMERA						$0
710-11	STILL PHOTOGRAPHER						$0
710-22	ADDITIONAL CAMERA OPERATO						$0
710-23	ADDITIONAL CAMERA FIRST						$0
710-24	ADDITIONAL CAMERA SECOND						$0
710-85	LOSS, DAMAGE AND REPAIR						$0
710-90	BOX RENTALS						$0
710-92	ADDITIONAL RENTALS						$0
710-93	RENTALS						$0
710-94	PURCHASES						$0
710-95	OTHER						$0
						Total For 710-00	$0
715-00	SET DESIGN						$0
715-01	PRODUCTION DESIGNER						
715-03	ASSISTANT ART DIRECTOR						$0
715-05	SET DESIGNERS						$0
715-06	CONSTRUCTION COORDINATOR						$0
715-10	ART DEPARTMENT RESEARCH						$0
715-89	CAR ALLOWANCE						$0
715-90	BOX RENTALS						$0
715-93	RENTALS						$0
715-94	PURCHASES						$0
715-95	OTHER						$0
						Total For 715-00	$0

Acct#	Description	Amount	Units	X	Rate	Subtotal	Total
720-00	SET CONSTRUCTION						
720-01	LABOR						$0
720-03	BACKINGS						$0
720-04	GREENS/NURSERY						$0
720-90	BOX RENTALS						$0
720-92	SET STORAGE						$0
720-93	RENTALS						$0
720-94	PURCHASES						$0
720-95	OTHER						$0
						Total For 720-00	$0
725-00	SET OPERATIONS						
725-01	KEY GRIP						$0
725-02	BEST BOY						$0
725-03	COMPANY GRIPS						$0
725-04	DOLLY GRIPS						$0
725-07	RIG & STRIKE LABOR						$0
725-09	CRAFT SERVICE PERSON						$0
725-12	GREENSPERSON						$0
725-13	STANDBY PAINTER						$0
725-15	FIRST AID						$0
725-24	DRESSING ROOM RENTALS						$0
725-85	LOSS, DAMAGE AND REPAIR						$0
725-89	CAR ALLOWANCE						$0
725-90	BOX RENTALS						$0
725-91	DOLLY RENTALS						$0
725-92	CAMERA CRANE RENTALS						$0
725-93	RENTALS						$0

Acct#	Description	Amount	Units	X	Rate	Subtotal	Total
725-00	SET OPERATIONS (CONT'D)						
725-94	PURCHASES						$0
725-95	OTHER						$0
						Total For 725-00	$0
730-00	ELECTRICAL						
730-01	GAFFER						$0
730-02	BEST BOY						$0
730-03	LAMP OPERATORS						$0
730-07	RIG & STRIKE LABOR						$0
730-09	GENERATOR OPER-LOCATION						$0
730-13	GLOBES						$0
730-16	POWER						$0
730-85	LOSS, DAMAGE & REPAIR						$0
730-90	BOX RENTALS						$0
730-92	GENERATOR RENTAL						$0
730-93	RENTALS						$0
730-94	PURCHASES						$0
730-95	OTHER						$0
						Total For 730-00	$0
735-00	SPECIAL EFFECTS						
735-01	SPECIAL EFFECTS PERSON						$0
735-02	ASSISTANT SPECIAL EFFECTS						$0
735-04	MANUFACTURING SPECIAL EFF						$0
735-85	LOSS, DAMAGE & REPAIR						$0
735-90	BOX RENTALS						$0
735-93	RENTALS						$0
735-94	PURCHASES						$0

Acct#	Description	Amount	Units	X	Rate	Subtotal	Total
735-00	SPECIAL EFFECTS (CONT'D)						
735-95	OTHER						$0
						Total For 735-00	$0
745-00	SET DRESSING						
745-01	SET DECORATOR						$0
745-02	LEADPERSON						$0
745-03	SWING GANG						$0
745-14	DRAPERY PURCHASE						$0
745-82	SET DRESSING MANUFACTURED						$0
745-85	LOSS, DAMAGE & REPAIR						$0
745-89	CAR ALLOWANCE						$0
745-90	BOX RENTALS						$0
745-93	RENTALS						$0
745-94	PURCHASES						$0
745-95	OTHER						$0
						Total For 745-00	$0
750-00	PROPERTIES						
750-01	PROPMASTER						$0
750-02	ASSISTANT PROPMASTER						$0
750-03	EXTRA PROP LABOR						$0
750-04	MANUFACTURE PROPS						$0
750-05	ANIMALS & LIVESTOCK						$0
750-06	ANIMAL WRANGLERS/TRAINERS						$0
750-07	ANIMAL FEED & STABLING						$0
750-85	LOSS, DAMAGE & REPAIR						$0
750-89	CAR ALLOWANCE						$0
750-90	BOX RENTALS						$0
750-93	RENTALS						$0

Acct#	Description		Amount	Units	X	Rate	Subtotal	Total
750-00	PROPERTIES (CONT'D)							
750-94	PURCHASES							$0
750-95	OTHER							$0
								Total For 750-00 $0
755-00	WARDROBE							
755-01	COSTUME DESIGNER							$0
755-02	MEN'S COSTUMERS							$0
755-03	WOMEN'S COSTUMERS							$0
755-04	ADDITIONAL COSTUME LABOR							$0
755-05	WARDROBE MANUFACTURE							$0
755-06	ALTERATIONS							$0
755-07	CLEANING & DYEING							$0
755-85	LOSS, DAMAGES & REPAIR							$0
755-89	CAR ALLOWANCE							$0
755-90	BOX RENTALS							$0
755-93	RENTALS							$0
755-94	PURCHASES							$0
755-95	OTHER							$0
								Total For 755-00 $0
760-00	MAKEUP & HAIRSTYLISTS							
760-01	KEY MAKE-UP ARTIST							$0
760-02	ADDITIONAL MAKE-UP ARTIST							$0
760-03	BODY MAKE-UP TECHNICIANS							$0
760-11	KEY HAIRSTYLIST							$0
760-12	ADDITIONAL HAIRSTYLISTS							$0
760-15	WIGS & HAIRPIECES							$0
760-85	LOSS, DAMAGE & REPAIR							$0
760-90	BOX RENTALS							$0

Acct#	Description	Amount	Units	X	Rate	Subtotal	Total
760-00	**MAKEUP & HAIRSTYLISTS (CONT'D)**						
760-93	RENTALS						$0
760-94	PURCHASES						$0
760-95	OTHER						$0
						Total For 760-00	$0
765-00	**PRODUCTION SOUND**						
765-01	SOUND MIXER						$0
765-02	BOOM OPERATOR						$0
765-04	CABLEMEN/UTILITY SOUND						$0
765-05	PLAYBACK OPER-AUDIO/VIDEO						$0
765-06	VIDEO ASSIST						$0
765-85	LOSS, DAMAGE & REPAIR						$0
765-90	BOX RENTALS						$0
765-92	PLAYBACK RNTL-AUDIO/VIDEO						$0
765-93	RENTALS						$0
765-94	PURCHASES						$0
765-95	OTHER						$0
						Total For 765-00	$0
770-00	**TRANSPORTATION**						
770-01	COORDINATOR						$0
770-02	CAPTAIN						$0
770-03	CO-CAPTAIN						$0
770-05	LOCATION DRIVERS						$0
770-07	PICTURE VEHICLE DRIVERS						$0
770-08	MAINTENANCE						$0
770-18	PARKING						$0
770-20	GAS AND OIL						$0
770-21	TRAILER/PUMPING/VEH WASH						$0

Acct#	Description	Amount	Units	X	Rate	Subtotal	Total
770-00	**TRANSPORTATION (CONT'D)**						
770-22	MILEAGE/CAR ALLOWANCE						$0
770-23	TAXIS AND TOLLS						$0
770-30	MESSENGERS/COURIERS						$0
770-85	LOSS, DAMAGE & REPAIR						$0
770-90	BOX RENTALS						$0
770-91	CRANE RENTAL (EXCL CAMERA						$0
770-92	LOCATION VEHICLE RENTALS						$0
770-94	PURCHASES						$0
770-95	OTHER						
							$0
						Total For 770-00	**$0**
772-00	**PICTURE VEHICLES**						
772-01	MANUFACTURING						$0
772-10	VEHICLES						$0
772-85	LOSS, DAMAGE & REPAIR						$0
772-93	RENTALS						$0
772-94	PURCHASES						$0
772-95	OTHER						$0
						Total For 772-00	**$0**
775-00	**LOCATION EXPENSE**						
775-01	SURVEY EXPENSE						$0
775-02	LOCATION MANAGER						$0
775-04	LOCATION SECURITY						$0
775-05	LOCATION POLICE						$0
775-06	LOCATION FIRE SAFETY OFF						$0
775-07	SITE RENTAL FEES						$0
775-08	PERMITS						$0

Acct#	Description	Amount	Units	X	Rate	Subtotal	Total
775-00	LOCATION EXPENSE (CONT'D)						
775-09	CATERING EXPENSE						$0
775-10	CRAFT SERVICE						$0
775-11	LOCATION OFFICE RENTAL						$0
775-12	LOCATION OFFICE EQUIP RTL						$0
775-13	PHONE/FAX INSTALL/RENT						$0
775-14	LOCATION SHIPPING						$0
775-15	LOCATION MEDICAL LABOR						$0
775-16	LOCATION MEDICAL SUPPLIES						$0
775-17	GRATUITIES						$0
775-51	AIRFARES						$0
775-52	HOTEL						$0
775-53	PER DIEM						$0
775-54	DRIVERS MEAL MONEY						$0
775-55	AIRPORT PICKUPS						$0
775-56	MISC. TRAVEL						$0
775-85	LOSS, DAMAGE & REPAIR						$0
775-89	CAR ALLOWANCE						$0
775-90	BOX RENTALS						$0
775-93	RENTALS						$0
775-94	PURCHASES						$0
775-95	OTHER						$0
						Total For 775-00	$0
785-00	PRODUCTION DAILIES						
785-01	NEGATIVE RAW STOCK						$0
785-02	"B" CAMERA RAW STOCK						$0
785-03	DEVELOP PHOTOGRAPHY						$0

Acct#	Description	Amount	Units	X	Rate	Subtotal	Total
785-00	**PRODUCTION DAILIES (CONT'D)**						
785-04	PRINT PHOTOGRAPHY						$0
785-05	SOUND STOCK						$0
785-06	TRANSFER SOUND DAILIES						$0
785-07	VIDEOTAPE TRANSFER						$0
785-10	STILLS RAW STOCK						$0
785-95	OTHER						$0
						Total For 785-00	$0
790-00	**LIVING EXPENSE**						
790-01	COMMISSARY CHARGES						$0
790-02	REWRITE/SIDELINE FOOD						$0
790-09	CATERING EXPENSE						$0
790-51	AIRFARES						$0
790-52	LIVING EXPENSE						$0
790-53	CAR AND OTHER TRAVEL						$0
						Total For 790-00	$0
795-00	**FRINGES**						
795-01	B-T-L FRINGES						$0
						Total For 795-00	$0
798-00	**FACILITIES FEES**						
798-01	STAGE CONSTRUCTION						$0
798-02	STAGE SHOOTING						$0
798-03	STAGE HOLDING						$0
798-04	STAGE STRIKING						$0
798-05	OFFICE SPACE						$0
798-06	TESTS/INSERTS/PROMOS						$0
798-08	POWER						$0
798-93	FACILITIES FEES-RENT						$0

Acct#	Description	Amount	Units	X	Rate	Subtotal	Total
798-00	FACILITIES FEES (CONT'D)						
798-95	OTHER						$0
						Total For 798-00	$0
795-00	Total Fringes						
						Total For 795-00	$0
	TOTAL PRODUCTION						$0
800-00	EDITING						
800-01	EDITORS						$0
800-09	POST PRODUCTION SUPERVIS						$0
800-13	ASSISTANT EDITOR						$0
800-14	APPRENTICE EDITOR						$0
800-30	OTHER CHARGES						$0
800-90	BOX RENTAL						$0
800-92	EDITORIAL FACIL-ROOM RENT						$0
800-93	EDITORIAL EQUIP RENTALS						$0
800-95	OTHER						$0
						Total For 800-00	$0
801-00	POST-PROD VIDEO EDITING						
801-02	OFFLINE EDITING						$0
801-03	ONLINE EDITING						$0
801-06	TAPE DUPLICATION						$0
801-08	TAPE STOCK						$0
801-11	MAIN TITLES						$0
801-12	COLOR CORRECTION						$0
801-94	PURCHASES						$0
801-95	OTHER						$0
						Total For 801-00	$0

Acct#	Description	Amount	Units	X	Rate	Subtotal	Total
810-00	MUSIC						
810-01	COMPOSER						$0
810-02	RECORDING MUSICIANS						$0
810-04	COPYISTS & PROOFREADERS						$0
810-05	SCORE (FACILITIES)						$0
810-06	STUDIO EQUIPMENT RENTALS						$0
810-07	MUSIC INSTRUMENT RENTALS						$0
810-08	MUSIC INSTRUMENT CARTAGE						$0
810-11	MUSIC PUBLISHING/LICENSES						$0
810-13	MUSIC SUPERVISOR						$0
810-94	PURCHASES						$0
810-95	OTHER						$0
						Total For 810-00	$0
820-00	POST-PROD SOUND						
820-01	DIALOGUE RECORDING						$0
820-02	NARRATION RECORDING						$0
820-03	SOUND EFFECTS RECORDING						$0
820-04	DUBBING SESSION						$0
820-05	MUSIC TRANSFERS						$0
820-06	PURCHASED SOUND EFFECTS						$0
820-07	TRANSFERS SOUND EFFECTS						$0
820-09	SOUND TRANS TO OPTICAL 35						$0
820-10	POST PROD MAG TAPE-SOUND						$0
820-11	OPTICAL NEGATIVE						$0
820-12	TEMP DUBS FOR PREVIEWS						$0
820-14	PREVIEWS						$0
820-95	OTHER						$0
						Total For 820-00	$0

Acct#	Description	Amount	Units	X	Rate	Subtotal	Total
830-00	STOCK SHOTS						
830-01	LIBRARY EXPENSE/LIBRARIAN						$0
830-02	LAB PROCESSING						$0
830-03	TAPE DUPLICATION-STOCK ST						$0
830-93	RENTAL-STOCK SHOTS						$0
830-94	PURCHASES						$0
						Total For 830-00	$0
840-00	TITLES						
840-01	AMORTIZATION OF TITLES						$0
840-02	MAIN TITLES						$0
840-03	END TITLES						$0
840-04	MISC TITLES & TRAILERS						$0
840-05	LAB PROCESSING						$0
840-06	CLOSED CAPTIONING						$0
840-07	TITLE DESIGNER						$0
						Total For 840-00	$0
850-00	OPTICALS, MATTES, INSERTS						
850-01	OPTICAL EFFECTS & DUPE NG						$0
850-02	MASTER POSITIVES/COLOR						$0
850-03	LAB PROCESSING						$0
850-04	SPECIAL PHOTO EFFECTS						$0
850-05	INSERTS						$0
850-06	OPTICAL TEST						$0
850-07	GENERAL EXPENSES						$0
850-94	PURCHASES						$0
850-95	OTHER						$0
						Total For 850-00	$0

Acct#	Description	Amount	Units	X	Rate	Subtotal	Total
870-00	FRINGES						
870-01	POST-PRODUCTION FRINGES						$0
						Total For 870-00	$0
870-00	Total Fringes						
						Total For 870-00	$0
	TOTAL POST PRODUCTION						$0
910-00	ADMINISTRATIVE EXPENSES						
910-01	ACCOUNTING/COMPUTER FEES						$0
910-02	MPAA CERTIFICATE/AMPTP						$0
910-03	OFFICE EXP,POSTAGE & SUPP						$0
910-04	XEROX (EXCEPT SCRIPTS)						$0
910-05	LEGAL FEES						$0
910-06	TELEPHONE AND FAX						$0
910-09	PARKING						$0
910-15	MESSENGER						$0
910-16	CATERING-OFFICE						$0
910-17	VIDEO/AUDIO RENTAL CHRGES						$0
910-22	OFFICE EQUIPMENT/REPAIRS						$0
910-23	COMPUTER SOFTWARE PURCHAS						$0
910-25	COMPUTER HARDWARE PURCHAS						$0
910-27	COMPUTER RENTALS						$0
910-30	INSURANCE PREMIUMS						$0
910-31	MEDICAL EXAMS						$0
910-40	RESEARCH SCREENINGS/SURV						$0
910-45	ENTERTAINMENT						$0
910-92	OFFICE EQUIPMENT RENT						$0
910-93	OFFICE RENT & OTHER EXP						$0

Acct#	Description	Amount	Units	X	Rate	Subtotal	Total
910-00	ADMINISTRATIVE EXPENSES (CONT'D)						
910-94	PURCHASES						$0
910-95	OTHER						$0
910-99	COSTS-TO-DATE						$0
						Total For 910-00	$0
920-00	PUBLICITY						
920-01	UNIT PUBLICIST						$0
920-02	STILL PHOTOGRAPHER						$0
920-03	STILL FILM & LAB PROCESS						$0
920-10	MISCELLANEOUS PROMOTION						$0
920-45	ENTERTAINMENT						$0
920-95	OTHER						$0
						Total For 920-00	$0
940-00	FRINGES						
						Total For 940-00	$0
940-00	Total Fringes						
						Total For 940-00	$0
	TOTAL OTHER						$0
	TOTAL ABOVE-THE-LINE						$0
	TOTAL BELOW-THE-LINE						$0
	TOTAL ABOVE & BELOW-THE-LINE						$0
	GRAND TOTAL						$0

VI. SUMMARY OF QUALIFICATIONS

List of all key people involved in producing your film. Include brief biographies.

B

Film Festivals

Dates may change from year-to-year, and there's no guarantee that any festival, even one that's been around for years, will be there indefinitely. So, before you make plans to enter your film anywhere, write or call the Film Commission in the city, state, and/or country in which you plan to take your work, and ask for detailed information.

Call several months in advance.

JANUARY

United States:
Nortel Palm Springs International Film Festival, Palm Springs, California
Miami Film Festival, Miami, Florida
Kid Film Festival, Dallas, Texas
Sundance Film Festival, Park City, Utah
Slamdance Film Festival, Park City, Utah
Women in Cinema Film Festival, Seattle, Washington
Sarasota French Film Festival, Sarasota, Florida

Non-U.S.:
International Film Festival, Brussels, Belgium
Würzburg Film Weekend (Internale Filmwochenende), Würzburg, Germany

Max Ophuls Preis Film Festival, Saarbruken, Germany
Clermont-Ferrand Short Film Festival, Clermont-Ferrand, France
Gerardmer Frantastic Arts, Neuilly, France
Festival International de Programmes, Paris, France
Premiere Plans, Paris, France
Midem (Film Market), Paris, France
Traveling, Rennes Film Festival, Rennes Cedex, France
International Film Festival of India, New Delhi, India
International Film Festival, Rotterdam, The Netherlands
Tromso Film Festival, Bergen, Norway
Göteborg Film Festival, Göteborg, Sweden
Solothurn Film Festival, Solothurn, Switzerland
International Film Festival, Belgrade, Yugoslavia

FEBRUARY

United States:
Pan-African Film Festival, Los Angeles, California
Cinequest Film Festival, San Jose, California
American Film Market, Santa Monica, California
Portland International Film Festival, Portland, Oregon

Non-U.S.:
Mardi Gras Film Festival, Sydney, Australia
European Youth Film Festival, Antwerp, Belgium
Brussels Cartoon & Animated Film Festival, Brussels, Belgium
Pan-African Film & TV Festival of Quagadougou, Quagadougou, Burkina Faso
Green Screen, London, England
Comedy Film Festival, Southampton, England
Milia (Film Market), Cannes, France
Berlin International Film Festival, Berlin, Germany
European Film Market, Berlin, Germany
International Forum of New Cinema, Berlin, Germany
Hungarian Film Week, Budapest, Hungary
Fajr Film Festival, Tehran, Iran
Imagina, Monaco
Cinemart (Market for Independent Films), Rotterdam, The Netherlands
Fantasporto, Oporto, Portugal

MARCH

United States:
Sedona Film Festival, Sedona, Arizona
San Francisco International Asian-American Film Festival,
San Francisco, California
Santa Barbara Film Festival, Santa Barbara, California
New England Film & Video Festival, Brookline, Massachusetts
Ann Arbor 16mm Film Festival, Ann Arbor, Michigan
New Directors/New Films, New York, New York
Remembering Krzysztof Kieslowski, New York, New York
Cleveland International Film Festival, Cleveland, Ohio
South by Southwest Film Festival & Conference, Austin, Texas

Non-U.S.:
Mar del Plata International Film Festival, Buenos Aires, Argentina
Brussels Festival of Fantasy, Thriller, & Sci-Fi, Brussels, Belgium
Viewpoint: Documentary Now, Ghent, Belgium
Local Heroes International Film Festival, Alberta, Canada
Moving Pictures/The Traveling Canadian Film Festival, Vancouver, Canada
Cartagena International Film Festival, Cartagena, Columbia
London Lesbian & Gay Film Festival, London, England
Tampere Short Film Festival, Tampere, Finland
Creteil International Festival of Women's Film, Creteil, France
Film Festival for Young People, Laon Cedex, France
Cinema du Reel (Interational Film Festival of Anthropology), Paris, France
Nordic Film Festival, Roven, France
Days of Independent Film, Augsburg, Germany
Hong Kong Film Festival, Kowloon, Hong Kong
Dublin Film Festival, Dublin, Ireland
Bergamo Film Meeting, Bergamo, Italy
Guadalajara Film Festival, Guadalajara, Mexico
Fribourg Film Festival, Fribourg, Switzerland
Istanbul International Film Festival, Istanbul, Turkey
Montevideo International Film Festival, Montevideo, Uruguay

APRIL

United States:
Santa Clarita International Film Festival, Santa Clarita, California
Hermosa Beach Film Festival, Hermosa Beach, California

Los Angeles Independent Film Festival, Los Angeles, California
Newport Beach International Film Festival, Newport Beach,
  California
San Francisco International Film Festival, San Francisco, California
Aspen Shortfest, Aspen, Colorado
Palm Beach International Film Festival, Palm Beach, Florida
Chicago Latino Film Festival, Chicago, Illinois
Minneapolis/St. Paul International Film Festival, Minneapolis/
  St. Paul, Minnesota
St. Louis Film Festival, Spring Sampler, Missouri
Taos Talking Picture Festival, Taos, New Mexico
The Gen Art Film Festival, New York, New York
Philadelphia Festival of World Cinema, Philadelphia, Pennsylvania
Weld-Fest, Charleston, South Carolina
USA Film Festival, Dallas, Texas
Worldfest, Houston, Texas
Filmfest DC, Washington D.C.

Non-U.S.:
National Film Festival, Copenhagen, Denmark
Munich International Documentary Film Festival, Munich,
  Germany
Oberhausen International Short Film Festival, Oberhausen, Germany
Grenzland Days, Wunsiedel, Germany
Cartoons on the Bay, Rome, Italy
Turin International Gay and Lesbian Film Festival, Turin, Italy
International Film Festival, Edinburgh, Scotland
Cape Town International Film Festival, Cape Town, South Africa
Golden Rokse of Montreux, Geneva, Switzerland
Visions de Reel (Nyon International Documentary Film Festival),
  Nyon, Switzerland

MAY

United States:
Los Angeles Asian-Pacific American Film & Video Festival,
  Los Angeles, California
Boston International Festival of Women's Cinema, Boston,
  Massachusetts
Seattle International Film Festival, Seattle, Washington
Showbiz Expo West, Los Angeles, California

Non-U.S.:
Inside/Out Lesbian & Gay Film & Video Festival of Toronto, Toronto, Canada
Balticum Film & TV Festival, Svaneke, Denmark
Cannes Film Festival, Cannes, France
Augsburg Short Film Festival, Augsburg, Germany
Emden Film Festival, Emden, Germany
Krakow International Short Film Festival, Krakow, Poland
Trios International Film Festival, Setobal, Portugal

JUNE

United States:
E-3, Los Angeles, California
Human Rights Watch Film Festival, New York, New York
Los Angeles Film Festival, Los Angeles, California
San Francisco International Lesbian & Gay Film Festival,
    San Francisco, California
Florida Film Festival, Maitland, Florida
U.S. International Film/Video Festival, Redondo Beach, California

Non-U.S.:
Sydney Film Festival, Glebe, Australia
Cinevision, Innsbruck, Austria
Banff TV Festival, Banff, Canada
Prague International Film Festival, Prague, Czech Republic
Bradford Animation Festival, Bradford, England
London Jewish Film Festival, London, England
Shots in the Dark, Nottingham, England
Midnight Sun Film Festival, Helsinki, Finland
Marseilles Documentary Film Festival, Marseilles, France
La Rochelle International Film Festival, Paris, France
Hamburg International Short Film Festival, Hamburg, Germany
Munich Film Festival, Munich, Germany
French Filmdays, Tuebingen, Germany
Il Cinema Ritrovato, Bologna, Italy
Mystfest (International Mystery Film Festival), Cattolica, Italy
Pesaro Film Festival, Rome, Italy
Norwegian Short Film Festival, Oslo, Norway
Oslo Gay & Lesbian Film Festival, Oslo, Norway
Vila Do Conde International Short Film Festival, Vila Do Conde, Portugal

Sochi International Film Festival, Moscow, Russia
Art Film, Bratislava, Slovak Republic

JULY

United States:
Outfest: The Gay & Lesbian Film Festival, Los Angeles, California
Wine Country Film Festival, Glen Ellen, California
Asian-American International Film Festival, New York, New York

Non-U.S.:
Melbourne International Film Festival, Melbourne, Australia
Cinedecouvertes, Brussels, Belgium
Kariovy Vary International Film Festival, Prague, Czech Republic
Cambridge Film Festival, Cambridge, England
Outdoor Short Film Festival, Grenoble, France
Jerusalem Film Festival, Jerusalem, Israel
Giffoni Film Festival, Giffoni, Italy
Wellington Film Festival, Wellington, New Zealand
Moscow International Film Festival, Moscow, Russia
Durban International Film Festival, Durban, South Africa
Vevey International Comedy Film Festival, Vevey, Switzerland
Montevideo International Film Festival, Montevideo, Uruguay

AUGUST

United States:
Telluride Film Festival, Telluride, Colorado

Non-U.S.:
Brisbane International Film Festival, Brisbane, Australia
Festival of Latino Film, Gramado, Brazil
Montreal International Festival of New Cinema, Montreal, Canada
Montreal Film/TV/Video Festival, Montreal, Canada
Montreal World Film Festival, Montreal, Canada
Odense International Short Film Festival, Odense, Denmark
Espoo Dine, Espoo, Finland
Venice International Film Festival, Venice, Italy
Drambuie Edinburgh Film Festival, Edinburgh, Scotland
Edinburgh International TV Festival, Edinburgh, Scotland

Festival Internacional de Cinema, Spain
Locarno International Film Festival, Locarno, Switzerland

SEPTEMBER

United States:
Temecula Valley International Film Festival, Temecula, California
Aspen Filmfest, Aspen, Colorado
Breckenridge Festival of Film, Breckenridge, Colorado
Boston Film Festival, Boston, Massachusetts
Independent Feature Film Market, New York, New York
New York Film Festival, New York, New York
Showbiz Expo East, New York, New York

Non-U.S.:
Toronto Worldwide Film Festival, Toronto, Canada
Rio de Janeiro Film Festival, Rio de Janeiro, Brazil
Toronto International Film Festival, Toronto, Canada
Cinefest: The Sudbury Film Festival, Canada
Sante Fe de Bogota Festival, Bogota, Columbia
Copenhagen Film Festival, Copenhagen, Denmark
Alexandria International Film Festival, Cairo, Egypt
British Short Film Festival, London, England
Latin America Film Festival, London, England
International Film Festival for Children and Young People, Frankfurt, Germany
Oldenburg International Film Festival, Oldenburg, Germany
Drama Short Film Festival, Athens, Greece
Focus on Asian Fukuoka International Film Festival, Fukuoka, Japan
Tokyo International Film Festival, Tokyo, Japan
Arsenais International Film Forum, Riga, Latvia
San Sebastian International Film Festival, San Sebastian, Spain
Umea International Film Festival, Umea, Sweden

OCTOBER

United States:
Heartland Film Festival, Indianapolis, Indiana
Lone Pine Film Festival, Lone Pine, California
Denver International Film Festival, Denver, Colorado
Ft. Lauderdale International Film Festival, Ft. Lauderdale, Florida
Chicago International Children's Film Festival, Chicago, Illinois

Chicago International Film Festival, Chicago, Illinois
New Orleans Film/Video Festival, New Orleans, Louisiana
Showeast, Atlantic City, New Jersey
Hamptons International Film Festival, Long Island, New York
Virginia Festival of American Films, Charlottesville, Virginia

Non-U.S.:
Montreal International Festival of New Cinema, Montreal, Canada
Festival du Cinema International en Abitibi-Temiscamique,
   Rouyn-Noranda, Canada
Festival De Cinema International, Therese/Sainte-Adele, Canada
Vancouver International Film Festival, Vancouver, Canada
Rencontres International De Cinema, Paris, France
International Leipzig Festival for Documentary/Animated Film,
   Leipzig, Germany
Mifed Film Market, Milan, Italy
Pondenone Silent Film Festival, Pondenone, Italy

NOVEMBER

United States:
Olympia Film Festival, Olympia, Washington
St. Louis Film Festival, St. Louis, Missouri
· AFI. L.A. International Film Festival, Los Angeles, California
Film Arts Festival, San Francisco, California
Israel Film Festival, Los Angeles, California
Hawaii International Film Festival, Honolulu, Hawaii
Northwest Film/Video Festival, Portland, Oregon

Non-U.S.:
Festival Internacional de Cine e Artes Audiovisuales, Buenos Aires, Argentina
Banff Festival of Mountain Films, Banff, Canada
London Film Festival, London, England
Amiens International Film Festival, Amiens, France
Augsburg Children's Film Festival, Augsburg, Germany
Duisburger Filmwoche, Duisburg, Germany
Cinanima, International Animation Film Festival, Espinho, Portugal
Film Art Fest, Lubliana, Slovenia
Ourense Film Festival, Ourense, Spain

DECEMBER

United States:
Hungarian Film Festival of Los Angeles, Los Angeles, California

Non-U.S.:
International Festival of Latin American Cinema, Havana, Cuba
Cairo International Film Festival, Cairo, Egypt
Rencontres D'Annecy du Cinema Italien, Annecy, France
Mip-Asia Film Market, Hong Kong
Noir In Festival, Courmayer, Italy
Pia Film Festival, Tokyo, Japan
The Forum, Amsterdam, The Netherlands

Foreign Distributors

Achab Film
Viale Gorizia 24C
00198 Rome, Italy
Phone: (39-06) 854-7229
Fax: (39-06) 853-5692

Alliance/Le Monde
808 Wilshire Blvd., 3rd Fl.
Santa Monica, CA 90404
Phone: (310) 899-8000, (416) 967-1174
Fax: (310) 899-8100

Alpine Pictures International
6919 Valjean Ave.
Van Nuys, CA 91406
Phone: (818) 909-5207
Fax: (818) 782-4565

Amazing Movies
7471 Melrose Avenue, Suite 7
Los Angeles, CA 90046.
Phone: (323) 852-1396
Fax: (323) 658-7265

American World Pictures
www.americanworldpictures.com
6355 Topaga Canyon Blvd., Ste. 428
Woodland Hills, CA 91367
Phone: (818) 715-1480
Fax: (818) 344-5685

Amsell Ent.
12001 Ventura Pl., Suite 404
Studio City, CA 91604
Phone: (818) 766-8500
Fax: (818) 766-7873

Angel Films
967 Highway 40
New Franklin, MO 65274
Phone: (573) 698-3900
Fax: (573) 698-3900

Arama Entertainment
www.aramaent.com
18034 Ventura Boulevard, Suite 435
Encino, CA 91316
Phone: (818) 344-4477
Fax: (818) 344-5685

Artedis
12 rue Raynouard
75016 Paris, France
Phone: (33-1) 5392-2929
Fax: (33-1) 5392-2920

Artist View Ent.
12500 Riverside Drive, Suite 201-B
North Hollywood, CA 91607
Phone: (818) 752-2480
Fax: (818) 752-9339

Atlas International Film
Rumfordstrasse 29-31
Munich, 80469 Germany
Phone: (49-89) 210-9750
Fax: (49-89) 224-332

Atmosphere Entertainment
www.atmosphereent.com
1828 Broadway
Santa Monica, CA 90404
Phone: (310) 449-9220
Fax: (310) 449-9240

August Ent.
838 North Fairfax Avenue
Los Angeles, CA 90046
Phone: (323) 658-8888

Aurum Productions
Avenida Burgos, 12, Tenth Floor
Madrid 28036, Spain
Phone: (34-91) 768-4800
Fax: (34-91) 768-4833

Behaviour Worldwide
1925 Century Park East, Suite 1700
Los Angeles, CA 90067
Phone: (310) 226-8300
Fax: (310) 226-8350

Beta Film
www.betacinema.com
Robert-Burkle-Strasse 3
Munich, 85737 Germany
Phone: (49-89) 9956-2345
Fax: (49-89) 9956-2703

Beyond Films
53-55 Brisbane Street
Surrey Hills
Sydney, NSW 2010 Australia
Phone: (612) 8217-2000,
    (212) 977-2480
Fax: (612) –8217-2035

Big Bear Licensing Corporation
1350 Abbot Kinney Boulevard
Venice, CA 90291
Phone: (310) 341-9919
Fax: (310) 314-8081

Blue Rider Pictures
2800 Twenty-eighth Street
Suite 105
Santa Monica, CA 90405
Phone: (310) 314-8246
Fax: (310) 581-4352

Buena Vista International (BVI)
500 South Buena Vista Street
Burbank, CA 91521-7383
Phone: (818) 972-3592
Fax: (818) 848-1322

Callisto Ent.
11684 Ventura Boulevard, # 512
Studio City, CA 91604
Phone: (818) 508-7619
Fax: (818) 508-1679

Capella Films
9200 Sunset Boulevard, Suite 315
Los Angeles, CA 90069
Phone: (310) 247-4700
Fax: (310) 247-4701

Capitol Films
23 Queensdale Pl.
London W11 4SQ
Phone: (44-171) 471-6000
Fax: (44-171) 471-6012

Celluloid Dreams
2rue Turgot
75009 Paris, France
Phone: (33-1) 4970-0370,
  (44-20) 7288-8422
Fax: (33-1) 4970-0371

C.E.O. Films
838 North Fairfax Avenue
Los Angeles, CA 90046
Phone: (323) 658-8888
Fax: (323) 658-7654

Adriana Chiesa Enterprises
Via Barnaba Oriana, 24/A
00197 Rome, Italy
Phone: (011) 39-06-8086-0520
Fax: (39-06) 806-7855

Cinema Arts Ent.
9350 Wilshire Boulevard, # 203
Beverly Hills, CA 90212
Phone: (310) 550-1085
Fax: (310) 550-1182

Cinequanon Pictures
  International
8057 Beverly Boulevard
Second Floor
Los Angeles, CA 90048
Phone: (323) 658-6043
Fax: (323) 658-6087

Cinetel Films
8255 Sunset Boulevard
Los Angeles, CA 90046
Phone: (323) 654-4000
Fax: (323) 650-6400

Cineville International
www.cineville.com
3400 Airport Avenue
Santa Monica, CA 90405
Phone: (310) 397-7150
Fax: (310) 397-7155

CLT-UFA International
45 Boulevard Pierre
Frieden L-1543, Luxembourg
Phone: (352) 42149-23935
Fax: (352-421) 423-771

Coast Entertainment
1530 Willina Lane
Santa Barbara CA 93108
Phone: (805) 969-2151
Fax: (805) 963-7590

Columbia/Tristar Home Video
10202 W. Washington Blvd.
Culver City, CA 90232
Phone: (310) 244-4000
Fax: (310) 244-2626

Concorde-New Horizons
11600 San Vicente Boulevard
Los Angeles, CA 90049
Phone: (310) 820-6733
Fax: (310) 207-6816

Crystal Sky International
1901 Avenue of the Stars, Suite 605
Los Angeles, CA 90067
Phone: (310) 843-0223
Fax: (310) 553-9895

Curb Entertainment International
3907 West Alameda Avenue
Burbank, CA 91505
Phone: (818) 843-8580
Fax: (818) 566-1719

Danehip Ent./Powersports
Millennium International
18226 Ventura Boulevard, # 102
Tarzana, CA 91356
Phone: (818) 708-9995
Fax: (818) 708-0598

Dimension Films
C/o Miramax Films
375 Greenwich St.
New York, NY 10013-2338
Phone: (212) 941-3800

Distant Horizon
8282 Sunset Boulevard, Suite A
Los Angeles, CA 90046
Phone: (323) 848-4140
Fax: (323) 848-4144

Dream Ent.
8489 West Third Street, Suite 1038
Los Angeles, CA 90048
Phone: (323) 655-5501
Fax: (323) 655-5603

Eurocine
33, Ave des Champs Elysees
75008 Paris, France
Phone: (33-1) 4225-6492
Fax: (33-1) 4225-7338

Film Bridge International
1316 Third Street Promenade
Suite 105
Santa Monica, CA 90401
Phone: (310) 656-8680
Fax: (310) 656-8683

The Film Company
25 Elizabeth Mews
London NW3 4UH
Phone: (44-207) 586-3686
Fax: (44-207) 586-3117

Channel Four International
124 Horseferry Road
London SW1P 2TX
Phone: (44-207) 306-8602
Fax: (44-207) 306-8361

FilmExport Group SRL
Via Polonia 9
Rome 00198, Italy
Phone: (39-06) 853-5432
Fax: (39-6) 855-0248

Films Distribution
6 rue L'Ecole de Medecine
Paris 75006 France
Phone: (33-1) 5310-33999
Fax: (33-1) 5310-3398

1st Miracle Pictures
3439 West Cahuenga Boulevard
Hollywood, CA 90068
Phone: (323) 874-7822
Fax: (323) 874-4252

Focus Features
417 Canal Street, Fourth Floor
New York, NY 10013
Phone: (212) 343-9230
Fax: (212) 343-9645

Forefront Films
507 17th Streeet
Brooklyn, NY 11215
Phone: (718) 832-3395
Fax: (718) 832-4951

Fortissimo Film Sales
www.fortissimo-films.com
Veemarkt 77-79
Amsterdam, 1019DA Netherlands
Phone: (31-20) 627-3215
Fax: (31-20) 626-1155

Franchise Pictures
8228 Sunset Boulevard, Suite 305
Los Angeles, CA 90046
Phone: (323) 848-3444
Fax: (323) 822-1442

Fries Film Group
22817 Ventura Boulevard, #909
Woodland Hills, CA 91364
Phone: (818) 888-3051
Fax: (818) 888-3042

Full Moon Pictures
1645 North Vine Street
Ninth Floor
Los Angeles, CA 90028
Phone: (323) 468-0599
Fax: (323) 468-0598

Futura Film
Rambergstrasse 5
80799 Munich, Germany
Phone: (89-38) 170-030
Fax: (89-38) 170-020

Gabriel Film Group
Tribeca Film Center
375 Greenwich Street
Suites 503-504
New York, NY 10013
Phone: (212) 941-2002
Fax: (212) 941-2439

Gaumont International
30 avenue de Gaulle
92200 Neuilly, France
Phone: (33-1) 4643-2000
Fax: (33-1) 4643-2033

Goldcrest Films International
65/66 Dean Street
London W1V 6PL
Phone: (44-207) 437-8696
Fax: (44-207) 437-4448

US Office:
1240 Olive Drive
Los Angeles, CA 90069
Phone: (323) 650-4551
Fax: (323) 650-4551

Golden Harvest
  Entertainment Company
www.goldenharvest.com
16F The Peninsula Office Tower
18 Middle Road
Tsimshatsui, Hong Kong
Phone: (011) 852-2352-8222
Fax: (011) 852-2351-1683

Golden Network Asia
Unit 1803A, Nanyang Plaza
57 Hung To Road
Kowloon, Hong Kong
Phone: (852) 2751-1886
Fax: (852) 2750-4862

Golden Sun Film
7B Dragon House
7-7B Cameron Rd., 4th Fl.
Tsimbatsui, Hong Kong
Phone: (852) 2385-5939
Fax: (852) 2782-6950

Green Communications
www.greenfilms.com
255 Parkside Drive
San Fernando, CA 91340
Phone: (818) 557-0050
Fax: (818) 365-0151

Gruppo Minerva International
Via Domenico Cimarosa, 18
00198 Rome, Italy
Phone: (39-06) 854-3841
Fax: (39-06) 855-8105

HBO Enterprises
1100 Avenue of the Americas
Suite G14-29
New York, NY 10036
Phone: (212) 512-7112
Fax: (212) 512-5698

Highland Crest Pictures
7471 Melrose Avenue, Suite 7
Los Angeles, CA 90046
Phone: (323) 852-9848
Fax: (323) 658-7265

IAC Films
Greencoat House, 15 Francis ST
London SW1P1DH
Phone: (44-207) 592-1620
Fax: (44-207) 592-1621

Icon Entertainment International
37 Soho Square
London W1V 5DG
Phone: (44-171) 543-4300
Fax: (44-171) 543-4301

IFD Films and Arts
Flat 4, Third Floor, Block B
Vigor Industrial Building
14-20 Cheung Tat Road
Tsing Yi
New Territories, Hong Kong
Phone: (852) 2730-0048
Fax: (852) 2730-8756

International Film Distributor
    Consultants (IFDC)
Water Garden
1601 Cloverfield Blvd., Suite 200,
    South Tower
Santa Monica, CA 90404
Phone: (310) 460-3537
Fax: (310) 460-3445

IFM Film Associates
www.ifmfilm.com
1328 East Palmer Rd.
Glendale, CA 91205
Phone: (818) 243-4976
Fax: (818) 550-9728

Initial Entertainment Group (IEG)
www.initial-ent.com/
3000 W. Olympic, Suite 1550
Santa Monica, CA 90404
Phone: (310) 315-1722
Fax: (31) 315-1723

Interlight Pictures
8981 Sunset Boulevard, Suite 101
West Hollywood, CA 90069
Phone: (323) 933-0312

Intermedia
9-13 Grosvenor Street
London S1X 9FB
Phone: (44-171) 495-3322
Fax: (44-171) 495-3993

Intermedia Films (LA)
www.intermediafilm.com
9350 Civic Center Drive
Suite 100
Beverly Hills, CA 90210
Phone: (310) 777-0007
Fax: (31) 777-0008

Intra Movies SRL/Intrafilms
Via E. Manfredi 15
00197 Rome, Italy
Phone: (39-06) 807-6157
Fax: (39-06) 807-6156

International Keystone
    Entertainment Inc.
www.keypics.com
23410 Civic Center Way, Suite E9
Malibu, CA 90265
Phone: (310) 317-4883
Fax: (310) 317-4903

Kandice King Productions
5995 Sepulveda Boulevard, # 201
Culver City, CA 90230
Phone: (310) 915-6695
Fax: (310) 915-6674

Kitsch Pictures
34-140 El Paseo, Suite 4-222
Palm Desert, CA 92260
Phone: (760) 346-6372
Fax: (760) 346-6632

Kushner-Locke Co.
11601 Wilshire Boulevard
Twenty-first Floor
Los Angeles, CA 90025
Phone: (310) 659-1508

KWA
Galeon 32, Bajo A
Madrid, 28042 Spain
Phone: (34-91) 747-3100
Fax (34-91) 747-7000

Lakeshore International
5555 Melrose Avenue
Gloria Swanson Building
Fourth Floor
Hollywood, CA 90038
Phone: (323) 956-4222
Fax: 9323) 862-1190

Largo Entertainment
925 Sunset Blvd. Ste. 717
Los Angeles, CA 90069
Phone: (310) 203-0055
Fax: (310) 203-0254

Lions Gate Films International
4553 Glencoe Avenue
Suite 200
Marina Del Rey, CA 90292
Phone: (310) 314-2000
Fax: (310) 392-0252

Lolafilms
Velazquez 12, Seventh Floor
28001 Madrid, Spain
Phone: (34-91) 436-74-00
Fax: (34-91) 435-5994

Magus Entertainment
Amperestraat 10, 1221 GH
Hilversum, The Netherlands
Phone: (31-35) 642-0677
Fax: (31-35) 642-0668

Mainline Releasing
1801 Avenue of the Stars
Suite 1200
Los Angeles, CA 90067
Phone: (310) 286-1001
Fax: (310) 286-0530

Matoni Films
214 Sullivan Street
New York, NY 10012
Phone: (212) 505-3366
Fax: (212) 941-2439

Media Films International
3832 Wilshire Boulevard
Los Angeles, CA 90010
Phone: (213) 736-6060
Fax: (213) 736-6066

Mercure Distribution
27, rue de la Butte aux Cailles
75013 Paris, France
Phone: (33-1) 4416-6844
Fax: (33-1) 4563-0747

Miramax International
99 Hudson Street, Fifth Floor
New York, NY 10013
Phone: (212) 941-3800
Fax: (212) 941-3836

MK2 International
55 rue Traversiere
75012 Paris, France
Phone: (33-1) 4467-3055
Fax: (33-1) 4307-2963

Monarch Films
368 Danforth Avenue
Jersey City, NJ 07305
Phone: (201) 451-3770
Fax: (201) 451-3877

Kathy Morgan International
12262 Sky Lane
Los Angeles, CA 90049
Phone: (310) 472-6300
Fax: (310) 472-6304

Motion International
376 Victoria Ave., Ste. 350
Montreal, Quebec H32 IC3
Phone: (514) 844-3542
Fax: (514) 985-4461

M6 Droits Audiovisuels
89, Avenue Charles de Gaulle
92575 Neuilly-sur-Seine Cedex
France
Phone: (33-1) 4192-6866
Fax: (33-1) 4192-6869

Mutual Film International
650 North Bronson Avenue
Clinton Building
Los Angeles, CA 90004
Phone: (323) 871-5690
Fax: (323) 960-4097

Myriad Pictures
www.myriadpictures.com
405 S. Beverly Drive, Fifth Floor
Beverly Hills, CA 90212
Phone: (310) 279-4000, (011-44)
207-580-9200
Fax: (310) 279-4001

NBC Enterprises
3500 West Olive Avenue
Fifteenth Floor
Burbank, CA 91505
Phone: (818) 526-6908
Fax: (818) 526-6921

New Line Cinema
116 North Robertson Boulevard
Los Angeles, CA 90048
Phone: (310) 854-5811
Fax: (310) 854-1824

New Zealand Film Commission
Post Office Box 11-546
Wellington, New Zealand
Phone: (64-4) 382-7680
Fax: (64-4) 384-9719

Nu Image/Millennium Films
6423 Wilshire Blvd.
Los Angeles, CA 90048
Phone: (310) 388-6900
Fax: (310) 388-6901

October Films
65 Bleecker Street
New York, NY 10012
Phone: (212) 539-4000
Fax: (212) 539-4099

Omni International
P.O. Box 264
Orangeville, ON L9W2Z6
Canada
Phone: (519) 941-0914

Overseas Filmgroup
www.firstlookmedia.com
8800 Sunset Boulevard
East Penthouse
Los Angeles, CA 90046
Phone: (323) 337-1000
Fax: (323) 337-1080

Pandora Films
4000 Warner Blvd.
Building 148, Suite 201
Burbank, CA 91522
Phone: (818) 954-5549
Fax: (818) 954-7713

Peakviewing Transatlantic
 Productions
The Wheelhouse
Bonds Mill
Stonehouse, GL10 3RF
Phone: (44-0) 1453-826300
Fax: (44-0) 1453-826303

PFG Entertainment
429 Santa Monica Blvd., Ste. 600
Santa Monica, CA 90401
Phone: (310) 393-5788
Fax: (310) 393-0882

Picture This! Entertainment
7471 Melrose Avenue, Suite 7
Los Angeles, CA 90046
Phone: (323) 852-1398
Fax: (323) 658-7265

Playboy Entertainment Group
www.playboy.com
2706 Media Center Drive
Los Angeles, CA 90065
Phone: (323) 276-4000
Fax: (323) 276-4500

PM Entertainment
 Sunland Entertainment
1185 W. Olympic Blvd., Suite 550
Los Angeles, CA 90064
Phone: (310) 444-4100
Fax: (31) 444-4102

Porchlight Entertainment
11777 Mississippi Avenue
Los Angeles, CA 90025
Phone: (310) 477-8400
Fax: (310) 477-5555

Portman Entertainment
167 Wardour Street
London W1V 3TA
Phone: (44-207) 468-3443
Fax: (44-171) 468-3469

Promark Entertainment Group
The Promark Center
3599 Cahuenga Boulevard West
Third Floor
Los Angeles, CA 90068
Phone: (323) 878-0404
Fax: (323) 878-0486

Quadra Entertainment
130 South El Camino Drive
Beverly Hills, CA 90212
Phone: (310) 205-6262
Fax: (310) 205-6264

Quantum Entertainment
3599 Cahuenga Boulevard West
Suite 316
Los Angeles, CA 90068
Phone: (323) 878-2578
Fax: (323) 878-0235

RAI Trade
www.raitrade.it
Via Umberto Novaro
Rome 00195 Italy
Phone: (39-06) 3749-8469
Fax: (39-06) 3751-6222

R.A.M.M. Entertainment
www.rammentertainment.com
221 W. Alameda Ave., Ste. 203
Burbank, CA 91502
Phone: (818) 558-3130

Redwood Communications
228 Main Street, Studio 17
Venice, CA 90291
Phone: (310) 581-9090
Fax: (310) 581-9093

Regent Entertainment
www.regententertainment.com
1401 Ocean Ave., Ste. 300
Santa Monica, CA
Phone: (310) 260-3333
Fax: (310) 260-3343

RGH/Lions Share Pictures
8831 Sunset Boulevard, Suite 300
Los Angeles, CA 90069
Phone: (310) 652-2893
Fax: (310) 652-6237

Santelmo Entertainment
901 Wilshire Blvd., Ste. 350
Santa Monica, CA 90401
Phone: (310) 656-0777
Fax: (310) 656-4611

Scanbox Intl.
11846 Ventura Blvd., # 120
Studio City, CA 91604
Phone: (818) 762-8662
Fax: (818) 762-0094

Sceneries International
1660 Ocean Avenue
Santa Monica, CA 90401
Phone: (310) 652-9900
Fax: (310) 652-9901

Shoreline Entertainment
www.shorelineentertainment.com
1875 Century Park East, Suite 600
Los Angeles, CA 90067
Phone: (310) 551-2060
Fax: (310) 201-0729

Showcase Entertainment
Warner Center
21800 Oxnard Street, Suite 150
Woodland Hills, CA 91637
Phone: (818) 715-7005
Fax: (818) 715-7009

Silhouette Film Dist.
67 Wall Street, Suite 2411
New York, NY 10005
Phone: (212) 323-8014
Fax: (212) 363-2260

Alain Siritzky Productions
23 rue Raynouard
75016 Paris, France
Phone: (33-1) 4224-5050
Fax: (33-1) 4224-6642

Soho Entertainment
105 Greene Street
New York, NY 10012
Phone: (212) 431-3737
Fax: (212) 431-3733

Southern Star Film Sales
8 West Street
NSW 2060, Australia
Phone: (61-2) 9202-8555
Fax: (61-2) 9956-6918

Spice Factory
81, The Promenade
Peacehaven, Brighton
East Sussex, BN10 8SL
Phone: (44-1273) 585-275
Fax: (44-1273) 535-304

Star Land Ent.
8306 Wilshire Boulevard, # 7032
Beverly Hills, CA 90211
Phone: (310) 651-1625
Fax: (310) 651-1627

Starway Entertainment
12021 Wilshire Boulevard, # 661
Los Angeles, CA 90025
Phone: (310) 458-6202
Fax: (310) 458-6102

Stone Canyon Investments
1800 Avenue of the Stars
Suites 430-450
Los Angeles, CA 90067
Phone: (310) 788-9555
Fax: (310) 788-9559

Storm Entertainment
127 Broadway Ste. 200
Santa Monica, CA 90401
Phone: (310) 656-2500
Fax: (310) 656-2510

Summit Entertainment
1630 Stewart Street, Suite 120
Santa Monica, CA 90404
Phone: (310) 309-8400
Fax: (310) 828-4132

TF1 International
www.tf1international.com
18 Quai du Point du Jour
Boulogne Billancourt
92100 France
Phone: (33-1) 41-41-1763
Fax: (33-1) 41-41-1769

THF Pictures
106 Palmetto Street, Suite D
Pasadena, CA 91105
Phone: (626) 683-9502
Fax: (626) 683-9814

Third Coast Ent.
8079 Selma Avenue
Los Angeles, CA 90046
Phone: (213) 650-3953
Fax: (213) 650-3859

Thompson/Starr Organization
270 North Canon Avenue, # 1705
Beverly Hills, CA 90210
Phone: (818) 998-8126
Fax: (818) 773-8962

Thunderhead Films
5010 North Parkway, Suite 104
Calabasas, CA 91302
Phone: (818) 591-6715
Fax: (818) 591-6717

Tomorrow Film Corporation
www.tomorrowfilms.com
9250 Wilshire Blvd., Suite 220
Beverly Hills, CA 90212
Phone: (310) 385-7900
Fax: (310) 385-7990

Trans-Pacific Media
   Consultants Group
8491 Sunset Boulevard, Suite 800
Los Angeles, CA 90069
Phone: (323) 654-4933
Fax: (323) 654-4921

Trident Releasing
8401 Melrose Place, Second Floor
Los Angeles, CA 90069
Phone: (323) 655-8818
Fax: (323) 655-0515

Trimark International
4553 Glencoe Ave., Ste. 200
Marina del Rey, CA 90292
Phone: (310) 314-2000
Fax: (310) 399-1570

Troma Ent.
733 Ninth Avenue
New York, NY 10019
Phone: (212) 757-4555
Fax: (212) 399-9885

Trust Film Sales
www.trust-film.dk
Filmbyen 12
Huidovre, 2650 Denmark
Phone: (45-36) 868-788
Fax: (45-36) 774-448

United Film Organization (UFO)
www.ufofilm.com
100 E. Cedar Ave.
Bldg. 16, 1st Floor
Burbank, CA 91502
Phone: (818) 846-0465
Fax: (818) 846-0256

Works
4 Great Portland Street, 4th Floor
London W1W8Qj
Phone: (44-207) 612-1080
Fax: (44-207) 612-1081

Cash Flow

CASH REQUIREMENTS ESTIMATE

	P Week 1	P Week 2	P Week 3	S Week 4	S Week 5	S Week 6	S Week 7	W Week 8	W Week 9	W Week 10		TOTAL
Deposits / Petty Cash Advances		25,000	25,000				(25,000)	(25,000)				----
A-T-L Labor		1,000	1,000	1,000	20,000	20,000	20,000	20,000				83,000
B-T-L Labor		60,000	60,000	60,000	140,000	140,000	140,000	140,000	40,000	40,000		820,000
Purchases/Rentals	50,000		80,000	80,000	80,000	80,000	35,000	35,000	35,000	35,000		510,000
Extras					8,000	8,000	8,000	8,000				32,000
Catering					8,000	8,000	8,000	8,000				32,000
Raw Stock				30,000		30,000						60,000
TOTALS	50,000	86,000	166,000	171,000	256,000	286,000	186,000	186,000	75,000	75,000		1,537,000

P - Prep Weeks
S - Shoot Weeks
W - Wrap Weeks

Sample Budget

PRODUCTIONS, INC.
BUDGET MASTER SUMMARY REPORT

RUN DATE

```
------------------------------------     SCRIPT DATE:
PRODUCER:                                 NO. OF PAGES: 114 PAGES
DIRECTOR:                                 SHOOTING DAYS: 20 - 12 HOURS EACH
UNIT MGR:                                              : 3-6 DAY WEEKS + 2 DAYS
SCHEDULE:                                 PRELIMINARY 2 HOUR M.O.W. BUDGET
COMMENTS:                                 -------------------------------------
------------------------------------
```

Acct #	Description	Page #			Total
815	STORY	1			97,905
825	PRODUCER	1			121,970
835	DIRECTOR	2			131,360
845	CAST	3			656,958
855	PAYROLL TAXES	4			26,684
	TOTAL ABOVE-THE-LINE	4			
919	EXTRA TALENT	4			1,034,877
921	PRODUCTION STAFF	4			37,204
923	CAMERA	6			199,665
927	ELECTRICAL	7			95,703
929	GRIP	8			68,291
931	PROPS	10			61,609
933	PRODUCTION SOUND	10			40,591
935	WARDROBE	11			29,458
937	MAKEUP & HAIRDRESSING	12			77,331
939	SPECIAL EFFECTS	13			27,378
941	SET OPERATIONS	13			10,152
945	SET DESIGN	14			18,700
947	SET CONSTRUCTION	14			33,135
951	SET DRESSINGS	14			51,450
955	SECOND UNIT	15			85,022
959	RAWSTOCK	16			30,000
					92,530

This budget is applicable for a two-hour movie-of-the-week or a low budget movie in the three-million-dollar range. It is designed for a present-day film, shot on location, with minimal special effects and stunt work.

(continued)

(continued from previous page)

Acct #	Description	Page #		Total
961	TRANSPORTATION	16		151,582
963	PICTURE CARS/ANIMALS	18		5,900
965	LOCATION EXPENSE	19		145,157
966	B-T-L FRINGE BENEFITS	20		172,809
	TOTAL PRODUCTION	20		1,433,667
968	EDITORIAL	20		168,100
969	MUSIC	21		50,000
971	SPECIAL PHOTOGRAPHIC F/X	21		15,500
973	TITLES	22		3,370
975	POST-PRODUCTION SOUND	22		12,500
978	DELIVERY MATERIALS	22		4,250
	TOTAL POST PRODUCTION	22		266,529
979	INSURANCE	22		20,000
981	PUBLICITY	22		3,500
983	MISCELLANEOUS	22		94,708
985	POST-PROD FRINGE BENEFITS	23		12,809
988	SECOND RUN	23		87,000
989	PACKAGING & OVERHEAD	23		175,000
	TOTAL OTHER	23		380,208
	TOTAL ABOVE-THE-LINE			1,034,877
	TOTAL BELOW-THE-LINE			2,080,404
	ABOVE & BELOW-THE-LINE			3,115,279
	TOTAL FRINGES			169,726
	GRAND TOTAL			3,115,279

PRODUCTIONS, INC.
BUDGET MASTER SUMMARY REPORT

Page 1

```
------------------------------------          RUN DATE
                                      ------------------------------------
PRODUCER:                             SCRIPT DATE:
DIRECTOR:                             NO. OF PAGES: 114 PAGES
UNIT MGR:                             SHOOTING DAYS: 20 - 12 HOURS EACH
SCHEDULE:                                        : 3-6 DAY WEEKS + 2 DAYS
COMMENTS:                             PRELIMINARY 2 HOUR M.O.W. BUDGET
------------------------------------  ------------------------------------
```

Acct #	Description	Amount	Units	X	Rate	Subtotal	Total
815	**STORY**						
815-03	WRITER						
	(CORP)	1	CONTR		75,000	75,000	75,000
815-07	WRITER'S TRAVEL EXPENSE						
	WRITER'S AIRFARE						
	AIRFARE	1	RNDTR		1,580	1,580	
	LIMO	1	RNDTR		200	200	1,780
815-08	WRITER'S LIVING EXPENSE						
	HOTEL	30	DAYS		100	3,000	
	PER DIEM	30	DAYS		100	3,000	
	AUTO	5	WEEKS		150	750	6,750
815-10	RESEARCH		ALLOW		1,500	1,500	1,500
815-11	SECRETARY/TYPIST						
	SCRIPT INPUT/REVISIONS		ALLOW		2,000	2,000	2,000
815-12	SCRIPT COPYING						
			ALLOW		1,500	1,500	1,500
815-21	WGA PH & W						
		0.125	%		75,000	9,375	9,375
					Total for 815		97,905
825	**PRODUCER**						
825-01	EXECUTIVE PRODUCER						
	ASSUMING CORPORATION	1	CONTR		75,000	75,000	75,000
825-02	PRODUCER						
	LINE PRODUCER		ALLOW		25,000	25,000	25,000
825-03	EXEC. PRODUCER SECRETARY						
	LOS ANGELES						
	PREP	3	WEEKS		650	1,950	
	WRAP	6	WEEKS		650	3,900	
	LOCATION						
	PREP	3	WEEKS		650	1,950	
	SHOOT	3.40	WEEKS		650	2,210	
	WRAP	1	WEEK		650	650	10,660

Acct #	Description	Amount	Units	X	Rate	Subtotal	Total
825	**PRODUCER** (Cont'd)						
825-05	PRODUCER TRAVEL EXPENSE						
	AIRFARES		2	RNDTR	1,580	3,160	
	LIMOS		2	RNDTR	200	400	3,560
825-06	PRODUCER LIVING EXPENSE						
	EXECUTIVE PRODUCER						
	HOTEL		30	DAYS	100	3,000	
	PER DIEM		30	DAYS	100	3,000	
	AUTO		5	WEEKS	150	750	6,750
825-25	OTHER CHARGES						
	ENTERTAINMENT			ALLOW	1,000	1,000	1,000
					Total for 825		121,970
835	**DIRECTOR**						
835-01	DIRECTOR						
	ASSUMING CORPORATION		1	CONTR	90,000	90,000	90,000
835-05	DIRECTOR'S TRAVEL EXPENSE						
	AIRFARES		2	RNDTR	1,580	3,160	
	LIMOS		2	RNDTR	200	400	3,560
835-06	DIRECTOR'S LIVING EXPENSE						
	HOTEL		49	DAYS	100	4,900	
	PER DIEM		49	DAYS	100	4,900	
	AUTO		7	WEEKS	150	1,050	10,850
835-09	CASTING DIRECTOR EXPENSE						
	ASSISTANT -		10	WEEKS	700	7,000	7,000
835-10	LOC. CASTING DIRECTOR						
				ALLOW	7,500	7,500	7,500
835-11	LOC. CAST. DIR. EXPENSES						
	MISC EXPENSES			ALLOW	1,000	1,000	1,000
835-21	DGA PH & W						
		0.125	%		90,000	11,250	11,250
835-25	OTHER CHARGES						
	PHYSICAL			ALLOW	200	200	200
					Total for 835		131,360

Acct #	Description	Amount	Units	X	Rate	Subtotal	Total
845	**CAST**						
845-01	PRINCIPAL CAST						
	ASSUMING CORP.	1	CONTR		205,000	205,000	
	ASSUMING CORP.	1	CONTR		205,000	205,000	
			ALLOW		45,000	45,000	
			ALLOW		45,000	45,000	500,000
845-02	SUPPORTING CAST						
			ALLOW		40,000	40,000	
							40,000
845-11	CAST OVERTIME		ALLOW		7,500	7,500	7,500
845-12	LOOPING ALLOWANCE		ALLOW		7,500	7,500	7,500
845-13	CAST TRAVEL EXPENSE						
	PRINCIPAL	4	RNDTR		1,580	6,320	
	PRINCIPAL	4	RNDTR		1,580	6,320	
	PRINCIPAL	2	RNDTR		1,580	3,160	
	PRINCIPAL	2	RNDTR		1,580	3,160	
	ALLOWANCE FOR SUPPORTING	4	RNDTR		1,580	6,320	
	STUNT COORDINATOR	0	RNDTR		1,580	0	
	STUNTS	0	RNDTR		1,580	0	
	LIMOS	16	RNDTR		200	3,200	28,480
845-15	CAST LIVING EXPENSE						
	HOTEL						
	PRINCIPALS	30	DAYS	4	100	12,000	
	SUPPORTING CAST	50	DAYS		50	2,500	
	PER DIEM						
	PRINCIPALS	30	DAYS	4	100	12,000	
	SUPPORTING CAST	50	DAYS		53	2,650	
	AUTO RENTAL						
	PRINCIPALS	4	WEEKS	4	150	2,400	31,550
845-17	STUNT COORDINATOR						
		2	WEEKS		2,500	5,000	5,000
845-19	STUNTS						
			ALLOW		6,000	6,000	6,000
845-21	SAG PH & W						
		0.128	%		226,000	28,928	28,928
845-25	OTHER CHARGES						
	CAST PHYSICALS		ALLOW		1,000	1,000	
	MISC		ALLOW		1,000	1,000	2,000
					Total for 845		656,958

Acct #	Description	Amount	Units	X	Rate	Subtotal	Total
855	**PAYROLL TAXES**						
855-01	A-T-L FRINGES						
	A-T-L FRINGES						0
855-	Fringes						
	A-T-L	16	%		7,850	1,256	
	CAL WORK COMP	3.37	%		182,000	6,133	
	WORKERS COMP	1.43	%		160,810	2,300	
	FICA	6.20	%		163,410	10,131	
	FUI	0.80	%		57,810	462	
	SUI	5.40	%		57,810	3,122	
	MEDICARE	1.45	%		192,810	2,796	
	PAYROLL FEE	0.25	%		192,810	482	26,682
					Total for 855		26,682
	TOTAL ABOVE-THE-LINE						1,034,877

919	**EXTRA TALENT**						
919-01	EXTRAS/STANDINS						
	STANDINS	28	DAYS	4	75	8,400	
	EXTRAS	400	DAYS		50	20,000	28,400
919-03	CASTING COMMISSION						
	EXTRAS CASTING FEE	0.15	%		28,400	4,260	
	PAYROLL TAXES	0.16	%		28,400	4,544	8,804
					Total for 919		37,204
921	**PRODUCTION STAFF**						
921-01	PRODUCTION MANAGER						
	(TRAVEL FROM L.A.)						
	PREP (INC. TRAVEL)	5	WEEKS		3,786	18,930	
	SHOOT	3.40	WEEKS		4,486	15,252	
	WRAP (INC. TRAVEL)	2	WEEKS		3,786	7,572	
	SEVERANCE	1	WEEK		3,786	3,786	45,540
921-02	1ST ASSISTANT DIRECTOR						
	PREP	3	WEEKS		2,569	7,707	
	SHOOT	3.40	WEEKS		3,044	10,350	
	SATURDAYS	3	DAYS		877.80	2,633	
	SEVERANCE	1	WEEK		2,569	2,569	23,259
921-03	2ND ASSISTANT DIRECTOR						
	PREP	2	WEEKS		1,722	3,444	
	SHOOT	3.40	WEEKS		2,085	7,089	
	SATURDAYS	3	DAYS		601.50	1,805	
	WRAP	0.20	WEEK		1,722	344	

Acct #	Description	Amount	Units	X	Rate	Subtotal	Total
921	**PRODUCTION STAFF** (Cont'd)						
921-03	2ND ASSISTANT DIRECTOR (Cont d)						
	SEVERANCE		ALLOW		1,722	1,722	14,404
921-04	2ND 2ND ASST DIRECTOR						
	PREP	0.40	WEEK		1,626	650	
	SHOOT	3.40	WEEKS		1,626	5,528	
	SATURDAYS	3	DAYS		468.90	1,407	
	WRAP	0.20	WEEK		1,626	325	
	SEVERANCE	1	WEEK		1,626	1,626	9,536
921-05	PRODUCTION ASSISTANT						
	P.A. #1						
	PREP	1	WEEK		500	500	
	SHOOT	3.40	WEEKS		500	1,700	
	SATURDAYS	3	DAYS		150	450	
	WRAP	2	WEEKS		500	1,000	
	P.A. #2						
	PREP	1	WEEK		500	500	
	SHOOT	3.40	WEEKS		500	1,700	
	SATURDAYS	3	DAYS		150	450	
	WRAP	2	WEEKS		500	1,000	
	P.A. #3						
	PREP	1	WEEK		500	500	
	SHOOT	3.40	WEEKS		500	1,700	
	SATURDAYS	3	DAYS		150	450	
	WRAP	2	WEEKS		500	1,000	
	P.A. #4						
	SHOOT	3.40	WEEKS		500	1,700	
	SATURDAYS	3	DAYS		150	450	
	OFFICE P.A.						
	PREP	3	WEEKS		500	1,500	
	SHOOT	3.40	WEEKS		500	1,700	
	SATURDAYS	3	DAYS		150	450	
	WRAP	2	WEEKS		500	1,000	17,750
921-06	SCRIPT SUPERVISOR						
	PREP	1	WEEK		1,650	1,650	
	SHOOT	3.40	WEEKS		1,650	5,610	
	SATURDAYS	3	DAYS		495	1,485	
	2 CAMERA DAYS	7	DAYS		40	280	
	OVERTIME	3.40	WEEKS	0.10	1,650	561	9,586
921-07	PRODUCTION COORDINATOR						
	COORDINATOR						
	PREP	5	WEEKS		1,200	6,000	
	SHOOT	3.40	WEEKS		1,200	4,080	
	SATURDAYS	3	DAYS		360	1,080	
	WRAP	2	WEEKS		1,200	2,400	
	ASS'T COORDINATOR						
	PREP	3	WEEKS		700	2,100	

Acct #	Description	Amount	Units	X	Rate	Subtotal	Total
921	**PRODUCTION STAFF (Cont'd)**						
921-07	PRODUCTION COORDINATOR (Cont'd)						
	SHOOT	3.40	WEEKS		700	2,380	
	SATURDAYS	3	DAYS		210	630	
	WRAP	2	WEEKS		700	1,400	20,070
921-08	PRODUCTION ACCOUNTANT						
	ACCOUNTANT - PREP	4	WEEKS		1,850	7,400	
	- SHOOT	3.40	WEEKS		1,850	6,290	
	- SATURDAYS	3	DAYS		555	1,665	
	- WRAP	4	WEEKS		1,850	7,400	
	1ST ASST - PREP	3	WEEKS		1,050	3,150	
	- SHOOT	3.40	WEEKS		1,050	3,570	
	- SATURDAYS	3	DAYS		315	945	
	- WRAP	3	WEEKS		1,050	3,150	33,570
921-09	LOCATION MANAGER						
	LOCATION MANAGER:						
	PREP	4	WEEKS		1,200	4,800	
	SHOOT	3.40	WEEKS		1,200	4,080	
	SATURDAYS	3	DAYS		360	1,080	
	WRAP	1	WEEK		1,200	1,200	
	ASS'T LOCATION MANAGER:						
	PREP	2	WEEKS		800	1,600	
	SHOOT	3.40	WEEKS		800	2,720	
	SATURDAYS	3	DAYS		240	720	16,200
921-13	TECHNICAL ADVISOR						
	MAGICIAN/ILLUSIONIST	4	WEEKS		1,500	6,000	
	(CONTRACTED)						6,000
921-22	CAR ALLOWANCE						
	LOCATION MANAGER	9	WEEKS		150	1,350	
	ASS'T LOCATION MANAGER	6	WEEKS		150	900	2,250
921-25	OTHER CHARGES						
	POLAROID FILM		ALLOW		1,500	1,500	1,500
					Total for 921		199,665
923	**CAMERA**						
923-01	D.P./OPERATOR						
	PREP/TRAVEL	1.40	WEEKS		5,000	7,000	
	SHOOT	3.40	WEEKS		5,000	17,000	
	SATURDAYS	3	DAYS		1,500	4,500	
	TRAVEL	0.20	WEEK		5,000	1,000	29,500
923-02	CAMERA OPERATOR						
	SHOOT	3.40	WEEKS		3,034.50	10,317	
	SATURDAYS	3	DAYS		910.35	2,731	13,048

Acct #	Description	Amount	Units	X	Rate	Subtotal	Total
923	**CAMERA** (Cont'd)						
923-03	1ST ASST CAMERAMAN						
	PREP	0.60	WEEKS		1,792	1,075	
	SHOOT	3.40	WEEKS		1,792	6,093	
	SATURDAYS	3	DAYS		537.60	1,613	
	WRAP	0.40	WEEK		1,792	717	
	OVERTIME	3.40	WEEKS	0.10	1,792	609	10,107
923-04	2ND ASST CAMERAMAN						
	PREP	0.60	WEEK		1,484	890	
	SHOOT	3.40	WEEKS		1,484	5,046	
	SATURDAYS	3	DAYS		445.20	1,336	
	WRAP	0.40	WEEK		1,484	594	
	OVERTIME	3.40	WEEKS	0.10	1,484	505	8,371
923-05	EXTRA OPERATOR						
	"B" CAMERA	5	DAYS		606.90	3,035	
	STEADICAM OPERATOR	3	DAYS		750	2,250	5,285
923-06	EXTRA ASSISTANTS						
	"B" CAMERA	5	DAYS		358.40	1,792	
	STEADICAM ASS'T	3	DAYS		400	1,200	2,992
923-10	EQUIPMENT RENTALS						
	CAMERA PACKAGE	3.40	WEEKS		5,000	17,000	
	ADD'L EQUIPMENT	3.40	WEEKS		1,500	5,100	
	STEADICAM	3	DAYS		750	2,250	24,350
923-11	MATERIALS & SUPPLIES						
			ALLOW		1,250	1,250	1,250
923-23	BOX RENTALS						
	1ST ASS'T CAMERA	4	WEEKS		100	400	
	2ND ASS'T CAMERA	4	WEEKS		100	400	800
					Total for 923		95,703
927	**ELECTRICAL**						
927-01	GAFFER						
	PREP	1	WEEK		1,410.50	1,411	
	SHOOT	3.40	WEEKS		1,410.50	4,796	
	SATURDAYS	3	DAYS		423.15	1,269	
	WRAP	0.60	WEEKS		1,410.50	846	
	OVERTIME	3.40	WEEKS	0.10	1,410.50	480	8,802
927-02	BEST BOY						
	PREP	1	WEEK		1,260	1,260	
	SHOOT	3.40	WEEKS		1,260	4,284	
	SATURDAYS	3	DAYS		378	1,134	

Acct #	Description	Amount	Units	X	Rate	Subtotal	Total
927	**ELECTRICAL (Cont'd)**						
927-02	BEST BOY (Cont'd)						
	WRAP	0.60	WEEKS		1,260	756	
	OVERTIME	3.40	WEEKS	0.10	1,260	428	7,862
927-03	LAMP OPERATORS						
	LAMP OP #1 - PREP	0.40	WEEK		1,151.50	461	
	- SHOOT	3.40	WEEKS		1,151.50	3,915	
	- SATURDAYS	3	DAYS		345.45	1,036	
	- WRAP	0.40	WEEK		1,151.50	461	
	- OVERTIME	3.40	WEEKS	0.10	1,151.50	392	
	LAMP OP #2 - PREP	0.40	WEEK		1,151.50	461	
	- SHOOT	3.40	WEEKS		1,151.50	3,915	
	- SATURDAYS	3	DAYS		345.45	1,036	
	- WRAP	0.40	WEEKS		1,151.50	461	
	- OVERTIME	3.40	WEEKS	0.10	1,151.50	392	
	LAMP OP #3 - SHOOT	3.40	WEEKS		1,151.50	3,915	
	- SATURDAYS	3	DAYS		345.45	1,036	
	- WRAP	0.40	WEEKS		1,151.50	461	
	- OVERTIME	3.40	WEEKS	0.10	1,151.50	392	
	LAMP OP #4 - SHOOT	3.40	WEEKS		1,151.50	3,915	
	- SATURDAYS	3	DAYS		345.45	1,036	
	- WRAP	0.20	WEEK		1,151.50	230	
	- OVERTIME	3.40	WEEKS	0.10	1,151.50	392	23,907
927-10	EQUIPMENT RENTALS						
	ELECTRIC PACKAGE	3.40	WEEKS		5,250	17,850	
	ADD'L EQUIPMENT	3.40	WEEKS		750	2,550	20,400
927-15	PRODUCTION GLOBES		ALLOW		1,200	1,200	1,200
927-17	MATERIALS & SUPPLIES						
			ALLOW		4,000	4,000	4,000
927-19	LOSS & REPAIR		ALLOW		1,000	1,000	1,000
927-23	BOX RENTAL						
	GAFFER	5.60	WEEKS		200	1,120	1,120
					Total for 927		68,291
929	**GRIP**						
929-01	KEY GRIP						
	PREP	1	WEEK		1,410.50	1,411	
	SHOOT	3.40	WEEKS		1,410.50	4,796	
	SATURDAYS	3	DAYS		423.15	1,269	
	WRAP	0.60	WEEKS		1,410.50	846	
	OVERTIME	3.40	WEEKS	0.10	1,410.50	480	8,802

Acct #	Description	Amount	Units	X	Rate	Subtotal	Total
929	**GRIP** (Cont'd)						
929-02	BEST BOY						
	PREP	1	WEEK		1,260	1,260	
	SHOOT	3.40	WEEKS		1,260	4,284	
	SATURDAYS	3	DAYS		378	1,134	
	WRAP	0.60	WEEKS		1,260	756	
	OVERTIME	3.40	WEEKS	0.10	1,260	428	7,862
929-03	DOLLY GRIP						
	PREP	0.20	WEEK		1,260	252	
	SHOOT	3.40	WEEKS		1,260	4,284	
	SATURDAYS	3	DAYS		378	1,134	
	WRAP	0.20	WEEK		1,260	252	
	OVERTIME	3.40	WEEKS	0.10	1,260	428	6,350
929-05	COMPANY GRIPS						
	GRIP #1 - PREP	0.40	WEEK		1,151.50	461	
	- SHOOT	3.40	WEEKS		1,151.50	3,915	
	- SATURDAYS	3	DAYS		345.45	1,036	
	- WRAP	0.40	WEEK		1,151.50	461	
	- OVERTIME	3.40	WEEKS	0.10	1,151.50	392	
	GRIP #2 - PREP	0.40	WEEK		1,151.50	461	
	- SHOOT	3.40	WEEKS		1,151.50	3,915	
	- SATURDAYS	3	DAYS		345.45	1,036	
	- WRAP	0.40	WEEKS		1,151.50	461	
	- OVERTIME	3.40	WEEKS	0.10	1,151.50	392	
	GRIP #3 - PREP	0.40	WEEK		1,151.50	461	
	- SHOOT	3.40	WEEKS		1,151.50	3,915	
	- SATURDAYS	3	DAYS		345.45	1,036	
	- WRAP	0.40	WEEK		1,151.50	461	
	- OVERTIME	3.40	WEEKS	0.10	1,151.50	392	18,795
929-10	EQUIPMENT RENTAL						
	GRIP PACKAGE	3.40	WEEKS		1,750	5,950	
	PEEWEE DOLLY	3.40	WEEKS		400	1,360	
	HYBRID DOLLY	3.40	WEEKS		600	2,040	
	ADD'L EQUIPMENT	3.40	WEEKS		750	2,550	
	CONDOR RENTAL	3	DAYS		500	1,500	13,400
929-17	MATERIALS & SUPPLIES						
			ALLOW		4,000	4,000	4,000
929-19	LOSS & REPAIR		ALLOW		1,000	1,000	1,000
929-23	BOX RENTALS						
	KEY GRIP	5.60	WEEKS		250	1,400	1,400
					Total for 929		61,609

Acct #	Description	Amount	Units	X	Rate	Subtotal	Total
931	**PROPS**						
931-01	PROPMASTER						
	PREP	3	WEEKS		1,410.50	4,232	
	SHOOT	3.40	WEEKS		1,410.50	4,796	
	SATURDAYS	3	DAYS		423.15	1,269	
	WRAP	1	WEEK		1,410.50	1,411	
	OVERTIME	3.40	WEEKS	0.10	1,410.50	480	12,188
931-02	ASST PROPMASTER						
	PREP	2	WEEKS		1,113	2,226	
	SHOOT	3.40	WEEKS		1,113	3,784	
	SATURDAYS	3	DAYS		333.90	1,002	
	WRAP	1	WEEK		1,113	1,113	
	OVERTIME	3.40	WEEKS	0.10	1,113	378	8,503
931-05	PURCHASES - RECOVERABLE						
			ALLOW		1,500	1,500	1,500
931-07	PURCHASES - EXPENDABLE						
			ALLOW		2,500	2,500	2,500
931-09	MANUFACTURING		ALLOW		1,500	1,500	1,500
931-10	PROP RENTALS						
			ALLOW		1,500	1,500	
	MAGIC RENTALS		ALLOW		10,000	10,000	11,500
931-12	LOSS & REPAIRS		ALLOW		500	500	500
931-22	CAR ALLOWANCE						
	PROPMASTER	8	WEEKS		125	1,000	1,000
931-23	BOX RENTALS						
	PROPMASTER - SHOOT ONLY	4	WEEKS		350	1,400	1,400
					Total for 931		40,591
933	**PRODUCTION SOUND**						
933-01	MIXER						
	PREP	0.20	WEEK		1,410.50	282	
	SHOOT	3.40	WEEKS		1,410.50	4,796	
	SATURDAYS	3	DAYS		423.15	1,269	
	WRAP	0.20	WEEK		1,410.50	282	
	OVERTIME	3.40	WEEKS	0.10	1,410.50	480	7,109
933-03	BOOM OPERATOR						
	PREP	0.20	WEEK		1,260	252	
	SHOOT	3.40	WEEKS		1,260	4,284	
	SATURDAYS	3	DAYS		378	1,134	
	WRAP	0.20	WEEK		1,260	252	
	OVERTIME	3.40	WEEKS	0.10	1,260	428	6,350

Acct #	Description	Amount	Units	X	Rate	Subtotal	Total
933	**PRODUCTION SOUND** (Cont'd)						
933-05	CABLEMAN						
	SHOOT	3.40	WEEKS		1,113	3,784	
	SATURDAYS	3	DAYS		333.90	1,002	
	OVERTIME	3.40	WEEKS	0.10	1,113	378	5,164
933-10	EQUIPMENT RENTAL						
	SOUND PACKAGE	3.40	WEEKS		1,400	4,760	
	WALKIE-TALKIES	3.40	WEEKS	25	15	1,275	
	PAGERS	2	MO.S	20	20	800	6,835
933-17	MATERIALS & SUPPLIES						
	1/4" TAPE, BATTERIES						
	BATTERIES, ETC.		ALLOW		1,000	1,000	1,000
933-25	OTHER CHARGES						
	VIDEO PLAYBACK		ALLOW		3,000	3,000	3,000
					Total for 933		29,458
935	**WARDROBE**						
935-01	COSTUME DESIGNER						
	PREP	3	WEEKS		2,250	6,750	
	SHOOT	3.40	WEEKS		2,250	7,650	
	SATURDAYS	3	DAYS		675	2,025	
	WRAP	1	WEEK		2,250	2,250	18,675
935-02	COSTUME SUPERVISOR						
	PREP	2	WEEKS		1,500	3,000	
	SHOOT	3.40	WEEKS		1,500	5,100	
	SATURDAYS	3	DAYS		450	1,350	
	WRAP	1	WEEK		1,500	1,500	
	OVERTIME	3.40	WEEKS	0.20	1,500	1,020	11,970
935-03	SET COSTUMER						
	PREP	1	WEEK		1,186.50	1,187	
	SHOOT	3.40	WEEKS		1,186.50	4,034	
	SATURDAYS	3	DAYS		355.95	1,068	
	WRAP	1	WEEK		1,186.50	1,187	
	OVERTIME	3.40	WEEKS	0.20	1,186.50	807	8,283
935-04	SET COSTUMER						
	PREP	1	WEEK		1,186.50	1,187	
	SHOOT	3.40	WEEKS		1,186.50	4,034	
	SATURDAYS	3	DAYS		355.96	1,068	
	WRAP	1	WEEK		1,186.50	1,187	
	OVERTIME	3.40	WEEKS	0.20	1,186.50	807	8,283
935-13	PURCHASES						
			ALLOW		13,000	13,000	13,000
935-15	RENTALS						
			ALLOW		5,000	5,000	

Acct #	Description	Amount	Units	X	Rate	Subtotal	Total
935	**WARDROBE** (Cont'd)						
935-15	RENTALS (Cont d)						5,000
935-17	ALTERATIONS		ALLOW		3,000	3,000	3,000
935-18	CLEANING & REPAIRS		ALLOW		3,000	3,000	3,000
935-20	LOSS & DAMAGE		ALLOW		1,000	1,000	1,000
935-21	SUPPLIES		ALLOW		750	750	750
935-22	CAR ALLOWANCE						
	COSTUME DESIGNER	8	WEEKS		150	1,200	
	COSTUME SUPERVISOR	7	WEEKS		150	1,050	
							2,250
935-23	BOX RENTAL						
	COSTUME DESIGNER	7.40	WEEKS		200	1,480	
	COSTUME SUPERVISOR	6.40	WEEKS		100	640	2,120
					Total for 935		77,331
937	**MAKEUP & HAIRDRESSING**						
937-01	MAKEUP ARTIST						
	PREP	0.20	WEEKS		1,550	310	
	SHOOT	3.40	WEEKS		1,550	5,270	
	SATURDAYS	3	DAYS		465	1,395	
	WRAP	0.20	WEEK		1,550	310	
	OVERTIME	3.40	WEEKS	0.20	1,550	1,054	8,339
937-02	EXTRA MAKEUP						
		12	DAYS		310	3,720	3,720
937-03	HAIRSTYLIST						
	PREP	0.20	WEEKS		1,550	310	
	SHOOT	3.40	WEEKS		1,550	5,270	
	SATURDAYS	3	DAYS		465	1,395	
	WRAP	0.20	WEEK		1,550	310	
	OVERTIME	3.40	WEEKS	0.20	1,550	1,054	
	ASSISTANT HAIRSTYLIST						
	SHOOT	8	DAYS		310	2,480	10,819
937-05	SUPPLIES						
			ALLOW		1,500	1,500	1,500
937-07	WIGS & HAIRPIECES						
			ALLOW		1,500	1,500	1,500
937-23	BOX RENTAL						
	MAKE-UP (SHOOT ONLY)	4	WEEKS		125	500	
	HAIR (SHOOT ONLY)	4	WEEKS		125	500	

Acct #	Description	Amount	Units	X	Rate	Subtotal	Total
937	**MAKEUP & HAIRDRESSING** (Cont'd)						
937-23	BOX RENTAL (Cont d)						
	ASS'T MAKEUP (SHOOT ONLY)	12	DAYS		25	300	
	ASS'T HAIR (SHOOT ONLY)	8	DAYS		25	200	1,500
					Total for 937		27,378
939	**SPECIAL EFFECTS**						
939-01	SPECIAL EFFECTS KEYMAN						
	PREP/SHOOT/WRAP	3	WEEKS		1,410.50	4,232	4,232
939-02	ASST SPECIAL EFFECTS						
	PREP/SHOOT/WRAP	2	WEEKS		1,260	2,520	2,520
939-10	EQUIPMENT RENTALS		ALLOW		1,000	1,000	1,000
939-17	MATERIALS						
			ALLOW		1,500	1,500	1,500
939-23	BOX RENTAL	3	WEEKS		300	900	900
					Total for 939		10,152
941	**SET OPERATIONS**						
941-05	CRAFTSERVICE PERSON						
	PREP	0.20	WEEK		927.50	186	
	SHOOT	3.40	WEEKS		927.50	3,154	
	SATURDAYS	3	DAYS		278.25	835	
	WRAP	0.20	WEEK		927.50	186	
	OVERTIME	3.40	WEEKS	0.20	927.50	631	
	ADD'L CRAFTSERVICE	5	DAYS		185.50	928	5,920
941-08	FIRST AID						
	SHOOT	3.40	WEEKS		927.50	3,154	
	SATURDAYS	3	DAYS		278.25	835	
	OVERTIME	3.40	WEEKS	0.20	927.50	631	4,620
941-16	CRAFT SERVICE SUPPLIES	4	WEEKS		1,500	6,000	6,000
941-18	FIRST AID SUPPLIES		ALLOW		500	500	500
941-22	CAR ALLOWANCE						
	CRAFTSERVICE	4.40	WEEKS		150	660	660
941-23	BOX RENTAL						
	CRAFT SERVICE-SHOOT ONLY	4	WEEKS		125	500	
	FIRST AID-SHOOT ONLY	4	WEEKS		125	500	1,000
					Total for 941		18,700

Acct #	Description	Amount	Units	X	Rate	Subtotal	Total
945	**SET DESIGN**						
945-01	PRODUCTION DESIGNER						
	PREP	4	WEEKS		3,000	12,000	
	SHOOT	3.40	WEEKS		3,000	10,200	
	SATURDAYS	3	DAYS		900	2,700	
	WRAP	0.40	WEEK		3,000	1,200	26,100
945-02	ART DIRECTOR						
	PREP	2	WEEKS		750	1,500	
	SHOOT	3.40	WEEKS		750	2,550	
	SATURDAYS	3	DAYS		225	675	
	WRAP	0.40	WEEK		750	300	5,025
945-12	BLUEPRINTS		ALLOW		250	250	250
945-14	MATERIALS & SUPPLIES		ALLOW		500	500	500
945-22	CAR ALLOWANCE						
	PRODUCTION DESIGNER	8.40	WEEKS		150	1,260	1,260
					Total for 945		33,135
947	**SET CONSTRUCTION**						
947-03	CONSTRUCTION LABOR		ALLOW		30,000	30,000	30,000
947-05	CONSTRUCTION MATERIALS						
			ALLOW		15,000	15,000	15,000
947-22	CAR ALLOWANCE						
	COORD. CREWCAB	6	WEEKS		300	1,800	
	PAINTER CREWCAB	6	WEEKS		300	1,800	3,600
947-23	BOX RENTALS						
	COORDINATOR	3	WEEKS		700	2,100	
	PAINTER	3	WEEKS		250	750	2,850
					Total for 947		51,450
951	**SET DRESSINGS**						
951-01	SET DECORATOR						
	PREP	3	WEEKS		1,500	4,500	
	SHOOT	3.40	WEEKS		1,500	5,100	
	SATURDAYS	3	DAYS		450	1,350	
	WRAP	1	WEEK		1,500	1,500	12,450
951-02	LEADMAN						
	PREP	2	WEEKS		1,260	2,520	
	SHOOT	3.40	WEEKS		1,260	4,284	
	SATURDAYS	3	DAYS		378	1,134	
	WRAP	1	WEEK		1,260	1,260	
	OVERTIME	3.40	WEEKS	0.10	1,260	428	9,626

Acct #	Description	Amount	Units	X	Rate	Subtotal	Total
951	**SET DRESSINGS** (Cont'd)						
951-03	SWING GANG						
	SWING GANG #1						
	PREP	2	WEEKS		1,113	2,226	
	SHOOT	3.40	WEEKS		1,113	3,784	
	SATURDAYS	3	DAYS		333.90	1,002	
	WRAP	1	WEEK		1,113	1,113	
	OVERTIME	3.40	WEEKS	0.10	1,113	378	
	SWING GANG #2						
	PREP	2	WEEKS		1,113	2,226	
	SHOOT	3.40	WEEKS		1,113	3,784	
	SATURDAYS	3	DAYS		333.90	1,002	
	WRAP	1	WEEK		1,113	1,113	
	OVERTIME	3.40	WEEKS	0.10	1,113	378	
	SWING GANG #3						
	PREP	1	WEEK		1,113	1,113	
	SHOOT	3.40	WEEKS		1,113	3,784	
	SATURDAYS	3	DAYS		333.90	1,002	
	WRAP	1	WEEK		1,113	1,113	
	OVERTIME	3.40	WEEKS	0.10	1,113	378	24,396
951-06	PURCHASES		ALLOW		5,000	5,000	5,000
951-07	GREENS		ALLOW		1,000	1,000	1,000
951-10	RENTALS		ALLOW		25,000	25,000	25,000
951-14	LOSS & DAMAGE		ALLOW		2,000	2,000	2,000
951-22	CAR ALLOWANCE						
	SET DECORATOR	8	WEEKS		150	1,200	
	LEADMAN	7	WEEKS		150	1,050	
	SHOPPER	7	WEEKS		150	1,050	3,300
951-23	BOX RENTAL						
	SET DECORATOR	8	WEEKS		150	1,200	
	LEADMAN	7	WEEKS		150	1,050	2,250
					Total for 951		85,022
955	**SECOND UNIT**						
955-25	OTHER CHARGES						
	ALL COSTS "ATLANTIC CITY"		ALLOW		30,000	30,000	30,000
					Total for 955		30,000

Acct #	Description	Amount	Units	X	Rate	Subtotal	Total
959	**RAWSTOCK**						
959-01	NEGATIVE RAW STOCK						
	A-CAMERA	5,000	FEET	20	0.502	50,200	
	B-CAMERA/STEADICAM	2,500	FEET	8	0.502	10,040	60,240
959-02	DEVELOPING						
	NORMAL DEVELOPING - 90%	108,000	FEET		0.117	12,636	12,636
959-06	TAPE DAILIES						
	TRANSFER TO TAPE - 55%	66,000	FEET		0.269	17,754	
	1" VIDEO TAPE	20	DAYS		95	1,900	19,654
					Total for 959		92,530
961	**TRANSPORTATION**						
961-03	DRIVERS						
	COORDINATOR						
	PREP	3	WEEKS		1,700	5,100	
	SHOOT	3.40	WEEKS		1,700	5,780	
	SATURDAYS	3	DAYS		510	1,530	
	WRAP	2	WEEKS		1,700	3,400	
	OVERTIME	3.40	WEEKS	0.20	1,700	1,156	
	DRIVER CAPT (TOWS WARDRB)						
	PREP	2	WEEKS		1,400	2,800	
	SHOOT	3.40	WEEKS		1,400	4,760	
	SATURDAYS	3	DAYS		420	1,260	
	WRAP	1	WEEK		1,400	1,400	
	OVERTIME	3.40	WEEKS	0.20	1,400	952	
	ELECTRIC/GRIP						
	PREP	0.60	WEEK		1,024.20	615	
	SHOOT	3.40	WEEKS		1,024.20	3,482	
	SATURDAYS	3	DAYS		307.26	922	
	WRAP	0.40	WEEK		1,024.20	410	
	OVERTIME	3.40	WEEKS	0.20	1,024.20	696	
	HONEYWAGON						
	PREP	0.60	WEEKS		1,159.20	696	
	SHOOT	3.40	WEEKS		1,159.20	3,941	
	SATURDAYS	3	DAYS		347.76	1,043	
	WRAP	0.40	WEEK		1,159.20	464	
	OVERTIME	3.40	WEEKS	0.20	1,159.20	788	
	STARWAGON #1						
	PREP	0.60	WEEKS		1,024.20	615	
	SHOOT	3.40	WEEKS		1,024.20	3,482	
	SATURDAYS	3	DAYS		307.26	922	
	WRAP	0.40	WEEK		1,024.20	410	
	OVERTIME	3.40	WEEKS	0.20	1,024.50	697	
	STARWAGON #2						
	PREP	0.60	WEEK		1,024.20	615	

Acct #	Description	Amount	Units	X	Rate	Subtotal	Total
961	**TRANSPORTATION** (Cont'd)						
961-03	DRIVERS (Cont'd)						
	SHOOT	3.40	WEEKS		1,024.20	3,482	
	SATURDAYS	3	DAYS		307.26	922	
	WRAP	0.40	WEEK		1,024.20	410	
	OVERTIME	3.40	WEEKS	0.20	1,024.20	696	
	MAXI VAN #1						
	PREP	1.80	WEEKS		964.90	1,737	
	SHOOT	3.40	WEEKS		964.90	3,281	
	SATURDAYS	3	DAYS		289.47	868	
	WRAP	1	WEEK		964.90	965	
	OVERTIME	3.40	WEEKS	0.20	964.90	656	
	MAXI VAN #2						
	PREP	0.60	WEEK		964.90	579	
	SHOOT	3.40	WEEKS		964.90	3,281	
	SATURDAYS	3	DAYS		289.47	868	
	WRAP	0.40	WEEK		964.90	386	
	OVERTIME	3.40	WEEKS	0.20	964.90	656	
	CAMERA/SOUND						
	PREP	0.60	WEEK		1,024.20	615	
	SHOOT	3.40	WEEKS		1,024.20	3,482	
	SATURDAYS	3	DAYS		307.26	922	
	WRAP	0.40	WEEK		1,024.20	410	
	OVERTIME	3.40	WEEKS	0.20	1,024.20	696	
	PROP TRUCK						
	PREP	0.60	WEEK		1,024.20	615	
	SHOOT	3.40	WEEKS		1,024.20	3,482	
	SATURDAYS	3	DAYS		307.26	922	
	WRAP	0.40	WEEK		1,024.20	410	
	OVERTIME	3.40	WEEKS	0.20	1,024.20	696	
	MAKEUP/HAIR TRAILER						
	PREP	0.20	WEEK		1,024.20	205	
	SHOOT	3.40	WEEKS		1,024.20	3,482	
	SATURDAYS	3	DAYS		307.26	922	
	WRAP	0.20	WEEK		1,024.20	205	
	OVERTIME	3.40	WEEKS	0.20	1,024.20	696	
	WARDROBE TRAILER						
	PREP	1	WEEK		1,024.20	1,024	
	SHOOT	3.40	WEEKS		1,024.20	3,482	
	SATURDAYS	3	DAYS		307.26	922	
	WRAP	1	WEEK		1,024.20	1,024	
	OVERTIME	3.40	WEEKS	0.20	1,024.20	696	
	CATERER	3.40	WEEKS		1,250	4,250	
	SATURDAYS	3	DAYS		375	1,125	
	ASST CATERER	3.40	WEEKS		750	2,550	
	SATURDAYS	3	DAYS		225	675	

Acct #	Description	Amount	Units	X	Rate	Subtotal	Total
961	**TRANSPORTATION (Cont'd)**						
961-03	DRIVERS (Cont'd)						
							100,231
961-07	VEHICLE RENTAL						
	STARWAGONS - 2 EACH	4.40	WEEKS	2	525	4,620	
	HONEYWAGON	4.40	WEEKS		1,470	6,468	
	MAKEUP/HAIR TRAILER	4.40	WEEKS		525	2,310	
	WARDROBE TRAILER	4.40	WEEKS		787.50	3,465	
	CAMERA/SOUND	4.40	WEEKS		472.50	2,079	
	ELECTRIC 5-TON	4.40	WEEKS		550	2,420	
	GRIP 5-TON	4.40	WEEKS		550	2,420	
	PROPS	4.40	WEEKS		315	1,386	
	SET DRESSING	6.40	WEEKS		315	2,016	
	CREWCAB (TOWS MAKEUP/HAIR	5.40	WEEKS		315	1,701	
	CREWCAB (TOWS WARDROBE)	5.40	WEEKS		315	1,701	
	CREWCAB (TOWS CAST TR #1)	5.40	WEEKS		315	1,701	
	FUEL TR (TOWS CAST TR #2)	5.40	WEEKS		367.50	1,985	
	COORDINATOR'S WAGON	8.40	WEEKS		135	1,134	
	MAXI VAN #1	7.40	WEEKS		200	1,480	
	MAXI VAN #2	6.40	WEEKS		200	1,280	
	U.P.M.	10.40	WEEKS		200	2,080	
	GENERATOR	3.40	WEEKS		325	1,105	41,351
961-10	GAS & OIL						
			ALLOW		4,000	4,000	4,000
961-13	TAXIS AND LIMOS		ALLOW		500	500	500
961-15	MILEAGE ALLOWANCE						
			ALLOW		1,000	1,000	1,000
961-16	PARKING		ALLOW		1,500	1,500	1,500
961-17	LOSS & DAMAGE						
	REPAIRS/MAINTENANCE		ALLOW		3,000	3,000	3,000
					Total for 961		151,582
963	**PICTURE CARS/ANIMALS**						
963-01	RENTALS & PURCHASES						
			ALLOW		5,000	5,000	5,000
963-15	TRAINER						
	RAVEN TRAINER	2	DAYS		250	500	500
963-17	ANIMAL RENTAL						
	RAVEN RENTAL	2	DAYS		200	400	400
					Total for 963		5,900

Acct #	Description	Amount	Units	X	Rate	Subtotal	Total
965	**LOCATION EXPENSE**						
965-01	SURVEY COST		ALLOW		1,000	1,000	1,000
965-03	LOCATION SITE RENTALS		ALLOW		40,000	40,000	40,000
965-04	LOCATION RESTORATION						
			ALLOW		1,500	1,500	1,500
965-05	AIRFARES						
	U.P.M.	1	RNDTR		1,580	1,580	
	DIRECTOR OF PHOTOGRAPHY	1	RNDTR		1,580	1,580	3,160
965-07	LODGINGS						
	U.P.M.	77	NITES		50	3,850	
	DIRECTOR OF PHOTOGRAPHY	40	NITES		50	2,000	5,850
965-09	PER DIEM						
	UPM	77	DAYS		50	3,850	
	DIRECTOR OF PHOTOGRAPHY	40	DAYS		50	2,000	5,850
965-11	CATERING COST						
	CREW MEALS	20	DAYS	80	11.50	18,400	
	2ND MEALS	5	DAYS	50	11.50	2,875	
	STANDINS/EXTRAS	428	MEALS		11.50	4,922	
	ICE, MISC FOR SET	20	DAYS		200	4,000	
	OFFICE FOOD,WATER,COFFEE	8	WEEKS		200	1,600	
	OFF-PRODUCTION MEALS	4	WEEKS		500	2,000	
							33,797
965-12	SHIPPING COST		ALLOW		5,000	5,000	5,000
965-13	TELEPHONE/TELEGRAPH						
	LONG DISTANCE	2	MO.S		3,500	7,000	
	CELLULARS	2	MO.S		2,000	4,000	11,000
965-14	OFFICE SPACE RENTAL						
	PRODUCTION OFFICES	11	WEEKS		900	9,900	
	OFFICE FURNITURE	2	MO.S		1,500	3,000	
	PARKING	2	MO.S		1,000	2,000	14,900
965-15	OFFICE EQUIPMENT RENTAL						
	COMPUTERS/PRINTERS/FAX	2	MO.S		2,000	4,000	
	TYPEWRITERS/STANDS	2	MO.S		300	600	4,600
965-16	OFFICE SUPPLIES/POSTAGE		ALLOW		3,000	3,000	3,000
965-17	COPYING						
		2	MO.S		1,000	2,000	
	EXCESS COPIES		ALLOW		2,000	2,000	4,000
965-21	LOCAL POLICE SERVICE		ALLOW		3,500	3,500	3,500
965-23	LOCAL WATCHMAN		ALLOW		4,000	4,000	4,000

Acct #	Description	Amount	Units	X	Rate	Subtotal	Total
965	**LOCATION EXPENSE** (Cont'd)						
965-24	COURTESY PAYMENTS		ALLOW		1,500	1,500	1,500
965-25	OTHER CHARGES		ALLOW		2,500	2,500	2,500
					Total for 965		145,157
966	**B-T-L FRINGE BENEFITS**						
966-01	B-T-L FRINGES						
	IA 479 ANNUITY	1,250	DAYS		22	27,500	
	NY CAMERA P.H & W	96	DAYS		65	6,240	
	TEAMSTERS	6	WEEKS	12	122.70	8,834	42,574
966-	Fringes						
	B-T-L	16	%		8,400	1,344	
	DGA V/H/PHW	21	%		92,739	19,475	
	CAL WORK COMP	3.37	%		98,723	3,327	
	TEAMSTERS	18	%		74,665	13,440	
	IA/CAMERA-VACATN	12	%		29,500	3,540	
	WORKERS COMP	1.43	%		577,821	8,263	
	FICA	6.20	%		675,616	41,888	
	FUI	0.80	%		443,098	3,545	
	SUI	5.40	%		443,098	23,927	
	MEDICARE	1.45	%		675,616	9,796	
	PAYROLL FEE	0.25	%		675,616	1,689	130,234
					Total for 966		172,808
	TOTAL PRODUCTION						1,433,667

968	**EDITORIAL**						
968-01	EDITOR		12	WEEKS		2,750	33,000	33,000
968-02	ASSISTANT EDITOR		12	WEEKS		1,150	13,800	13,800
968-05	SOUND EFFECTS PACKAGE		ALLOW		50,000	50,000	50,000
968-06	LAYDOWN		ALLOW		3,000	3,000	3,000
968-07	LAYBACK		ALLOW		1,000	1,000	1,000
968-08	2" AUDIO STOCK		2	HOURS		600	1,200	1,200
968-09	VIDEO CASSETTE STOCK		2	HOURS		1,650	3,300	3,300
968-10	ON-LINE ASSEMBLY						
			ALLOW		8,600	8,600	8,600

Acct #	Description	Amount	Units	X	Rate	Subtotal	Total
968	**EDITORIAL** (Cont'd)						
968-11	COLOR CORRECTION		ALLOW		6,000	6,000	6,000
968-12	ON-LINE COMPLETION						
			ALLOW		500	500	500
968-13	MUSIC EDITING-CONTRACT		ALLOW		7,500	7,500	7,500
968-17	EQUIP/ROOM RENTAL	12	WEEKS		250	3,000	3,000
968-19	OFF-LINE SYSTEM	12	WEEKS		2,400	28,800	28,800
968-20	DAILIES CASSETTES/DISKS	20	DAYS		187.50	3,750	3,750
968-21	MISC. SUPPLIES						
			ALLOW		500	500	500
968-23	POST-PRODUCTION RUNNER						
	SPLIT	10	WEEKS		375	3,750	3,750
968-24	POST-PROD RUNNER EXPENSE						
	MILEAGE		ALLOW		400	400	400
					Total for 968		168,100
969	**MUSIC**						
969-01	COMPOSER						
	COMPLETE PACKAGE		ALLOW		45,000	45,000	45,000
969-16	MUSIC RIGHTS & CLEARANCE		ALLOW		5,000	5,000	5,000
					Total for 969		50,000
971	**SPECIAL PHOTOGRAPHIC F/X**						
971-03	OPTICALS						
			ALLOW		6,000	6,000	6,000
971-10	INSERT SHOOTING		ALLOW		2,000	2,000	2,000
971-11	STOCK SHOTS - LICENSE		ALLOW		4,000	4,000	4,000
971-12	FILM & LAB CHARGES		ALLOW		3,500	3,500	3,500
					Total for 971		15,500

Acct #	Description	Amount	Units	X	Rate	Subtotal	Total
973	**TITLES**						
973-03	TITLE FILMING						
			ALLOW		2,500	2,500	2,500
973-07	SUB TITLES						
	CLOSED CAPTIONING		ALLOW		870	870	870
					Total for 973		3,370
975	**POST-PRODUCTION SOUND**						
975-04	MUSIC RECORDING/POST-PROD		ALLOW		6,500	6,500	6,500
975-06	FOLEY/SND F/X - STUDIO		ALLOW		5,250	5,250	5,250
975-16	POST-PROD SOUND TRANSFERS		ALLOW		750	750	750
					Total for 975		12,500
978	**DELIVERY MATERIALS**						
978-10	NETWORK: 1" & 1/2"		ALLOW		4,250	4,250	4,250
					Total for 978		4,250
	TOTAL POST PRODUCTION						266,529
979	**INSURANCE**						
979-01	INSURANCE						
	ALL COSTS		ALLOW		20,000	20,000	20,000
					Total for 979		20,000
981	**PUBLICITY**						
981-05	ALL COSTS		ALLOW		3,500	3,500	3,500
					Total for 981		3,500
983	**MISCELLANEOUS**						
983-01	LEGAL FEES		ALLOW		17,500	17,500	17,500
983-04	OFFICE RENTAL		2	MO.S	3,750	7,500	7,500
983-05	OFFICE FURNITURE/EQUIP		2	MO.S	2,500	5,000	5,000
983-06	PARKING						
	10 UCP - CASTING		2	MO.S	1,375	2,750	2,750
983-07	OFFICE SUPPLIES		2	MO.S	1,750	3,500	3,500
983-08	COPYING - NONSCRIPT						
			2	MO.S	2,500	5,000	

Acct #	Description	Amount	Units	X	Rate	Subtotal	Total
983	**MISCELLANEOUS (Cont'd)**						
983-08	COPYING - NONSCRIPT (Cont'd)						5,000
983-09	TELEPHONE/TELEX/POSTAGE						
			2	MO.S	4,750	9,500	9,500
983-10	NON-LOCATION SHIPPING						
			2	MO.S	2,250	4,500	4,500
983-11	MEALS/ENTERTAINING		2	MO.S	3,250	6,500	6,500
983-14	M.P. ASSOCIATION FEE		ALLOW		1,208	1,208	1,208
983-20	ACCOUNTING SERVICES						
	E.P. SOFTWARE LICENSE		ALLOW		1,500	1,500	
	BOARD & BREAKDOWN		ALLOW		4,000	4,000	
	COMPUTER RENTALS		ALLOW		3,750	3,750	9,250
983-25	OTHER CHARGES		ALLOW		22,500	22,500	22,500
					Total for 983		94,708
985	**POST-PROD FRINGE BENEFITS**						
985-01	POST-PROD FRINGES						
	POST-PROD FRINGES						0
	Fringes						0
					Total for 985		0
988	**SECOND RUN**						
988-25	FRINGES						
	LIFETIME CAP		ALLOW		75,000	75,000	
	FRINGES		ALLOW		12,000	12,000	87,000
					Total for 988		87,000
989	**PACKAGING & OVERHEAD**						
989-02	PRODUCTION FEES						
	PRODUCTIONS		ALLOW		175,000	175,000	175,000
					Total for 989		175,000
	TOTAL OTHER						380,208
	TOTAL ABOVE-THE-LINE						1,034,877
	TOTAL BELOW-THE-LINE						2,080,404
	ABOVE & BELOW-THE-LINE						3,115,279

Acct #	Description	Page #	Total
	TOTAL FRINGES		169,726
	GRAND TOTAL		3,115,279

Miscellaneous Forms and Information

Office Rental

If you are renting production offices in a full-service building, the following will probably be covered by the actual office lease or can be arranged through the building management office:

- Garbage pick-up (please use special bins for recycling paper, plastics, etc.)
- Janitorial
- Duplicate keys
- Parking and security
- Telephones (may or may not be part of the services provided)

Check to see if utilities and/or furniture are included in the lease of your building. If not, you will have to arrange for the following:

- Office furniture (check moving hours and use of elevators)
- Water and power (most water and power companies require notice and a deposit to turn on utilities)

General Office Start-Up

- Coffee services
- Computers, fax machine, photocopy machines
- Office supplies

- Paper goods
- Purchase orders, petty cash envelopes, invoices
- Telephones
- Video equipment
- Water service
- Travel agency
- Shipping—air freight
- Shipping—overnight mail service

Office Wrap Checklist

Contact:

_____ Post Office with change of address

Return:

_____ Duplicate keys
_____ Parking entry card

Arrange for pick-up:

_____ Office furniture
_____ Coffee service
_____ Computers
_____ Fax
_____ Calculators
_____ Copiers
_____ Video equipment
_____ Water cooler

Disconnect:

_____ Water & power
_____ Telephones

Inventory and box for transfer:

_____ Office supplies
_____ Paper goods (cups, paper towels, toilet paper, etc.)
_____ Production files

Guilds and Unions

SCREEN ACTORS GUILD		323/954-1600
5757 Wilshire Boulevard		
Los Angeles, CA 90036	Station 12	323/549-6794
	Station 12 Fax	323/549-6792
	Contracts	323/549-6835
	Membership	323/549-6768
	Residuals	323/549-6505
	Taft-Hartley	323/549-6770
	Artist Agents	323/549-6737
DIRECTORS GUILD OF AMERICA		310/289-2000
7920 Sunset Boulevard	Fax	310/289-2029
Los Angeles, CA 90046	Artist Agents	213/851-3671
ART DIRECTORS LOCAL 876		818/762-9995
AMERICAN FEDERATION OF MUSICIANS		
LOCAL 47		323/462-2161
CAMERA LOCAL 659		323/876-0160
COSTUME DESIGNERS GUILD IA 892		818/905-1557
COSTUMERS IA 705		323/851-0220
I.B.T. LOCAL 399 /TEAMSTERS		818/985-7374
Call Board		818/985-7550
I.A.T.S.E. LOCAL 122		619/640-0042

EDITORS IA 776	323/876-4770
FIRST AID IA 767	310/352-4485
LIGHTING IA 728	818/891-0728
MAKEUP/HAIR IA 706	818/984-1700
Fax	818/980-8561
SCENIC ARTISTS IA 816	323/965-0957
SCRIPT SUPERVISORS IA 871	818/509-7871
SET DECORATORS LOCAL 44	818/769-2500
SET DESIGNERS IA 847	818/784-6555
SET PAINTERS IA 729	818/842-7729
SOUND TECHNICIANS IA 695	818/985-9204
STUDIO GRIPS IA 80	818/526-0700
STUDIO TEACHERS	310/652-5330

Estimated Cost Report

The following page is an Estimated Cost Report. This form is used by the production accountant to update the cost of a film on a daily basis. It shows if the project is over- or underbudget.

ESTIMATED PRODUCTION COST REPORT

SERIES	PRODUCTION #	TITLE	DIRECTOR
PRODUCTION MANAGER	PATTERN		BUDGET THIS SHOW
ESTIMATOR	CURRENT UNDER (OVER) PATTERN		CURRENT UNDER (OVER) BUDGET

STAGE ☐
LOCAL LOCATION ☐
DISTANT LOCATION ☐

DATE OF REPORT
DATE OF SHOOTING

DAY	EST FINAL COST	HOURS BUD	ACTUAL HOURS WORKED	SCHED PAGES	PAGES SHOT
1ST					
2ND					
3RD					
4TH					
5TH					
6TH					
7TH					
8TH					
9TH					
10TH					
11TH					
12TH					
13TH					
14TH					
15TH					
16TH					
17TH					
18TH					
19TH					

NOTES	DAILY TOTALS	EPISODE TOTALS
LABOR VARIANCES		
CREW		
CREW MEAL PENALTIES		
CREW O.T.		
DRIVER O.T.		
CAST		
CAST MEAL PENALTIES		
CAST O.T.		
STUNTS		
STUNT ADJ		
STUNT O.T.		
STANDINS/EXTRAS		
EXTRAS O.T.		
NON LABOR VARIANCES		
FILM FOOTAGE - RAW STOCK		
FILM DEVELOP - PRINT/TRANSFERS		
CAMERA RENTALS		
GRIP RENTALS		
ELECTRIC RENTALS		
PROPS		
LOCATIONS		
WARDROBE		
CATERING		
SET DRESSING		
SET CONSTRUCTION		
VEHICLE RENTALS		
PICTURE CARS		
TOTALS	0	0

Daily Production Report

The following two pages are the front and back of the Daily Production Report. This is an extremely important document for every production company. It is an accurate record of what took place on that day on the shooting company. It lists all of the cast and crew, their "in" times and "out" times, lunch breaks, minutes of film shot, scene numbers, amount of film used, numbers of extras, time of first shot of the day, shooting call, wrap time, and anything out of the ordinary that occurred during the shooting day.

All of the above is used to compute wages and may also be used should any disputes with unions come up at a later date.

DAILY PRODUCTION REPORT

		1st Unit	2nd Unit	Reh.	Test	Travel	Holidays	Change-Over	Retakes& Add.Scs.	Total	SCHEDULE	
	No. Days Scheduled										Ahead	
	No. Days Actual										Behind	

Title _____ Prod. # _____ Date: _____

Producer _____ Director _____

Date Started _____ Sch. Finish Date _____ Est. Finish Date _____

Sets _____

Locations _____

Crew Call _____ Shooting Call _____ First Shot _____ Lunch _____

First Shot After Lunch _____ Dinner _____ Till _____

Company Dismissed: At Studio _____ On Location _____ Last Person Out _____

SCRIPT SCENES AND PAGES			MINUTES	SET-UPS	ADDED SCENES	RETAKES	
							SCENES
	SCENES	PAGES	Prev.	Prev.	Prev.	Prev.	
			Today	Today	Today	Today	
Script			Total	Total	Total	Total	
Taken Prev.			Scene No.				SOUND ROLLS
Taken Today							Prev.
Total to Date			Added Scenes				Today
To be Taken			Retakes				Total

FILM USE	5296 GOOD	5296 NO GOOD	5296 WASTE	5296 TOTAL USED	5296 FILM INVENTORY	
Prev.					Starting Inventory	
					Received +	
Today					Shortends +	
					Loaded -	
To Date					On Hand	
FILM USE	5297 GOOD	5297 NO GOOD	5297 WASTE	5297 TOTAL USED	5297 FILM INVENTORY	
Prev.					Starting Inventory	
					Received +	
Today					Shortends+	
					Loaded -	
To Date					On Hand	
FILM USE	5248 GOOD	5248 NO GOOD	5248 WASTE	5248 TOTAL USED	5248 FILM INVENTORY	
Prev.					Starting Inventory	
					Received +	
Today					Shortends +	
					Loaded -	
To Date					On Hand	
FILM USE	TOTAL GOOD	TOTAL NO GOOD	TOTAL WASTE	TOTAL USED	TOTAL FILM INVENTORY	
Prev.					Starting Inventory	
					Received +	
Today					Shortends+	
					Loaded -	
To Date					On Hand	

CAST	Test-T	W H	MAKEUP	WORK TIME		MEALS		NBD	TRAVEL TIME			
Worked-W Rehearse-R		S F	Report	Report	Dismiss			X	Leave	Arrive	Leave	Arrive
Started-S Hold-H		R T	to	on	on	Out	In		for	on	from	at
Travel-TR Finished-F		TR	Makeup	Set	Set				Location	Location	Location	Hotel

EXTRA TALENT

No.	Rate	1st Call	Final Dismiss	Adj.	O.T.	Type	No.	Rate	1st Call	Final Dismiss	Adj.	O.T.	Type

Assistant Directors _____ Production Manager _____

TITLE: **PRODUCTION REPORT**   Prod #   **DAY**   **DATE**

PRODUCTION	IN	OUT	PROPS	IN	OUT
Director	O/C		Property Master	O/C	
UPM	O/C		Assistant Prop	O/C	
First Assistant Director			Props		
2nd Asst Director			Prop Buyer	O/C	
2nd 2nd Asst Director			Prop Intern	O/C	
Key Production Assistant			WARDROBE		
Production Assistant			Costume Designer	O/C	
Production Assistant			Asst Costume Designer	O/C	
SCRIPT			Wardrobe Supervisor		
Script Supervisor			Costumer		
CAMERA			Seamstress	O/C	
Director of Photography			Wardrobe Asst		
Camera Operator			MAKE-UP / HAIR		
"B" Camera Operator			Key Make-up Artist		
1st Assistant Camera			Makeup Artist		
"B" Camera 1st Asst Camera			Add. Makeup Artist		
2nd Assistant Camera			Key Hair Stylist		
SOUND			Add. Hair Stylist		
Sound Mixer			LOCATIONS		
Boom Operator			Location Manager	O/C	
Cableman			Asst Location Manager		
ELECTRIC			Location Assistant		
Gaffer			Police		
Best Boy			CATERING + KEN & ARTS / CRAFT SERVICE		
Electrician			Crew Lunches		
Electrician			Extras Lunches		
Electrician			2nd Meals		
Electrician			Craft Service		
Add Electrician			SET OPERATIONS		
GRIP			SPFX Coord.		
Key Grip			Construction Coordinator	O/C	
Best Boy Grip			Construction Foreman	O/C	
Dolly Grip			Construction Buyer	O/C	
Dolly Grip			Lead Painter	O/C	
Grip			On Set Painter		
Grip			MEDIC		
Add Grips			Medic		
OFFICE			TRANSPORTATION DEPARTMENT		
Prod Coord	O/C		Transportation Coordinator		
Asst. Prod. Coord.	O/C		Transportation Captain		
Office P.A.	O/C		Co-Captain / Prop Truck		
ACCOUNTING			Star Trailer / A. Griffith		
Accountant	O/C		Honeywagon		
Assistant Accountant	O/C		Genny / Mechanic		
Accounting Assistant	O/C		Star Tlr / Fuel Truck		
ART DEPARTMENT			Electric		
Production Designer	O/C		Star Trailer		O/C
Set Decorator	O/C		Hair / Mu Trailer		O/C
Assistant Art Director	O/C		Grip Truck		O/C
Leadman	O/C		Wardrobe Trailer		O/C
Art Dept. Asst.	O/C		Van		O/C
Set Buyer	O/C		Van		O/C
Dresser	O/C		Van		O/C
Set Dresser P.A.	O/C		Camera Truck		O/C
On Set Dresser					
NOTES			MORE NOTES		

SPECIAL EQUIPMENT

Call Sheet

This page and the following page show the front and back of the Call Sheet. The Call Sheet is published on a daily basis, one day in advance (so that Tuesday's schedule is available some time on Monday, for example). The Call Sheet provides a full description of what will be shot, where it will be shot, who will be in each scene, and what crew and equipment will be needed.

Productions		**CALL SHEET**				MON Mar. 20, 2000		
Exec Prods.:						2ND Day out of: 7		
Supervising Prod.:		Producer:						
Director		**1ST UNIT**				**CREW CALL:**		
Prod Office #		Prod # 156				**SHOOTING CALL:**		
Fax#		**CREW PARKING:**						
SET DESCRIPTION			**SCENES**	**CAST**	**D/N**	**PGS**	**LOCATION**	
							City Studios	
							7700 Balboa Blvd	
							VAN NUYS	
							"	
							"	
							"	
							"	
							"	
							"	
							"	
							"	
							"	
					Total Pages			
CAST & DAY PLAYERS		**PART OF**	**ST**	**MAKEUP**	**ON SET**		**REMARKS**	
1.								
2.							PU @	
3.							Report to STAGE	
4.							"	
							"	
							CREW PARKING	
							"	
							"	
							"	
							"	
							"	
ATMOSPHERE & STAND INS				**SPECIAL INSTRUCTIONS**				
ADVANCE SHOOTING SCHEDULE								
1ST AD	Key 2ND AD	2ND 2ND AD		UPM				
Production office								

1ST UNIT   PROD #156   **DATE MON MAR 20, 2000**

PRODUCTION		
1	Director	
1	U.P.M.	O/C
1	1st A.D.	
1	2nd A.D.	
1	2ND 2ND AD	
1	DGA Trainee	
1	Script Supr	

CAMERA		
1	DP	
1	Camera Op	
1	1ST AC	
	B CAM Op	
1	1ST AC B Cam	
1	2ND AC	
1	Loader	
X	Cameras	
1	SteadiCam Op	
	Still Photog	
1	Crane AC	

GRIP		
1	Key Grip	
1	Best Boy Grip	"
1	Dolly Grip	"
3	Grips	"
		"
3	Xtra Grips	"
	ADD Grip	
X	Crab Dolly	TRK
	Rigging Grips	

ELECTRICAL		
1	Gaffer	
1	Best Boy Elec	"
4	Lamp Op.	"
2	Xtra Elec	"
	Rigging Elec	
	ADD Elec	

SPECIAL EFFECTS		
1	SFX	

SOUND/VIDEO		
1	Sound Mixer	
1	Boom Op	"
1	Utility Sound T.	
X	Walkie Talkies	TRK

ART DEPT		
1	Prod. Designer	O/C

SET DRESSING		
1	Set Decorator	O/C
1	Leadman	"
3	Set Dressers	"
		"
	Greensman	

CONSTRUCTION		
1	Const. Coord.	O/C
1	Const. Foreman	"
1	Prop Foreman	"
1	Painter Foreman	"
1	Set Painter	"
1	Prop Gang Boss	"
1	Prop Maker	"
1	Labor Foreman	"
1	Laborer	"

PROPERTY		
1	Prop Master	O/C
1	Prop Master	
1	Prop Asst	"

WARDROBE		
1	Costume Supr	O/C
1	Men's Costumer	"
1	Mr DVD Ward	O/C
1	Set Costumer	
		"
1	Set Cost	"
	Xtra Costume	
1	Tailor	O/C

MU/HAIR		
1	Makeup	
1	Makeup	
	Xtra MakeUp	
1	Makeup	
1	Hair Stylist	
1	Hair Stylist	
	Xtra Hair	

EDITORIAL		
1	Editor	O/C
1	Editor	"
1	Asst. editor	"
1	Asst. Editor	"
1	Post Coord	"
1	Prod Acct	"
1	Asst Acct	"
1	Payroll	"

SET OPERATIONS		
1	Craft Service	
1	X Craft Service	"
1	Medic	

LOCATION		
1	Loc. Mgr.	O/C
X	Police	Per Loc
X	Security	"
X	FSO	"

MISCELLANOUS		
	Computer Tech	
	Med Tech	
	Welfare Worker	

PRODUCTION OFFICE		
1	Prod Coord	O/C
1	Asst to Prod	"
1	Sec to UPM	"
1	PA	"
1	Assoc. Prod	"
1	Script Coord	"
1	Assistant	"

TRANSPORTATION		
1	Coordinator	O/C
1	Captian	"
1	Electric Truck w Tow Plant	
1	Grip Truck	
1	Camera Truck	
1	Prop Truck	
X	Crew Cabs	
1	Fueler	
1	Honeywagon (8)	
X	Maxivans	
3	Single Rm Star Trailers	
X	Dbl Rm Star Trailer	
1	DVD Cast Trailer	
1	MU Trailer	
1	Ward Trailer	
X	Set Dressing Trucks	
1	Const Crew Cab	
1	DVD Van	
2	3-Room Trailers	
1	Crane	OC
1	EZ Power	"
1	AC Unit	

ANIMALS		

PICTURE CARS		

CATERING		
X	Breakfast on Loc Rdy @	
	Lunches Rdy @	WN
	(Mario's Catering-Arturo/Victor)	
	Xtra Servers	

Station 12 Procedures

...arance though Station 12 determines whether a S.A.G. actor or stunt ...erformer is in good standing (dues paid, etc.). Even if you know the actor worked last week, you must clear him through Station 12. Failure to clear an actor can result in expensive fines.

All actors and stunt performers, whether members of S.A.G. or not, must be cleared through S.A.G. Station 12 *prior* to employment. This includes Taft-Hartley Waiver applications. Tell Station 12 that the actor is a non-member for whom you will be filing a Taft-Hartley.

TO CALL:
- The Station 12 direct dial is 213/549-6794. Fax: 213/549-6792
- It is important to write down the name of the Station 12 representative from whom you request clearances.
- You will be asked the following questions:
  - Your name
  - The name of the signatory company
  - The name of the movie
  - The address to which the clearance paperwork should be sent
  - The location of the shoot

For each actor you wish to clear, you will need to provide the following:
- The actor's name as listed with the Guild
- The actor's Social Security number
- The start date for the actor

The Station 12 representative will inform you whether the actor is cleared for work or not.

→ If YES, make sure you have the name of the representative who has given you verbal clearance. *Written clearance will follow and should be filed with the actor's contract and the talent memo.*

If NO, contact the actor and inform him that he is not clear with S.A.G. (If you cannot reach the Actor, contact his agent.) The actor must contact S.A.G., determine why he cannot be cleared, and rectify the situation. Once the actor has cleared up his status with S.A.G., run his name through Station 12 again.

DO NOT USE AN UNCLEARED ACTOR OR STUNT PERFORMER.

Taft-Hartley Procedure

Before hiring anyone for S.A.G. work, you must check membership status by contacting S.A.G.'s Station 12.

- A TAFT-HARTLEY APPLICATION MUST BE FILED ON THE SAG FORM. It must be completed and filed within fifteen consecutive days (including weekends) from the first day of employment (twenty-five days on overnight locations). S.A.G. allows no grace period in this matter.

- A résumé must be submitted with the application.

- In the application, state the exact circumstance of hire:
  - Station 12 was notified.
  - The actor in question intends to pursue an acting career in the motion picture industry.
  - No S.A.G. member met the qualifications of the producer. (It is not sufficient to simply state that the actor was the best for the role.)

- Your Assistant Director must notify casting or the production office immediately should the director give a background extra a non-script line or stunt, or use him or her to replace a no-show. These must be reported on a Taft-Hartley application.

- There is a separate fine involved when a member of the production staff is hired as a non-S.A.G. actor. Check with S.A.G. Labor Relations for proper guidelines.

Even when a Taft-Hartley is granted, the production company will still be levied a Preference of Employment fine for not hiring a S.A.G. member, unless the applicant is/are:

- A member of named or famous specialty group (i.e., Elton John)
- A person portraying himself (e.g., Bill Clinton)
- Extras adjusted for non-script lines
- Persons having special skills or abilities who uses said skills in the motion picture
- Children under 18 (if a child is under 4 years old, you do not have to file a Taft-Hartley)
- The owner/operator of a special or unique vehicle
- Qualified professional actors
- Military or government personnel

#15
4/30/99

SCREEN ACTORS GUILD
TAFT/HARTLEY REPORT

Resume ____
Photo ____

**Please be advised that it is the Producer's responsibility to complete
this report in its entirety or it will be returned for completion.**

EMPLOYEE INFORMATION

Name: _____   SS#: _____

Address: _____   Date of Birth: _____

City/State: _____ Zip: _____   Phone: _____

EMPLOYER INFORMATION

Name: _____   Phone: _____

Address: _____ City: _____   State: _____ Zip: _____

Check one: _____ Ad Agency   _____ Studio   _____ Production Co.   _____ Other: _____

EMPLOYMENT INFORMATION *(check one selection from each)*

CONTRACT TYPE	ENGAGEMENT CONTRACT	PERFORMER CATEGORY
____ TV/Theatrical	____ Daily	____ Actor ____ Stunt
____ Commercial	____ 3-Day	____ Singer ____ Other: _____
____ Industrial/Interactive	____ Weekly	

Work Date(s): _____   Salary: _____

Production Title: _____   Prod./Commercial. #: _____

Shooting Location(s) (City & State): _____

Reason for Hire (be specific): _____

_____

_____

Employer is aware of General Provision, Section 14 of the Screen Actors Guild Codified Basic Agreement of 1995 for Independent Producers, as amended, that applies to Theatrical and Television production; Schedule B of the 1997 Commercials Contract; and Section 13 of the 1996 Codified Industrial and Educational Contract, wherein Preference of Employment shall be given to qualified professional actors (except as otherwise stated). Employer will pay to the Guild, as liquidated damages, the sums indicated for each breach by the Employer of any provision of those sections.

Signature: _____   Date: _____

Print Name: _____ Producer / Casting Dir.   Phone: _____
                                     (circle one)

PLEASE BE CERTAIN RESUME LISTS ALL TRAINING AND/OR EXPERIENCE IN THE ENTERTAINMENT INDUSTRY. ATTACH PHOTO FOR PRINCIPAL TALENT.

PLEASE SUBMIT THIS REPORT TO THE TAFT/HARTLEY DEPARTMENT.
SCREEN ACTORS GUILD • 5757 WILSHIRE BLVD. • LOS ANGELES, CA 90036-3600 • FAX: (323) 549-6886

Actor's Daily Time Report

- S.A.G. requires an Actor's Daily Time Report (Exhibit G) to be completed, providing a written report of all the actor's hours, including those spent in travel, wardrobe, makeup, and on meal breaks. (Sample enclosed on the following page.)
- The report must be signed by the actor at the end of the day.
- The Unit Production Manager must also sign the completed report.
- A copy should be kept with the original Production Report in the production files.
- *Send the original to S.A.G.* Failure to submit accurate and timely reports will result in fines and/or other S.A.G. action.

SCREEN ACTORS GUILD PERFORMERS PRODUCTION TIME REPORT

17

Exhibit G

Picture Title _____ Prod. No. _____ Date _____ Contact _____ Phone No. ( ) _____

Shooting Location _____

Please Complete in Ink

Is Today a Designated Day Off? * Yes ___ No ___

CAST	PHONE# CHARACTER:	WORK-W START-S REHEARSAL-R HOLD-H FITTING-FT TEST-T TRAVEL-TR FINISH-F W S R T H F T TR FT	WORK TIME Report Makeup W/Dbe.	Report on set	Dismiss on set	Dismiss Makeup Wardrobe	In Out ND Meal	MEALS 1st Meal Start / Finish	2nd Meal Start / Finish	TRAVEL TIME Leave for Location	Arrive on Location	Leave Location	Arrive at Studio	Stunt Adj.	Minors Tutoring Time	Wardrobe Provided No. of Outfits	Forced Call / MPV:	PERFORMER'S SIGNATURE

The next five forms are actor contracts.

The first is an Artist Deal Memo. This is filled out by the casting department, and copies are sent to accounting and the production office.

The second is a sample of an Actor's Day Player Contract. This form is used for actors who are hired for one or two days of work.

The third is an Actor's Three-Day or Weekly Contract and is used for those actors who are hired for three or more days of work.

The fourth is an Actor's Loan-out Agreement. This is for actors who have their own personal corporations.

The last deals with actors' billing and credit placement.

** SAMPLE **

ARTIST DEAL MEMO

CASTING DIRECTORS: _____

PROJECT: _____

PROJECT #: _____
DATE: _____

ARTIST'S NAME: _____

SS#: _____

LOAN-OUT CORP: _____

FED ID#: _____

ADDRESS: _____

CITY/STATE/ZIP: _____

OTHER ADDRESS OR CONTACT: _____

TELEPHONE: _____

SERVICE: _____

ROLE: _____

TRAVEL DATE: _____

START DATE: _____

COMPENSATION: _____

BILLING: _____

OTHER TERMS (LOOPING, REHEARSAL, 2ND RUN, ETC.): _____

TRANSPORTATION: _____

HOTEL & PER DIEM: _____

AGENT INFO: _____

ACTORS TELEVISION MOTION PICTURE
DAY PLAYERS CONTRACT

Producer		Date of Agreement	
Player		Date Employment Starts	
Player's Address		Name of Series	
Player's Telephone No.		Production Number & Episode Title	
Social Security No.		Role	
Weekly Conversion Rate		Daily Rate	

1. This agreement covers the employment of the above-named Player by Producer in the above production, produced primarily for exhibition over free television (herein "photoplay"), and at the rate of compensation set forth above and is subject to and shall include, for the benefit of Player and Producer, all of the applicable provisions and conditions contained or provided for in the Screen Actors Guild Television Agreement (herein called the "Television Agreement"). Player's employment shall include performance in non-commercial openings, closings, bridges, etc., and no added compensation shall be payable to Player so long as such are used in the role and episode covered hereunder in which Player appears; for other use, Player shall be paid the added minimum compensation. if any, required under the provisions of the Television Agreement.

2. Producer shall have all the rights in and to the results and proceeds of Player's services rendered hereunder, as are provided with respect to "photoplays" in the Producer-Screen Actors Guild Codified Basic Agreement, and the unlimited right throughout the world to telecast the photoplay and exhibit the photoplay theatrically and in Supplemental Markets in accordance with the terms and conditions of the Television Agreement. Producer shall have the right to use Player's name, voice and likeness in connection with the photoplay and series and in the advertising, publicizing or other exploitation thereof by any means now or hereafter known. If such use is in connection with any merchandising or publishing activities, including covers for phonograph albums and books commercially published for sale to the public, Player hereby consents thereto and Producer shall pay Player 5% of the net receipts (after deducting a 50% distributor fee plus Producer's expenses) derived from such activities; provided, however, that if Player's name, voice or likeness is used jointly with that of other members of the cast, then Player's aforesaid percentage shall be divided by the number of cast members, including Player, whose names, voices or likenesses are used.

3. If the photoplay is rerun on television in the United States or Canada and contains any of the results and proceeds of Player's services, Player will be paid the minimum compensation prescribed therefor by the Television Agreement.

4. If there is foreign telecasting of the photoplay as defined in Section 18(c) of the Television Agreement, and such photoplay contains any of the results and proceeds of Player's services, Player will be paid the amount in the blank space below for each day of employment hereunder, or if such blank space is not filled in. then Player will be paid the minimum additional compensation prescribed therefor by the Television Agreement.
$_____

5. If the photoplay is exhibited theatrically anywhere in the world and contains any of the results and proceeds of Player's services, Player will be paid for each day of employment hereunder $_____, or, if this blank is not filled in, then Player will be paid the minimum additional compensation prescribed therefor by the Television Agreement.

6. If the photoplay is exhibited in Supplemental Markets anywhere in the world and contains any of the results and proceeds of Player's services, Player will be paid minimum Supplemental Markets fees in accordance with Section 20 of the Television Agreement.

7. Producer may require Player to perform in a television trailer during the term hereof (whether to promote a single episode or a television series) and for such services Player shall be entitled to the additional minimum compensation provided in Section 35 of the Television Agreement. If Player initials this paragraph in the space herein provided, Player hereby authorizes Producer to use portions of film clips and/or sound track of Player's services in the above photoplay as a trailer to promote another episode or the television series as a whole, upon payment to Player of the minimum additional compensation, if any, provided in Section 35 of the Television Agreement. If not, and Player would be entitled to any additional compensation for a contemplated use of a trailer pursuant to Section 35 of the Television Agreement, then prior to such use Producer shall bargain with Player for the additional compensation to be paid therefor. Notwithstanding the foregoing, if Player is engaged hereunder at a salary equivalent to or more than $2,000.00 per week, Producer shall have the right to utilize film clips or sound track of Player's services in trailers and/or may require Player to perform in trailers during the term hereof (whether such trailers are used to promote a single episode or to promote the television series) and Player shall not be entitled to any additional compensation therefor.

Initial

8. Player acknowledges that it is a crime to accept or pay any money, service or other valuable consideration for the inclusion of any plug, reference, product identification or other matter as a part of a television program unless there is full disclosure as required by the applicable sections of the Federal Communications Act. Player will not accept or pay any such consideration or agree to do so, and any breach of such undertaking will give Producer the right to terminate this agreement.

9. Time cards are available on the set for initialing or signature at the end of each day.

IN WITNESS WHEREOF, the parties hereto have executed this agreement on the day and year first above written.

For Screen Credit purposes, Player's name shall appear as follows:

_____
(please print clearly)

_____
Player

(Producer)
By: _____

Form #761 (Rev. 5/95) Blank

ACTORS TELEVISION MOTION PICTURE CONTRACT
MINIMUM THREE-DAY OR WEEKLY

Producer	Date of Agreement / Starting Date On or about**
Player	Series
Role	Production Title & Number
Player's Address	Guaranteed Employment Period
Player's Telephone / Social Security Number	Guaranteed Compensation (see also Paragraph 4)

1. EMPLOYMENT: This agreement covers the employment of the above-named Player by Producer in the above production, produced primarily for exhibition over free television (herein "photoplay"), and is subject to and shall include, for the benefit of Player and Producer, all of the applicable provisions and conditions contained or provided for in the Screen Actors Guild Television Agreement (herein called the "Television Agreement"). Player's employment shall include performance in non-commercial openings, closings, bridges, etc., and no added compensation shall be payable to Player so long as such are used in the role and episode covered hereunder in which Player appears; for other use, Player shall be paid the added minimum compensation, if any, required under the provisions of the Television Agreement.

2. RIGHTS: Producer shall have all the rights in and to the results and proceeds of Player's services rendered hereunder, as are provided with respect to "photoplays" in the Producer-Screen Actors Guild Codified Basic Agreement, and shall have the unlimited right throughout the world to telecast the photoplay and exhibit the photoplay theatrically and in Supplemental Markets in accordance with the terms and conditions of the Television Agreement.

3. SALARY: Producer will pay to Player, and Player agrees to accept the Guaranteed Compensation for the Guaranteed Employment Period, and pro rata thereof for each additional day thereafter.

4. RERUNS: If the photoplay is rerun on television in the United States or Canada and contains any of the results and proceeds of Player's services, Player will be paid the minimum additional compensation prescribed therefor by the Television Agreement. The Guaranteed Compensation provided above includes the following for the reruns indicated: *_____

_____

5. FOREIGN TELECASTING: If there is foreign telecasting of the photoplay as defined in Section 18(c) of the Television Agreement, and such photoplay contains any of the results and proceeds of Player's services, Player will be paid the minimum additional compensation prescribed therefor by the Television Agreement.

6. THEATRICAL EXHIBITION: If the photoplay is exhibited theatrically anywhere in the world and contains any of the results and proceeds of Player's services, Player will be paid the minimum additional compensation prescribed therefor by the Television Agreement.

7. SUPPLEMENTAL MARKETS: If the photoplay is exhibited in Supplemental Markets anywhere in the world and contains any of the results and proceeds of Player's services, Player will be paid minimum Supplemental Markets fees in accordance with Section 20 of the Television Agreement.

8. TERM: The term of employment hereunder shall begin on the date hereinabove specified and shall continue thereafter until completion of the photography and recordation of said role.

9. ARBITRATION OF DISPUTES: Should any dispute or controversy arise between the parties hereto with reference to this contract, or the employment herein provided for, such dispute or controversy shall be settled and determined by conciliation and arbitration in accordance with and to the extent provided in the conciliation and arbitration provisions of the Television Agreement, and such provisions are hereby referred to and by such reference incorporated herein and made a part of this agreement with the same effect as though the same were set forth herein in detail.

10. PLAYER'S ADDRESS: All notices which Producer is required or may desire to give to Player may be given either by mailing the same addressed to Player, or such notice may be given to Player personally, either orally or in writing.

11. PLAYER'S TELEPHONE: Player must keep Producer's casting office or the assistant director of said photoplay advised as to where the Player may be reached by telephone without unreasonable delay.

12. FURNISHING OF WARDROBE: Player agrees to furnish all modern wardrobe and wearing apparel reasonably necessary for the portrayal of said role; it being agreed, however, that should so-called "character" or "period" costumes be required, Producer shall supply the same.

13. TRAILERS: Producer may require Player to perform in a television trailer during the term hereof (whether to promote a single episode or a television series) and for such services Player shall be entitled to the additional minimum compensation, if any, provided in Section 35 of the Television Agreement. If Player initials this paragraph in the space herein provided, Player hereby authorizes Producer to use portions of film clips and/or sound track of Player's services in the above photoplay as a trailer to promote another episode or the television series as a whole, upon payment to Player of the minimum additional compensation, if any, provided in Section 35 of the Television Agreement. If not, and Player would be entitled to any additional compensation for a contemplated use of a trailer pursuant to Section 35 of the Television Agreement, then prior to such use Producer shall bargain with Player for the additional compensation to be paid therefor. Not-withstanding the foregoing, if Player is engaged hereunder at a salary equivalent to or more than $2,000.00 per week, Producer shall have the right to utilize film clips or sound track of Player's services in trailers and/or may require Player to perform in trailers during the term hereof (whether such trailers are used to promote a single episode or to promote the television series) and Player shall not be entitled to any additional compensation therefor.

Initial [   ]

14. NAME AND LIKENESS; MERCHANDISING AND PUBLICATIONS: Producer shall have the right to use Player's name, voice and likeness in connection with the photoplay and series and in the advertising, publicizing or other exploitation thereof by any means now or hereafter known. If such use is in connection with any merchandising or publishing activities, including covers for phonograph albums and books commercially published for sale to the public, Player hereby consents thereto and Producer shall pay Player 5% of the net receipts (after deducting a 50% distributor fee plus Producer's expenses) derived from such activities; provided, however, that if Player's name, voice or likeness is used jointly with that of other members of the cast, then Player's aforesaid percentage shall be divided by the number of cast members, including Player, whose names, voices or likenesses are used.

15. PLUGOLA AND PAYOLA: Player acknowledges that it is a crime to accept or pay any money, service or other valuable consideration for the inclusion of any plug, reference, product identification or other matter as a part of a television program unless there is full disclosure as required by the applicable sections of the Federal Communications Act. Player will not accept or pay any such consideration or agree to do so, and any breach of such undertaking will give Producer the right to terminate this agreement.

16. TIME CARDS: Time cards are available on the set for initialing or signature at the end of each day.

IN WITNESS WHEREOF, the parties hereto have executed this agreement on the day and year first above written.

For Screen Credit purposes, Player's name shall appear as follows:

_____   (Producer)
(please print clearly)

Player _____   By _____

* Advance Payments for residuals shall be subject to the limitations thereon set forth in the Television Agreement.
** The "on or about" clause may only be used when the contract is delivered to Player at least seven (7) days before the starting date.
(Player may not waive any provisions of the foregoing contract without the written consent of the Screen Actors Guild, Inc.)

Form #763 (Rev. 5/95)

SAG LOANOUT AGREEMENT

AGREEMENT made this _____ day of _____, 19 ____, by and between
(herein called "Producer") and_____
_____ (herein called "Contractor"), is as follows:

1.   Contractor hereby agrees to loan to Producer the services of _____
(herein called "Player") as an Actor in connection with the program entitled _____ .
of the program series entitled _____

2.   Reference is hereby made to that certain employment agreement, a copy of which is attached hereto as Exhibit "A" and hereby made a part hereof. All provisions of Exhibit "A" shall be deemed included as part of this agreement as though fully set forth herein; it being understood, however, that:

   (a)   wherever reference is made to payments to Player, such reference shall be deemed to refer to payments to Contractor;

   (b)   notwithstanding anything to the contrary contained in Exhibit "A" attached hereto, for the purpose of computing over-time, residual and all other payments to Contractor (other than initial compensation), Producer's obligation shall be based upon Contractor's minimum obligation to Player under the Screen Actors Guild Television Agreement (herein called the "Television Agreement"); provided, however, in no event shall Producer be required to make payments in excess of the minimum Television Agreement payments which it would have been obligated to make had Producer employed Player directly;

   (c)   all rights granted by Player hereunder shall be deemed granted by Contractor as well, and all warranties, agreements, duties, liabilities, obligations and indemnifications given, made and/or assumed by Player shall be deemed given, made and/or assumed by Contractor as well.

3.   As compensation in full for services of Player to be furnished by Contractor hereunder and for all rights granted and agreed to be granted herein, Producer will pay to Contractor directly, without payroll deductions of any kind whatsoever, except as may be required by any federal, state or local law, regulation or ordinance, all monies which may become due and payable pursuant to Exhibit "A", as, when and to the extent such payments become payable.

4.   The parties hereto are entering into this agreement as independent contractors, and no partnership or joint venture or other association shall be deemed created by this agreement. Contractor will have the entire responsibility of employer of Player and will discharge all of the obligations of employer under any federal, state or local laws, regulations or orders now or hereafter in force, including, but not limited to, those relating to taxes, unemployment compensation or insurance, social security, disability pensions, tax withholding and including the filing of all returns and reports required of employer and the payment of all taxes, assessments and contributions and other sums required of employer. Contractor will deduct and withhold from the consideration payable by Contractor to Player all amounts required to be deducted and withheld under employment agreements under the provisions of any statute, regulation, ordinance or order requiring the withholding or deduction of compensation. Further, it is agreed that Producer will pay directly all contributions to the Screen Actors Guild-Producers Pension and Welfare Plans on behalf of Contractor required by reason of the services rendered hereunder by Player. It is understood and agreed, however, that Producer's maximum obligation for such payment shall be subject to such limitations thereon as are set forth in the current Television Agreement.

5.   (a) Contractor warrants that Player is under an exclusive services contract with Contractor and will continue to be throughout the term of this agreement; that Contractor has and will have the right to furnish Player's services to Producer hereunder for the term of this agreement; and that Contractor has and will have the right to grant all rights of whatsoever nature in and to the results and proceeds of such services.

   (b) Contractor warrants that Player is or will become, and shall remain during the term of this agreement, a member in good standing of each labor union having jurisdiction over Player's services with which Producer may at any time have agreement(s) lawfully requiring such union membership.

   (c) Contractor warrants that Contractor will discharge all duties as employer of Player under and pursuant to the terms of the Television Agreement.

   (d) Contractor hereby agrees to indemnify and hold harmless Producer, its successors, transferees, assigns and licensees, and the respective agents, associates, directors, officers and employees of each, free and clear from and against any and all damages, costs, expenses, claims and causes of action (including, but not limited to, reasonable attorneys' fees and costs in the defense and disposition of such matters) in any way arising by reason of (i) any claim for compensation by Player and/or claims for payment by any third party related in any way to Player's employment by Contractor, (ii) any failure on Contractor's part to make or pay the required deductions and/or withholdings from the compensation payable by Contractor to Player, and/or (iii) the breach by Contractor and/or Player of any provision, agreement and/or warranty contained in this agreement.

   (e) Notwithstanding anything to the contrary set forth above, Contractor and Player hereby warrant and represent that for the purpose of any applicable workers' compensation statutes (the "Statutes"): the employment relationship exists between Producer and Player; Player is Producer's special employee; Producer is Player's special employer; and Contractor is Player's general employer (as the terms "Special employee", "special employer" and "general employer" are understood for purposes of the Statutes). In this regard, Contractor and Player warrant and represent that (a) any rights and remedies of Player (or Player's heirs, executors or administratorsharm) against Producer (or Producer's principals, officers, agents and/or employees, including, without limitation, any other special employee of Producer) by reason of any injury, illness, disability or death of Player (collectively "harm to Player") covered by the statutes and arising out of and in the course of Player's services hereunder, will be limited to those rights and remedies provided under the Statutes; (b) Producer (and Producer's principals, officers, agents, and/or employees, including, without limitation, any other special employee of Producer) shall have no obligation or liability to Contractor (or Contractor's principals, assignees, licensees, transferees or designees) by reason of harm to Player; and (c) neither Contractor nor Player (or the successors in interest of either) shall assert any claim arising out of harm to Player against any other entity which furnishes to Producer the services of any other special employee. Producer and Contractor hereby make any election whatsoever necessary to render the Statutes applicable to Producer's engagement of Contractor and/or to Player's services hereunder. Producer, Contractor and Player expressly agree that the California Worker's compensation Act shall apply to Player's services hereunder.

   (f) The warranties and indemnities set forth herein are in addition to, and not in limitation of, those contained in Exhibit "A."

IN WITNESS WHEREOF, the parties hereto have executed this agreement on the day and year first above written.

CONTRACTOR'S PLACE OF INCORPORATION, IF DIFFERENT
FROM CALIFORNIA:_____

CONTRACTOR:_____
                  FEDERAL ID #_____

                                                           _____
                                                           (Producer)
BY: _____   By: _____
         (SIGNATURE OF CORPORATE OFFICER)

The undersigned, _____ ("Player"), hereby acknowledges that Player has read and is familiar with each and every provision of this agreement, including Exhibit "A" attached thereto. Player hereby endorses and approves this agreement and agrees to be bound thereby and to perform all the terms and conditions thereof insofar as the same are to be performed by Player in the same manner as if Player had executed this agreement with Producer. Furthermore, Player acknowledges that Producer would not, without this endorsement and approval, have entered into said agreement.

                                                           _____
                                                           (Player)

RIDER ATTACHED TO AND HEREBY MADE
A PART OF THE AGREEMENT BETWEEN

_____

AND _____

DATED _____

1. <u>BILLING</u>:

Upon condition that Player fully and faithfully performs all of Player's obligations and covenants under this agreement, and that the photoplay as finally edited and released contains any of the results of Player's services, Producer agrees that Player shall receive the following billing on the positive prints of the original English language version of the photoplay, the style, nature and placement of which shall be within the sole discretion of Producer, subject only to such limitations as are expressly set forth herein, if any, and to such limitations as are imposed by applicable collective bargaining agreements.

In the event Player is accorded a designated credit placement, such placement shall apply only to the placement of Player's credit in relationship to other free lance performers (credit accorded regular series performers expressly excluded):

If the photoplay is combined with one or more other photoplays or is substantially cut or expanded, or is televised as a part of a television series other than the series for which originally intended or in which first televised, or exhibited in a different medium from that for which it was initially produced or on which it was first exhibited, Producer may make such changes in Player's credit and any other credits involved as Producer deems reasonable under the circumstances including but not limited to changes to resolve any conflicts in the credit requirements for such photoplays.

It is understood that no inadvertent or unintentional failure to give such billing, whether due to lack of time or otherwise, shall be deemed to be a breach of this agreement. Nothing herein contained shall be construed to prevent so-called "trailer", "teaser" or other advertising in connection with the photoplay without mentioning the name of Player. If Player shall have committed or does commit any act, or if Player shall have done or does anything which shall be an offense involving moral turpitude under federal, state or local laws, or which might tend to bring Player into public disrepute, contempt, scandal or ridicule, or which might tend to reflect unfavorably upon Producer, its assigns or licensees, including but not limited to, the sponsors, if any, or their advertising agencies, if any, of the photoplay, or otherwise injure the success of the photoplay, Producer shall have the right to delete the billing provided for herein from any broadcasts or other uses which are thereafter made of the photoplay.

2. <u>ADDITIONAL PROVISIONS</u>:

Initial Here	

Department of Justice Form

The following form is a federal government requirement and is self-explanatory.

U.S. Department of Justice
Immigration and Naturalization Service

OMB No. 1115-0136
Employment Eligibility Verification

Please read instructions carefully before completing this form. The instructions must be available during completion of this form. **ANTI-DISCRIMINATION NOTICE.** It is illegal to discriminate against work eligible individuals. Employers CANNOT specify which document(s) they will accept from an employee. The refusal to hire an individual because of a future expiration date may also constitute illegal discrimination.

Section 1. Employee Information and Verification. To be completed and signed by employee at the time employment begins

Print Name: Last	First	Middle Initial	Maiden Name

Address (Street Name and Number)	Apt. #	Date of Birth (month/day/year)

City	State	Zip Code	Social Security #

I am aware that federal law provides for imprisonment and/or fines for false statements or use of false documents in connection with the completion of this form.

I attest, under penalty of perjury, that I am (check one of the following):
☐ A citizen or national of the United States
☐ A Lawful Permanent Resident (Alien # A_____)
☐ An alien authorized to work until____/____/____
(Alien # or Admission #_____)

Employee's Signature _____   Date (month/day/year) _____

Preparer and/or Translator Certification. (To be completed and signed if Section 1 is prepared by a person other than the employee.) I attest, under penalty of perjury, that I have assisted in the completion of this form and that to the best of my knowledge the information is true and correct.

Preparer's/Translator's Signature	Print Name

Address (Street Name and Number, City, State, Zip Code)	Date (month/day/year)

Section 2. Employer Review and Verification. To be completed and signed by employer. Examine one document from List A OR examine one document from List B and one from List C as listed on the reverse of this form and record the title, number and expiration date, if any, of the document(s)

List A	OR	List B	AND	List C

Document title: _____
Issuing authority: _____
Document #: _____
Expiration Date (if any): ___/___/___
Document #: _____
Expiration Date (if any): ___/___/___

CERTIFICATION - I attest, under penalty of perjury, that I have examined the document(s) presented by the above-named employee, that the above-listed document(s) appear to be genuine and to relate to the employee named, that the employee began employment on (month/day/year) ___/___/___ and that to the best of my knowledge the employee is eligible to work in the United States. (State employment agencies may omit the date the employee began employment).

Signature of Employer or Authorized Representative	Print Name	Title

Business or Organization Name	Address (Street Name and Number, City, State, Zip Code)	Date (month/day/year)

Section 3. Updating and Reverification. To be completed and signed by employer

A. New Name (if applicable)	B. Date of rehire (month/day/year) (if applicable)

C. If employee's previous grant of work authorization has expired, provide the information below for the document that establishes current employment eligibility.

Document Title:_____ Document #:_____ Expiration Date (if any):___/___/___

I attest, under penalty of perjury, that to the best of my knowledge, this employee is eligible to work in the United States, and if the employee presented document(s), the document(s) I have examined appear to be genuine and to relate to the individual.

Signature of Employer or Authorized Representative	Date (month/day/year)

Form I-9 (Rev. 11-21-91) N

I-9 FORM - MUST BE COMPLETED PRIOR TO BEING PAID

The following four forms deal with below-the-line crew.

The first form is a sample of a crew time card and is self-explanatory.

The second form is for those individuals who, like some actors, have personal corporations. It confirms their employment with the producing company.

The third form is a straight employee start form.

The fourth form is for "box rentals." The gaffer, the key grip, and some key employees in wardrobe, makeup, and hairdressing will rent certain personal equipment, such as tools and supplies, to the producing company.

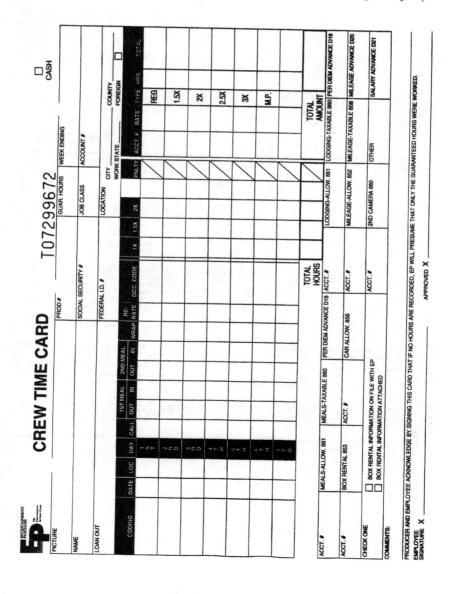

EP

LOAN-OUT
START/CLOSE FORM

PRODUCING COMPANY	PICTURE TITLE	ACCNT-MAJOR/MINOR

NAME OF LOAN-OUT CORPORATION	FEDERAL EMPLOYER'S I.D. NO.	START DATE	JOB CLASS	UNION NO.

ADDRESS

CHECK ONE:

DAILY EMPLOYEE ☐   WEEKLY EMPLOYEE ☐

CITY	STATE	ZIP CODE	TERMS OF EMPLOYMENT	STUDIO	LOCATION

NAME OF LOANED-OUT EMPLOYEE — RATE PER HOUR

SOCIAL SECURITY NUMBER - LOANED-OUT EMPLOYEE — RATE PER WEEK

GUARANTEED HOURS

STATE OF INCORPORATION	DATE INCORPORATED	IF RATE DOES NOT INCLUDE IDLE		PAY SATURDAY AT $ PAY SUNDAY AT $

STATE CORPORATE NUMBER — BOX RENTAL

CAR RENTAL

HAS CORPORATION QUALIFIED TO DO BUSINESS IN

CALIFORNIA   NEW YORK   FLORIDA

☐ YES   ☐ YES   ☐ YES
☐ NO   ☐ NO   ☐ NO

ENTER NAMES OF ALL STATES IN WHICH LOAN-OUT CORPORATION HAS QUALIFIED TO DO BUSINESS.

UNDER PENALTIES OF PERJURY, AS AN AUTHORIZED OFFICER OF THE ABOVE-STATED LOAN-OUT CORPORATION, I CERTIFY THAT, TO THE BEST OF MY KNOWLEDGE AND BELIEF, THE ABOVE-STATED INFORMATION CONCERNING THE LOAN-OUT CORPORATION IS TRUE, CORRECT AND COMPLETE. I HEREBY ACKNOWLEDGE RECEIPT OF "FACTS ABOUT WORKERS COMPENSATION" REQUIRED BY THE STATE OF CALIFORNIA TO BE PROVIDED TO ALL EMPLOYEES WORKING UNDER IT'S JURISDICTION.

SIGNATURE	DATE	TITLE OF AUTHORIZED OFFICER

Section 2. Employer Review and Verification. To be completed and signed by employer. Examine one document from List A OR examine one document from List B and one from List C as listed on the reverse of this form and record the title, number and expiration date, if any, of the document(s)

List A	OR	List B	AND	List C

Document title: _____

Issuing authority: _____

Document #: _____

Expiration Date (if any): ___/___/___   ___/___/___   ___/___/___

Document #: _____

Expiration Date (if any): ___/___/___

CERTIFICATION - I attest, under penalty of perjury, that I have examined the document(s) presented by the above-named employee, that the above-listed document(s) appear to be genuine and to relate to the employee named, that the employee began employment on (month/day/year) ___/___/___ and that to the best of my knowledge the employee is eligible to work in the United States. (State employment agencies may omit the date the employee began employment).

Signature of Employer or Authorized Representative	Print Name	Title
Business or Organization Name	Address (Street Name and Number, City, State, Zip Code)	Date (month/day/year)

Section 3. Updating and Reverification. To be completed and signed by employer

A. New Name (if applicable)	B. Date of rehire (month/day/year) (if applicable)

C. If employee's previous grant of work authorization has expired, provide the information below for the document that establishes current employment eligibility.

Document Title: _____   Document #: _____   Expiration Date (if any): ___/___/___

I attest, under penalty of perjury, that to the best of my knowledge, this employee is eligible to work in the United States, and if the employee presented document(s), the document(s) I have examined appear to be genuine and to relate to the individual.

Signature of Employer or Authorized Representative	Date (month/day/year)

Form I-9 (Rev. 11-21-91) N

START/CLOSE FORM

PRODUCING CO.	PICTURE TITLE		ACCT # MAJOR/MINOR
EMPLOYEE NAME	SOCIAL SECURITY NUMBER - -	UNION #	OCC CODE	JOB CLASS

EMPLOYEE ADDRESS	CITY	STATE	ZIP	SEX M F	TELEPHONE ( )

| ETHNIC CODE | 1 = WHITE 3 = HISPANIC 5 = NATIVE AMERICAN | START DATE |
| | 2 = BLACK 4 = ASIAN 6 = OTHER | |

NOTE: (This statement must be filled out prior to payment being made.)
UNDER THE PENALTIES OF PERJURY, I CERTIFY THAT I AM A RESIDENT OF THE STATE OF _____ .

WORK STATE/CITY/COUNTY

	TERMS OF EMPLOYMENT		DO NOT USE SHADED AREAS - FOR OFFICE USE ONLY		
DAILY EMPLOYEE	STUDIO RATE	GUAR HOURS	LOCATION RATE	GUAR HOURS	G/L CODING
HOURLY RATE *					
1.5x in excess of guar.					
2x in excess of guar.					
___x in excess of ___					
6TH DAY					
7TH DAY					
IDLE 6TH					
IDLE 7TH					

WEEKLY EMPLOYEE	STUDIO RATE	GUAR HOURS	LOCATION RATE	GUAR HOURS	G/L CODING
WEEKLY RATE *					
HOURLY RATE *					
1.5x in excess of guar.					
2x in excess of guar.					
___ x in excess of ___					
'TH DAY				__/__	
7TH DAY				__/__	
IDLE 6TH					
IDLE 7TH					

* NOTE: Overtime of not less than 1.5x paid for hours worked in excess of 8 per day or 40 per week as required by law or contract.

ALLOWANCE	STUDIO RATE	LOCATION RATE	SEPARATE CHECK	G/L CODING
BOX RENTAL			Y N	
CAR ALLOW			Y N	
MEAL ALLOW			Y N	
MEAL PENALTY			Y N	
PER DIEM ALLOW			Y N	
PER DIEM TAXBL			Y N	
PER DIEM ADV			Y N	
MILEAGE ALLOW			Y N	
MILEAGE TAXBL			Y N	
MILEAGE ADV				

"By signing this form, I agree that EP may take deductions from my earnings to adjust previous overpayments if and when said overpayments may occur"
I HEREBY ACKNOWLEDGE RECEIPT OF "FACTS ABOUT WORKERS COMPENSATION" (CA ONLY)

FORM W4 EMPLOYEE'S WITHHOLDING ALLOWANCE CERTIFICATE

MARITAL STATUS ☐ SINGLE ☐ MARRIED ☐	Married, but withhold at higher Single rate Note: If married, but legally separated, or spouse is a nonresident alien, check the single box.	1. TOTAL NUMBER OF DEPENDENTS CLAIMED

2. Additional amount, if any, you want deducted from each pay. $

3. I claim exemption from withholding because (see instructions and check boxes below that apply):
   a. ☐ Last year I did not owe any Federal income tax and had a right to a full refund of ALL INCOME TAX WITHHELD, AND
   b. ☐ This year I do not expect to owe any Federal income tax and expect to have a right to a full refund of ALL
       income tax withheld. If both a and b apply, enter "EXEMPT" here _____   3b. [   ]
   c. ☐ If you entered "EXEMPT" on line 3b, are you a full-time student?   ☐ Yes   ☐ No

Under the penalties of perjury, I certify that I am entitled to the number of withholding allowances claimed on this certificate, or if claiming exemption from withholding, that I am entitled to claim the exempt status.

AGREED-EMPLOYEE SIGNATURE	DATE	AUTHORIZED SIGNATURE

EMPLOYER

EP COPY

BOX RENTAL INFORMATION

PRODUCTION COMPANY _____

EMPLOYEE _____ **S.S.#** _____

LOAN OUT COMPANY _____

FEDERAL ID# _____

RENTAL RATE: $ _____ **PER WEEK/DAY**

(Must be recorded on employee time card each week)

RENTAL COMMENCES ON: _____

INVENTORY: (Attach additional pages if necessary):

_____

_____

_____

_____

_____

_____

_____

_____

_____

_____

Employee/Loanout agree that the equipment listed herein is rented to Production Company for use under Employee/Loanout's direction and control. Employee/Loanout are solely responsible for any damage to or loss of such equipment and hereby waive any claims against Entertainment Partners for any loss or damage of any kind and agree to look solely to Production Company to resolve any such claims. Entertainment Partners shall have no obligation to indemnify Employee/Loanout against any losses or damage, or to provide any insurance coverage for the benefit of Employee/Loanout covering the equipment herein described.

I attest that the above described equipment represents a valid rental for this production.

_____   _____

EMPLOYEE SIGNATURE   DATE

_____   _____

APPROVAL SIGNATURE   DATE

D.G.A. Deal Memorandum

Every employee who is a member of the Directors Guild of America must complete a D.G.A. Deal Memo. D.G.A. personnel are as follows:

- Unit Production Managers
- First and Second Assistant Directors
- Second Second Assistant Directors
- Stage Managers
- Associate Directors
- Technical Coordinators
- Some Associate Producers

D.G.A. Trainees are not required to fill out D.G.A. Deal Memos.

Directors Guild of America Reports

The following must be submitted:

To the D.G.A. National Office Reports Compliance Department:

- Deal Memos for all individuals employed in D.G.A.-covered categories, due prior to commencement of employment.
- Quarterly Gross Earnings Report, due within fifteen days after the close of each calendar quarter, listing all individuals employed in D.G.A.-covered categories, Social Security numbers, projects, and total gross earnings for the quarter. Such gross shall not include residual payments of any kind, per diem, travel allowance, profit participation, gross participation, and reimbursements that are not compensation for services rendered under the Basic Agreement.
- Quarterly Employment Data Report, due within thirty days after the close of each quarter. (See enclosed report form and instruction sheet, which detail reporting requirements.)
- Weekly Work List, listing all persons employed in D.G.A.-covered categories during the previous week, categories worked, project, and dates of employment.

To the Credits Department:

- Proposed Main and End Title Credits for approval.
- Copies of all press books and advertising materials for approval.

To the Residuals Department:

- Buy's or Distributor's Assumption Agreement, if your company arranges an assumption deal. Please contact the Guild for the appropriate form.

****

Please send the above to:

Director's Guild of America, Inc. • 7920 Sunset Boulevard
Los Angeles, CA 90046 • Phone: (310) 289-2000 • Fax: (310) 289-2029

Directors Guild of America
7920 Sunset Blvd.
Los Angeles, CA 90046
310-289-2000 / FAX 310-289-2029

Director Deal Memorandum - FILM

his confirms our agreement to employ you to direct the project described as follows:

DIRECTOR INFORMATION

Name: _____   SSN#: _____

Loanout: _____   Tel.#: _____

Address: _____

Salary: $_____ ☐ per week   Additional Time: $_____ ☐ per week
                      ☐ per day   ☐ per day
                      ☐ per show   ☐ per show

Start Date _____   Guaranteed Period: _____   pro rata: ☐ Yes ☐ No

PROJECT INFORMATION

Picture or Series Title: _____

Episode/Segment Title: _____   Episode #: _____

Length of Program: ☐ 30 min   ☐ 120 min
                      ☐ 60 min.   ☐ Other_____
                      ☐ 90 min.

Is this a Pilot?   ☐ Yes   ☐ No

Produced Primarily for: ☐ Theatrical   ☐ Disc/Cassette
                          ☐ Network   ☐ Syndication
                          ☐ Basic Cable   ☐ Pay-TV (service)_____

Theatrical Film Budget: ☐ Under $500,000
                          ☐ Between $500,000 and $1,500,000
                          ☐ Over $1,5000,000

Free/Pay Television: ☐ Network Prime Time
                       ☐ Other than Network Prime Time
                       ☐ Pay-TV -------------------------->

Number of subsrcibers to the pay television services to which
the program is licensed at the time of employment:
☐ Less than 1,500,000   ☐ 1,500,000 - 1,999,999
☐ 2,000,000 - 2,999,999   ☐ 3,000,000 or more
Is the budget $5,000,000 or more?   ☐ Yes ☐ No

Check one (if applicable)   ☐ Second Unit

The **INDIVIDUAL** having final cutting authority over the film is: _____

Other conditions:
(inc. credit above min.)   _____
                           _____

This employment is subject to the provisions of the Directors Guild of America Basic Agreement of 1993.

Accepted and Agreed: Signatory Co: _____

Employee: _____   By: _____

Date: _____   Date: _____

DIRECTOR.DM.9506

Directors Guild of America
7920 Sunset Blvd.
Los Angeles, CA 90046
310-289-2000 / FAX 310-289-2029

Unit Production Manager and Assistant Director Deal Memorandum - FILM

This confirms our agreement to employ you on the project described as follows:

AD/UPM INFORMATION

Name: _____ SSN#: _____

Loanout: _____ Tel.#: _____

Address: _____

Category:
☐ Unit Production Manager
☐ First Assistant Director
☐ Key Second Assistant Director
☐ 2nd Second Assistant Director
☐ Additional Second Assistant Director
☐ Technical Coordinator
☐ Asst. Unit Production Manager

Photography: ☐ Principal ☐ Second Unit ☐ Both

Salary (dollar amt.) $ _____ $ _____ ☐ per week
(Studio) (Location) ☐ per day

Production Fee (dollar amt): $ _____ $ _____
(Studio) (Location)

Start Date: _____ **Guaranteed Period:** _____

PROJECT INFORMATION

Film or Series Title: _____

Episode/Segment Title: _____

Length of Program:
☐ 30 min
☐ 60 min.
☐ 90 min.
☐ 120 min
☐ Other_____

Produced Primarily for:
☐ Theatrical
☐ Network
☐ Basic Cable
☐ Syndication
☐ Disc/Cassettes
☐ Pay-TV (service)_____

Other conditions:
(e.g., credit, suspension, per diem, etc.) _____
_____

☐ Studio ☐ Distant Location ☐ Both ☐ Check if New York Amendment Applies

This employment is subject to the provisions of the Directors Guild of America Basic Agreement of 1993.

Accepted and Agreed: Signatory Co: _____

Employee: _____ By: _____

Date: _____ Date: _____

AD-UPM.DM:9506

Directors Guild of America
7920 Sunset Blvd.
Los Angeles, CA 90046
310-289-2000 / FAX 310-289-2029

**Addendum to the
Director's Deal Memorandum
Post Production Schedule
(For a Theatrical Motion Picture or Television
Motion Picture 90 Minutes or Longer)**

Director's Name: _____

Project Title: _____

Company Name: _____

Director's Cut: Start Date: _____

 Finish Date: _____

Date For Special Photography & Processes (If Any): _____

Date For Delivery Of Answer Print: _____

Date Of Release (Theatrical Film): _____

Date Of Network Broadcast (If Applicable): _____

The following two forms are used when the rental of an airplane or boat is necessary for filming. These forms are self-explanatory and are used for insurance purposes.

AIRCRAFT QUESTIONNAIRE

Title of Production : _____

The Owner of the Aircraft should provide the Production Company with a Certificate of the Owner's Aviation Liability and Hull Insurance, naming the Production Company as Additional Insured. Such evidence must be signed by the Insurance Company (not the broker) and faxed to 213/862-5999.

For any use of non-scheduled aircraft, please supply the following information:

Date(s) of Use: _____

Make and Model: _____

FAA "N" Number: _____ Number of Seats: _____

Value of Aircraft: _____ Year Built: _____

Owner's Name: _____

Owner's Address: _____

Owner's City, State, Zip: _____

Owner's Phone Number: _____

Aircraft Based at (City, State): _____

Owner's Insurance: Liability Limit: _____ Hull Limit: _____

Aircraft to be operated by: __Our employee(s) OR __Owner or Owner's Employee(s)

Describe Locations, Activities, Passengers and Crew: _____

_____

_____

WATERCRAFT QUESTIONNAIRE

Title of Production: _____

The Owner of the Watercraft should provide the Production Company with a Certificate of the Owners Liability and Hull Insurance, naming the Production Company as Additional Insured. Such evidence must be signed by the Insurance Company (not the broker) and faxed to 213/862-5999.

For any use of watercraft, please supply the following information:

Date(s) of Use: _____

Name of Boat: _____

Length & Make/Model: _____

Value of Vessel: _____   Registration CF Number: _____

Hull Type: _____   Year Built: _____

Owner's Name: _____

Owner's Address: _____

Owner's City, State, Zip: _____

Owner's Phone Number: _____

Owner's Insurance: Liability Limit: _____   Hull Limit: _____

Vessel usually moored at (Home Port): _____

Watercraft to be operated by: __ Our employee(s)   OR   __ Owner or Owner's Employee(s)

Using any pyrotechnics?   ___ Yes   ___ No

Describe Locations, Activities, Passengers and Crew: _____

_____

_____

The following form is a standard Location Agreement. This form is a must, as it protects both the owner of the specific location and the producing company from any legal actions. For any location you go to—whether it is a private home, an office building, or an empty lot—be sure you get a signed location agreement from the owner or duly authorized representative of that property.

PROJECT:_____

CHARGE #:_____

LOCATION AGREEMENT

The undersigned grants to _____ Productions, Inc. _____ its successors and assigns, the right and license to enter upon, to make photographs (stills, film, tape or otherwise) and use for so-called "location" purposes the property located at: _____ (hereinafter referred to as "the property") on:_____ in consideration of the sum of $_____, (provided that the property is actually utilized). If such photography is prevented or hampered by weather or occurrences beyond _____ control, it will be postponed to or completed at a mutually agreeable time without further compensation.

The undersigned hereby grants to _____, its successors, assigns and licensees, the irrevocable, perpetual right in all media throughout the universe to use the photographs of the property taken by _____ hereunder in connection with motion picture and television photoplays in such manner and to such extent as _____ may desire, including without limitation, the right to use such photographs for advertising and publicity purposes as well as in on-line or interactive computer media. The rights herein granted include the right to photograph all structures and signs located on the property (including the exterior and interior of such structures and the names, logos and verbiage contained on such signs), the right to refer to the property by its correct name or any fictitious name, the right to attribute fictitious events as occurring on the property and the right to replicate the property including the right to use and dispose of such replication in any manner_____in its sole discretion deems appropriate.

The undersigned hereby warrants that the undersigned is the owner or lessee of said property and has the right to grant the license herein contained.

_____ agrees to hold the undersigned harmless from and against any and all costs, fees, expenses and damages (except as may relate to negligence of the undersigned) which may arise in connection with _____ use of the property as described herein._____ shall leave the property in the same condition as it was prior to _____ use hereunder, reasonable wear and tear, force majeure and the use permitted hereunder excepted.

The undersigned hereby releases _____ and its licensees, successors, assigns, all networks, stations, sponsors and advertising agencies from any and all claims, demands or causes of action which the undersigned, its heirs, successors or assigns may now have or hereafter acquire by reason of _____ photographing and using the photographs taken of the property, including but not limited to all buildings (exterior and interior), equipment, facilities and signs thereon. I understand this document and freely agree thereto.

By:_____   Date:_____

_____   _____
Address   City, State and Zip Code

Social Security or Federal I.D. No._____

We hereby approve and accept the above.

_____ PRODUCTIONS, INC.

By:_____

The following form is used when you are going to photograph an individual who happens to be visiting or working at a location that you are shooting. This form indemnifies your production company from any lawsuits arising out of any invasion-of-privacy claims.

Viacom Productions Inc.
10 Universal City Plans
Universal City, CA 91608

    I understand that you are producing a television
series/pilot/M.O.W. entitled _____
                                        (show name)
As an inducement to you to photograph me in connection for possible
use in connection with such television series, and without any payment
of any compensation:

1. I hereby give you my consent to photograph me and to record and
use my name and/or likeness in connection with the production,
distribution, exhibition, advertising and exploitation of one or more
episodes of such series or otherwise as you may elect throughout the
universe in perpetuity by any and all methods and means now known or
hereafter devised.

2. I hereby waive any and all right of privacy and/or publicity
and/or defamation or any other rights in connection with said use of my
likeness, photograph and/or name or otherwise in connection with said
television series. However, you shall not be obligated to produce
such series or to make use of any of the rights herein granted by me.

3. The permission, waiver and rights granted by me are without any
limitation of any nature whatsoever and will inure to the benefit of
your successors, assigns and licensees.

4. I understand that you are photographing me and will use my name,
likeness and/or photograph in express reliance on the foregoing.

_____   _____
DATE   SIGNATURE

                                   _____
                                   PRINT NAME

                                   _____
                                   STREET ADDRESS

                                   _____
                                   CITY, STATE, AND ZIPCODE

As parent or legal guardian of the above-named minor, I consent and
agree to the foregoing in all respects.

                                   _____
                                   SIGNATURE

                                   _____
                                   PRINT NAME

1

Gentlepersons:

You have the irrevocable permission of the undersigned to photograph the undersigned on _____, 1987 at _____
_____

and to use or license the use of such film in any manner whatsoever, including (without limitation) in connection with your motion picture activities.

The undersigned acknowledges that you will own all rights in and to all film in which the undersigned may appear, and you, your successors, assigns and/or licensees may (but will not be obligated to) use or license the use of such film in all kinds of motion pictures, and the advertising and publicity thereof, and further acknowledges that the same may be exhibited and/or exploited throughout the universe in perpetuity by any means or methods now or hereafter known.

In accordance with Section 507 of the Federal Communications Act (which makes it a criminal offense for anyone related to the production or preparation of a program intended for broadcast, to pay or accept money, service or other valuable consideration for the inclusion of any material in such program, unless certain disclosures are made), the undersigned affirms that he/she has neither given nor received any consideration for the inclusion of any "plug", reference, or product identification or of any other material in the program for which said film is intended.

The undersigned represents that he/she is over the age of eighteen and has the full right and is free to execute this permission.

NAME: ADDRESS: DATE SIGNED:

_____   _____   _____
Print Name

_____   _____
Signature

_____   _____   _____
Print Name

_____   _____
Signature

_____   _____   _____
Print Name

_____   _____
Signature

_____   _____   _____
Print Name

_____   _____
Signature

0581B

Script Color Revisions

The following shows the color order in which script revisions are distributed. Every time a script revision is printed, it is printed on a different color paper. This is done so that everyone will be able to keep current with the numerous revisions that are common with every script.

WHITE

BLUE

PINK

YELLOW

GREEN

GOLD

BUFF

SALMON

CHERRY

TAN

BACK TO WHITE

Index

Books from Allworth Press

Allworth Press is an imprint of Allworth Communications, Inc. Selected titles are listed below.

Shoot Me: Independent Filmmaking from Creative Concept to Rousing Release
by Roy Frumkes and Rocco Simonelli (paperback, 6 × 9, 240 pages, 56 b&w illus., $19.95)

The Directors: Take Four
by Robert J. Emery (paperback, 6 × 9, 256 pages, 10 b&w illus., $19.95)

The Health & Safety Guide for Film, TV & Theater
by Monona Rossol (paperback, 6 × 9, 256 pages, $19.95)

Technical Film and TV for Nontechnical People
by Drew Campbell (paperback, 6 × 9, 256 pages, $19.95)

Creative Careers in Hollywood
by Laurie Scheer (paperback, 6 × 9, 240 pages, $19.95)

Directing for Film and Television, Revised Edition
by Christopher Lukas (paperback, 6 × 9, 256 pages, 53 b&w illus., $19.95)

Documentary Filmmakers Speak
by Liz Stubbs (paperback, 6 × 9, 240 pages, $19.95)

The Filmmaker's Guide to Production Design
by Vincent LoBrutto (paperback, 6 × 9, 216 pages, 15 b&w illus., $19.95)

Making Independent Films: Advice from the Filmmakers
by Liz Stubbs and Richard Rodriguez (paperback, 6 × 9, 224 pages, 42 b&w illus., $16.95)

Makin' Toons: Inside the Most Popular Animated TV Shows and Movies
by Allan Neuwirth (paperback, 6 × 9, 288 pages, 82 b&w illus., $21.95)

Animation: The Whole Story
by Howard Beckerman (paperback, 6⅞ × 9¾, 320, 210 b&w illus, $24.95)

Acting for Film
by Cathy Hasse (paperback, 6 × 9, pages, $19.95)

An Actor's Guide: Your First Year in Hollywood, Revised Edition
by Michael Saint Nicholas (paperback, 6 × 9, 272 pages, $18.95)

Please write to request our free catalog. To order by credit card, call 1-800-491-2808 or send a check or money order to Allworth Press, 10 East 23rd Street, Suite 510, New York, NY 10010. Include $5 for shipping and handling for the first book ordered and $1 for each additional book. Ten dollars plus $1 for each additional book if ordering from Canada. New York State residents must add sales tax.

To see our complete catalog on the World Wide Web, or to order online, you can find us at
www.allworth.com.